"Imaginative culture – a [...]
we anticipate the future [...]
Treating culture as an industry doesn't make any more sense
than treating healthcare the same way. O'Connor's brilliant
book argues for a holistic, ecological vision of culture in which
it is seen as an essential part of the maintenance of a functioning society."

Brian Eno

"Radically remakes the case for culture and cultural policy
in the twenty-first century. Rejecting the trend for culture's
depoliticisation and the illusions of the 'creative industries',
O'Connor proposes a dynamic new approach where culture is
recentred as foundational to citizenship, democracy, and a new
kind of economy."

Mark Banks, Professor of Cultural Economy,
University of Glasgow

"A passionate and well-argued 'corrective' that seeks to rebal-
ance the cultural scales away from the economic to a larger
sense of social purpose. The book's central argument is that we
must reclaim art, give it place and recognition in all and every
society that wishes to live well and without fear. I'll buy that…"

Josephine Burns, Co-Founder of BOP Consulting

"In an era of culture wars and governmental disdain for 'mickey
mouse degrees' and anything that can't have a price tag placed
on it, O'Connor makes a brave and important argument that
culture – high and low – is important for its *own* sake."

Owen Hatherley, author of *Clean Living*
Under Difficult Circumstances

"The way we talk about culture in society has become narrow and stale, concerned only with economics or questions of representation. This book offers a broader critique that does not neglect these questions but deepens them. With scholarship, wit, and a clarity of thought, it promises to reset the cultural conversation in the years ahead."

Kate Oakley, Professor of Cultural Policy, University of Glasgow

"O'Connor restores culture to its rightful place as the embodiment of meaning. He shows how it is a public good that needs to be treasured and nurtured. He throws down the gauntlet to the prevailing dogma and points to ways that culture can be better valued, not as a tool of industry or politics – but the essence of our humanity and a pillar of any successful society."

Julianne Schultz, Professor Emerita, Media and Culture, Griffith University

"O'Connor's book is a hugely important cultural act in itself, lifting our sights beyond the 'damaged present' and imagining new foundations, with culture at the heart of a renewed democracy and a collective future reoriented around the common good."

Dan Hill, Director of Melbourne School of Design

Culture is not an industry

Manchester University Press

The *Manchester Capitalism* book series

Manchester Capitalism is a series of short books that follow the trail of money and power across the systems of financialised capitalism. The books make powerful interventions about who gets what and why, with rigorous arguments that are accessible for the concerned citizen. They go beyond simple critiques of neoliberalism and its satellite knowledges to reframe our problems and offer solutions about what is to be done.

Manchester was the city of both Engels and Free Trade where the twin philosophies of collectivism and free market liberalism were elaborated. It is now the home of this venture in radical thinking that primarily aims to challenge self-serving elites. We see the provincial radicalism rooted here as the ideal place from which to cast a cold light on the big issues of economic renewal, financial reform and political mobilisation.

Books in the series so far have covered diverse but related issues. How technocratic economic thinking narrows the field of the visible while popular myths about the economy spread confusion. How private finance is part of the extractive problem not the solution for development in the Global South and infrastructural needs in the UK. How politics disempowers social housing tenants and empowers reckless elites. How foundational thinking about economy and society reasserts the importance of the infrastructure of everyday life and the priority of renewal.

General editors: Julie Froud and Karel Williams

Already published:

The end of the experiment: From competition to the foundational economy

What a waste: Outsourcing and how it goes wrong

Licensed larceny: Infrastructure, financial extraction and the global South

The econocracy: The perils of leaving economics to the experts

Reckless opportunists: Elites at the end of the establishment

Foundational economy: The infrastructure of everyday life (2nd edition)

Safe as houses: Private greed, political negligence and housing policy after Grenfell

The spatial contract: A new politics of provision for an urbanized planet

The pound and the fury: Why anger and confusion reign in an economy paralysed by myth

Reclaiming economies for future generations: Foundational economy

Bankruptcy, bubbles and bailouts: The inside history of the Treasury since 1976

Derailed: How to fix Britain's broken railways

When nothing works: From cost of living to foundational liveability

Culture is not an industry

Reclaiming art and culture for the common good

Justin O'Connor

MANCHESTER UNIVERSITY PRESS

Published by Manchester University Press
Oxford Road, Manchester, M13 9PL
www.manchesteruniversitypress.co.uk

British Library Cataloguing-in-Publication Data
A catalogue record for this book is available from the British Library

ISBN 978 1 5261 7126 9 paperback
ISBN 978 1 5261 7806 0 hardback

First published 2024

The publisher has no responsibility for the persistence or accuracy of
URLs for any external or third-party internet websites referred to in this
book, and does not guarantee that any content on such websites is, or will
remain, accurate or appropriate.

Typeset by Newgen Publishing UK

For May Linn and Kai Wen

Contents

Introduction

Culture and democracy

This book is about what happens when we turn culture into an industry, and how we can fix this. Culture is central to what it is to be human, to live in a social world. There certainly are cultural industries, the large-scale organised production of cultural goods and services, and these need to be taken very seriously. But culture is not itself an industry, nor is its function to produce "jobs and growth" or "catalyse innovation". It is part of our democratic citizenship, an inalienable element of our universal human rights, and essential for our reimagining of the future.

The key argument of the book is that culture, as an object of public policy, should be moved out of "industry" and back into the sphere of public responsibility alongside health, education, social welfare, and basic infrastructure. This will mean overturning the dominant discourse of the last thirty years and convincing both mainstream politicians and their progressive challengers of the importance of culture to the social foundations of any equitable and free society.

"Creative industries" is one of New Labour's most enduring legacies. While many of its signature initiatives have faded into the past, or been written over by Conservative austerity, Brexit, and pandemic mismanagement, the "creative industries" enjoys a flourishing afterlife.[1] The idea itself was ill thought out, a quick policy fix for a newly established culture department. But it stuck. A concept impossible to pin down, morphing between art and software, pop music and industrial design, it became the default terminology for a whole mass of activities deemed "creative". The term extended from the UK along the global trade routes of an ascendent neoliberalism. First the Netherlands and Nordic countries, on to the countries of the former Eastern bloc, and then leapfrogging to Hong Kong, Singapore, Taiwan, and the megalopolis of Shanghai.[2] By 2010, alongside its "creative economy" alter ego, it was being promoted by United Nations agencies, including UNESCO, which now led the charge in South-East Asia, Africa, and South America. By the time of the 2020 Covid-19 pandemic, it had become the global cultural policy paradigm.[3]

The creative industries promised jobs and prosperity in a new kind of post-industrial economy, one that valued knowledge and creativity as essential. After two decades of hanging around the backdoor with its begging bowl it could now talk directly to "the wealth-creating portfolios, the emergent industry departments and the enterprise support programmes".[4] But it has not delivered on these economic promises, and cultural policy is now more marginalised and irrelevant than ever. The "good" jobs and export-oriented innovation systems it promised have not materialised. Most of cultural consumption is delivered by a commercial system dominated by global corporations larger and more concentrated than at any time in history. Cultural workers did not get the keys to the kingdom of the knowledge economy but are loaded with debt, excluded from the "asset economy", facing cost-of-living hikes, low-paid and insecure work, and experiencing the disdain of those who suggest they retrain for a better-paid job.

Yet the cultural sector still cleaves to the image of itself as "creative industries", and that with the right metrics it might just convince government to invest in art as a kind of R&D, and creativity as a key economic driver. The language of culture-as-industry has hollowed out the self-understanding of the cultural sector. Even those who barely use the term in their day-to-day work still huddle under its umbrella, happy to bundle its social and cultural benefits as "creative industry" when addressing their paymasters. The term has colonised the very language in which art and culture understand and express their true function, and their value for us, leaving confusion and demoralisation in its wake.

The political and socioeconomic system established in the late 1980s is in crisis. The global financial crisis of 2008–10 opened a period in which the dominant model of market-led reforms – deregulation, privatisation, shrinking public services, tax cuts, globalised production and distribution chains, and so on – was increasingly compromised. Growing inequality, insecurity of work, rising indebtedness, stalled wages and rising living costs, and stagnation of growth and investment, along with a hollowing out of democratic institutions amid a deepening cynicism and a volatile populist "anti-politics". Martin Wolf, of the *Financial Times*, doyen of the global economic commentariat, has declared neoliberalism a failed experiment, though it is by no means clear what is to replace it.

In the wake of this growing crisis a whole slew of alternative ideas has emerged. These seek not only to reorient our socioeconomic system to environmental sustainability but also to various forms of "wellbeing". For these, the fetishisation of GDP as a unique measure of prosperity has driven global warming, hollowed out our social services, and allowed growth to accrue to the wealthiest ten per cent. Many propose instead a focus on those social foundations essential to our collective wellbeing – health, education, care, social services, essential infrastructure, housing, food systems. These agendas have seriously dented the economic orthodoxy of neoliberalism, opening space for heterodox and alternative economics based on sustainability, wellbeing, social equity, care, and democratic empowerment. Culture is notable for its absence.

While reformers and radicals call for a new social contract based on securing these basic services, rarely do they include culture. The cultural sector, still hoping to be taken seriously as a growth industry, remains one of the last bastions of the old neoliberal dispensation. This book will attempt an explanation of just why this is. Though rarely commented on, the cultural sector was one of the first targets for the 1980s neoliberal revolution. The global "big bang" of the 1980s in which communications, computing, and "content" converged, and that continued apace with the new internet platforms, saw this new public sphere given over almost entirely to the private sector. Hard-headed economists in the Treasury now repositioned culture not as a public good but as a private commodity economy, driven by individual sovereign consumers. In response, those promoting the "creative industries" reimagined this privatisation as a knowledge economy in which art and creativity would be at a premium. This was not simply about bowing down to "bean counters" but a full, unto-the-hilt buy-in to a powerful new political imaginary in which art and culture's transformational promise was hitched to a post-industrial economic vision.

4

Introduction: culture and democracy

In this book I argue that culture needs to be radically divested from its identification with "creative industry". Instead, it should take its place alongside the social foundations of health, education, welfare, and infrastructure. To do this requires a systematic critique of the "creative industries" idea but also the elaboration of an alternative vision. It requires a clear recognition of the political effects of the creative industries performed as a crucial prelude to the repoliticisation of culture. By which I do not mean an absorption into politics per se, progressive or otherwise, but a clear rearticulation of the role culture plays in the polis, in the demos. For one of the most damaging impacts of culture-as-industry has been to seriously undermine the case for any concerted policy for art and culture outside of its instrumental value. As the case for the creative industries recedes, we can see a new range of social and "wellbeing" benefits emerge in its wake, which in their own way also reduce culture to an instrumental value. How did we get here?

"Cool Britannia": de-politicising culture

That party at Tony Blair's has been much ridiculed, a youthful prime minister mixing it with the Britpop glitterati. But the moment it symbolised should not be so quickly dismissed. New Labour wanted to embrace the energy of a pop culture in which music, fashion, film, football, and contemporary art blurted out a raucous "we're coming home".[5] "Cool Britannia" proclaimed the arrival in power of a "Gen X" whose youth and early adulthood had been spent almost entirely under the eighteen-year rule of the Conservatives. Completely at home in the pyroclastic explosion of 1990s media and popular culture, the Union Jack guitars connected this youthful cohort to a previous moment of pop modernism in the "Swinging Sixties". Once-revolutionary Thatcherism had become moribund in its turn, so here was a chance to renew the white heat of innovation, now driven by creativity as much as science.

For those working in the cultural sector, as well as its "passionate" consumers, the creative industries moment spoke to real aspirations and hopes. It articulated, however briefly, an aspiration to a different future, tapping a seam of modernising optimism that had been forced underground since the late 1970s. The creative industries spoke to this generation, validating everything they watched and read, listened and danced to, played with and mashed up. It turned out, despite the admonishment of their concerned parents, they had chosen proper jobs after all. ABBA outsold Volvo. Music was bigger than steel, bigger than farming and mining. Popular culture had been validated, and its democratic force parlayed as a creativity that would power the whole economy.

Owen Hatherley, speaking of both Britpop and New Labour, remembers that "in both cases ... it seemed like 'our' side had won, but it soon became clear that, in pursuit of success at any costs, it had internalised every single one of its opponents' values".[6] The creative industries moment was born of that brief utopian flicker. It drew not just on the energies of a post-sixties popular culture but on a longer history of radical cultural politics born of the same dynamic social transformation. Creative industries presented itself as an apotheosis of a cultural democracy, the real substance of which it disavowed and made purely gestural. Robert Hewison wrote later: "New Labour's democracy was the democracy of the market. The hegemony of Thatcherite values survived New Labour's rebranding". The creative industries, Hewison continued, spoke to the freedom and autonomy of the new "citizen consumer".[7]

Indeed, the agenda of the "creative cultural industries" (CCI) represented a massive de-politicisation of culture, the damaging effects of which have been profound, and persist to this day. Cultural policy is given over to creativity gurus, TED Talkers, and the big four accountancy firms. Mapping documents, Venn diagrams, employment figures, multipliers, and value-added charts now provide the accoutrements of a policy area in which economic growth becomes an uncontested good. The economic benefits of the CCI simply require the standard tools of neoliberal economic policy – skills training, access to finance, infrastructure – whose delivery is a purely technical-administrative question best answered by McKinsey and Co.

Any residual politics mostly concerned the equitable representation of class, gender, and ethnicity in these creative industries, together with their geographical dispersal within nations or between the Global North and South. More recently, there has been growing concern about the remuneration and conditions of those working in the sector. These are all important questions, as we will see. But they do not by themselves challenge the creative industries narrative, that this sector primarily exists to deliver jobs, growth, and innovation.

The global financial crisis of 2008–10, followed by austerity, wage stagnation, rising debt, the chaos of Brexit, and the catastrophe of Covid-19, marked a demoralising period for the cultural sector. It became increasingly marginalised, battered, and scorned yet remained wedded, in a kind of Stockholm syndrome, to an economic language of creativity and innovation, markets, and entrepreneurship that its neoliberal captors had long since abandoned. As we enter an epoch of deep instability

7

and change, when one system is giving way to something as yet undecided, culture's radical political energies – fatally compromised or just simply forgotten – are tellingly absent.

I will argue in this book that the current interregnum opens a space for a revived notion of culture as essential to society as health, education, welfare, and infrastructure, one of the basic requirements for a decent, equitable, and sustainable life in common. Its essential contribution is distinct, not reducible to how it might impact on these other areas of public policy. Equally, its contribution is indispensable to any transformative programme, its absence hobbling our ability to reimagine a more viable human future. The repoliticisation requires us to return to the problematic of culture and democracy which was at the heart of post-war debates, and whose evisceration was so central to the neoliberal project. Hence the "utopian flicker", a momentary return of a radical agenda for culture that so quickly evaporated. Central to these hopes and to their disappointment was the idea of "creativity".

Creativity, art, and culture

The sudden rise to prominence of the word "creativity" has been well documented.[8] As I argue in the next chapter, creativity as "input" was crucial to how culture was absorbed into a language of economy. It was central to the construction of the new, self-directed subjects of "creative capitalism", with their "always-on" networked personas and blurred line between living and working. But creativity was also an answer to art and culture's "democratic deficit". If art was seen as elitist, with culture too acquiring the patina of something "worthy" to be acquired, creativity was an inalienable part of every human being. Creativity was something we all had and so we were all potential members of the new "creative class" that Richard Florida had espoused to universal applause. Creativity emphasised process over product, the future over the past, active life over deathly congealment. Most importantly, it had now been recognised as economically useful. The new economy was to be built on divergent concepts and radical innovation, not making stuff through incremental improvements.

The "new economy" annexed specifically artistic creativity. The radical non-linear, inspirational working processes of the "romantic artist" was melded with Joseph Schumpeter's creatively disruptive entrepreneur. The result is with us still, in a million start-up seminars and corporate beanbag and *fussball* chill-out zones. The "art" in question referred to a European modernist tradition, in which "the shock of the new" represented a power that might be productively harnessed if accompanied by the right "business model". In response, many critics have emphasised the collective or co-creative nature of the "cultural and creative industries", the ecosystems and social milieu rather than the inspired individual. Others, critical of the whole economic turn, urge us to take back our everyday creativity as a community activity, one that provides us with wellbeing outside of any economic benefit. Often these two perspectives are melded into "social and economic benefits" of creativity.

What all of this fails to register is the distinct space occupied by art and culture as separate to the "economy" but also as something more than "everyday life". Underlying the democratic charge of the creative industries is the idea that art and culture (conceived as a set of distinct practices and artefacts) are elitist. Not because they are dominated by middle-class people (though that too) but because they are somehow set above or apart from everyday culture, from culture as a "way of life". It might be that art and culture should not be valued economically, but to set them apart from community, from everyday life, is equally egregious.

Why is this important? Because if art and culture are mainly about exercising creativity, about building social bonds, about mental wellbeing, then they can more or less be folded into social and wellbeing policies. In this book I will argue that culture certainly should be part of those social foundations, but that it represents a distinct area of practice and knowledge. That it contributes not just to "mental wellbeing" but is essential to our citizenship, as autonomous, flourishing individuals in a strong democratic polis.

Art and culture provide a distinct space in which our individual freedom is facilitated and constantly examined. This freedom is positive – it is freedom to do, to become – and requires a social and cultural infrastructure to make it possible. This freedom is not simply about desires and wants, but about deciding who we ought to be and what we ought to do. It is ethical or spiritual freedom. Art and culture allow us to act and reflect on this spiritual freedom in the particular space of "what if", of metaphor, of fiction and fabulation rather than rational and analytic thought. As such it inevitably involves our whole sensorium, making sense of our experience through sounds and images, movements and word-signs. All of art and culture is made up; it's fiction, an insubstantial pageant, style, a making of shapes and rhythms. Yet it is concerned with the truth of things. And because it is concerned with the truth of things it is a communal act, inconceivable outside the social, no matter how arcane or in-your-face it appears.

This is why the annexation of creativity to economy is so damaging, as it refuses to allow this space of freedom the autonomy it necessarily requires. Critics of the "romantic artist" in the creative industries want to assert the social and co-creative nature of work in that sector. Teamwork and collective practice are indeed to be valued, but that "romantic" tradition is not solely nor primarily about the ineffable artistic genius. It evokes a space in which the imagination is given freedom to follow a line of enquiry, to pursue a particular vision, constrained only by the nature of the artistic material itself. This is about shapes and sounds, word-signs and movement, but ultimately it is about an ethical truth. As Martin Amis wrote in *Experience*, "style is morality: morality detailed, configured, intensified".[9] It is the restriction of artistic freedom which underlay Adorno's critique of the "cultural industries" rather than an elitist distain for popular culture (though there was that too).

The autonomy of art is not about the individual genius, social irresponsibility, or a refusal of collective co-creation but a space of practical attentiveness that emerged at the beginning of modernity, notably in the eighteenth century. This social separation of art as a distinct sphere is now commonly represented by proponents of community arts and modern cultural studies as an elitist move. As one community arts advocate recently put it, "it is the Enlightenment's invention of the Fine Arts that implicitly (and carelessly) relegated most human culture to a subordinate position as the 'not-fine arts'".[10] In which case, a democratic cultural policy is a "bottom-up" act of taking back "art" from its highfalutin autonomous realm and returned to the community where it belongs.

This distinction between an elitist "art" and a democratic "culture as a whole way of life" has been a crucial stake in post-war debates on culture and democracy. In fact, rather than art being ripped out of a holistic culture by the bourgeois enlightenment, the two became identified as distinct areas of social practice at the same historical moment; that is, at the end of the eighteenth century as commercial capitalism was turbocharged by the Industrial Revolution. Indeed, while something akin to art can be identified in ancient Greece, as in Persia, the Ottoman Empire, and classical India and China, something called "culture" would not be recognised in these older civilisations. Culture would be folded into religion, traditional mores, forms of administration, and patterns of agriculture and commerce. Culture, a distinct, nameable part of the social whole, only emerged in the sixteenth century, and outside of Europe, in the mid-nineteenth century.

Art and culture came to be identified as distinct areas of social experience and practice mainly because of the invention of economics, itself based on the modern scientific method developed in the seventeenth century (Descartes and Hobbes especially)[11]. Adam Smith identified a distinct economic realm governed by rational self-interested individuals whose behaviours could be codified scientifically. The kinds of fictional and metaphorical knowledge represented by "the arts" was relegated to the domain of sensual pleasures and a matter of taste, not objective knowledge. Of course, even Adam Smith recognised that while the "hidden hand" would provide prosperity for all, there were "moral sentiments", sympathy for others' feelings, that helped strengthen social bonds. This was the basis for a whole "civilising mission" which underpinned much nineteenth and early twentieth-century cultural policy, using "the arts" to stick together the society that industrial capitalism was assiduously ripping asunder. And of course, it allowed the new bourgeoise to display their civilised manners and dispositions, in ways that constantly reaffirmed their distinction from the unruly masses they sought to tame.

My argument is two-fold. First, that this space of art was social-structural not some bourgeois conspiracy. This separate sphere of knowledge and experience called art increasingly asserted its own autonomous space. Exemplified by the new generation of "romantic" artists and philosophers, it was a rejection of, or attempted escape from, this new economic-rational world, an evocation of a more "human" world of art and imagination.[12] This aesthetic or artistic autonomy was either linked to the rise of the bourgeoise (Pierre Bourdieu) or that of the new modern state (Michel Foucault). But it was a crucial historical gain. As Raymond Williams suggested: "The attempt to distinguish 'art' from other, often closely related, practices is a quite extraordinarily important historical and social process. The attempt to distinguish 'aesthetic' from other kinds of attention and response is, as a historical and social process, perhaps even more important".[13]

Art was more than some historical division of labour, performed by the bourgeoise while the new working class slaved in the factories. Of course, it was that too, but it also began a questioning of values and traditions long sanctified by God, State, and one's social betters. It formed part of that complex set of values and ethics called "enlightenment", which at its best (and it had its darker sides) was foundational for the new kinds of radical democratic questions being asked from the end of the eighteenth century onwards. Art was by no means democratic, but in putting sanctified traditions into question it became an essential part of the modern democratic tradition that itself was turbocharged by the French Revolution.

Specifically, art was concerned with all those elements of human life outlawed by the mechanistic scientism of economics and the principles of public administration derived from them. It saw in the senses, in the imagination, and in the intimation of a humanist ethics beyond the brick wall of mechanical rationalism a pathway to a different kind of understanding of human life.

Art, culture, and popular culture

My second argument is that it makes no sense to counterpose "art" as a distinct set of ideas or objects to culture as a "way of life". That is, counterposing what Matthew Arnold in 1869 defined as "the best which has been thought and said in the world" to what the anthropologist Edward Tyler in 1871 called "culture as a whole way of life". Given Arnold's privileged position at the heart of the British imperial elite, and how "the canon" has long been used to position popular culture as "lower", Tyler's anthropological definition has often been taken as a democratic counterweight to Arnold.[14]

But these were not opposing views. Arnold and Tyler were talking about two very different things. As outlined by Tyler, there could be no society without culture because human society was defined as that which was not naturally determined. We were, as a species, about culture not nature, our societies organised around shared symbolic meanings, passed on by learning not instinct. But culture viewed as a "whole way of life" is not intrinsically democratic or anti-elitist. It simply takes as its object the system as a whole. Indeed, Tyler was dealing with what he called "primitive cultures" (the title of the book), and naturally assumed that the culture of "advanced" societies

14

would be at its most evolved in "art". Just as "primitive culture" could be found in its least evolved spaces, such as the urban slums at the heart of the big cities.[15]

The confusion lies in identifying a "whole way of life" with the "ordinary" or with "popular culture". Raymond Williams' "culture is ordinary" is a claim that we all share a common creative capacity. Culture as a "whole way of life" is about a complex and historically evolved structure of social meanings and practices.[16] The class-based separation of art and popular culture which marked nineteenth-century Europe was therefore an expression of its "whole way of life". So too the monopolisation of imperial culture by the mandarins in China, or written texts by the priests of ancient Egypt or of medieval Europe, was part of their whole way of life.[17] Equally, "popular culture" – the songs, dances, images, stories, rituals, and so on of "the people" and the "everyday life" in which their practices were embedded – is merely one aspect of a "whole way of life" which can be highly unequal.[18]

However elitist and rarefied we may consider it, "fine art" is of the same ontological order as the symbolic forms of popular culture, both part of a sub-system within this wider "way of life". We can't make an essentialist distinction between "popular culture" and "art", between "art" and the ordinary making and enjoying of the symbolic, aesthetic, expressive goods of music, games, TV shows, films, books, stories, images, and so on. Which is not to say that they are not differently implicated in all sorts of social distinctions and exclusions, nor that we cannot make value distinctions amongst them.

Raymond Williams' statement that "culture is ordinary", and his radical claims that creativity is essential to all our lives, part of the "long revolution" towards a democratic, socialist society, has been foundational to my – and many others' – thinking.[19] This does not mean that art is to be abolished, or that it is a petrified, elitist trophy needing to be folded back into the vibrant, grassroots communal lifeworld of ordinary every-day culture. Rejecting art as intrinsically elitist abandons the important range of values, functions, and forms of life which have historically been attached to it.

Art relates to the acceleration and complexification of social change that came with industrial capitalism. In the eighteenth century, art was separated out from other aspects – legal, religious, political, economic, the "social" itself – in a manner that characterises modernity.[20] "All that is solid melts into air", declared Marx and Engels, in *The Communist Manifesto*. The rapid dissolution of people's everyday coordinates; the opening of local, bounded spaces to new forces; the complex flux of social life; new forms of knowledge, new values, and potential identities – all these are the historical realities of a modernity in which the practice of art moved into a separate social space. "Separate" does not necessarily entail "elite", as Marshall Berman persuasively argued.[21] Art became part of a "public sphere" that was separated from local social, political, and religious worlds, often as oppressive as they could be life sustaining. This separation created a space of relatively autonomous symbolic and political mediation crucial both to the idea of a democratic polity and of the modern city.[22]

Artistic autonomy is an essential political gain of modernity. This is not about artists being geniuses, or "special", or freeing them from social interests or responsibilities. Rather, without the autonomy of the space of art by which to mediate and reflect on a rapidly evolving society, modernity threatens to become oppressive and technocratic, leaving humanity spiritually blank before the instrumental reason of state power and industrial capital.

In short, if art was simply about class distinction, then its disappearance would be either welcome or of only limited historical interest. On the contrary, I would argue that the values at stake in the historical space of art are a crucial part of our democratic life and its disappearance damaging to our life on the planet.[23]

Arts and cultural policy

In the book I use "art" and "culture" interchangeably, because the couplet describes this historical accumulation of different forms and values around art, which includes elitism *and* the struggles against that elitism. It includes art and popular culture, a distinction that is unworkable in the present day. It keeps in play the fluid relations between the particular symbolic forms of art and culture, and the wider anthropological "way of life" that changes through history. "Art and culture" describes the production and consumption of symbolic forms and practices, a complex, evolving system central to modern societies. Their importance lies not just in the rights of individuals to access them but also in their systemic contribution to society. They are part of how societies work.

Though the boundaries with a general "culture as a way of life" are always fluid, art and culture can be more or less distinguished as an object of policy. This was covered by the term "arts" from the mid-nineteenth century, supplemented by policies around public broadcasting and mass entertainment in the interwar years, and included under "cultural policy" in last third of the twentieth century. This trajectory was associated with an extension – however uneven and contradictory – of social citizenship and democracy, in which culture was deemed important.

The post-war expansion of "art" into "culture" involved a complex sociological transformation in which "art" proliferated beyond its traditional sites and spread across the social whole, disrupting traditional boundaries and connecting with new aspirations to social change. But if art's character and its sites of production and consumption changed as it expanded into a wider cultural field, the historical values contained in the idea of "art" also changed that culture.

This was the context in which culture and democracy were to encounter each other from 1945. Cultural policy was by no means coherent. It engaged in an unsteady combination of protecting art and protecting traditional ways of life, promoting both modernism and versions of "Merrie England", projecting the nation-state and the cosmopolitanism of universal humanist culture. As the tradition of British cultural studies revealed, the working classes were themselves undergoing a radical social and cultural transformation. Michael Denning wrote that culture had now become an economic realm,

> encompassing the mass media, advertising, and the production and distribution of knowledge. Moreover, it came to signify not only the cultural industries and state cultural apparatuses but the forms of working-class subsistence and consumption, both the goods and services supplied by the welfare state or purchased on the market, and the time of leisure and social reproduction outside the working day.[24]

Working-class cultures were increasingly about renegotiating their own lives, individually and collectively, through various forms of popular culture. It was in this context of rapid social change that "culture" became central to a reinvented politics, a "new left" and the "counterculture", but also the kinds of radical popular cultures that exploded in the 1960s.

As key proponents of "cultural studies", Raymond Williams and Stuart Hall saw that the distinction between "high" art and "low" culture could not survive the new forms of the 1960s – the books, comics, music, film, clothes, TV, radio and their related objects, spaces, networks, economies, and emotional investments. "Everyday life" was transformed by these new "popular arts", which gave expression to its new aspirations, energies, and contestations.[25] Mark Fisher's notion of "popular modernism", whereby the transformative power associated with modernism and the avant-garde was appropriated and transformed within popular culture, also expresses this idea.[26]

These new forms blurred the lines between art and popular culture, just as they helped redefine the shape and dynamics of our "whole way of life". This "whole way of life" was never settled or unitary; it was continuously being fractured and transformed in a manner which has only accelerated since the 1960s.[27] Cultural studies tried to articulate this politically, identifying new forms of symbolic struggle (famously, popular music and its sub-cultures) within a wider process of social and political transformation.

By the 1970s it was recognised that the public sphere of culture, which acts as a complex mediation of our shared social horizon of experience and imagination, was increasingly dominated by what were called "the cultural industries", and the formal "arts" were only part of this expanding ecosystem.[28] The cultural industries were often called "popular" culture but it was only in part made by those who enjoyed it, as much of it was to be dominated by large corporate entities, something that has progressed in the last forty years. The calls by Williams, Hall, and others for creative freedom, for popular participation, and for democratic control were certainly made against the formal official arts system but they went beyond these. For them the whole system of cultural production and distribution, including the "cultural industries" and public media, was a key site of a political struggle for an expanding democratic, social citizenship.[29]

How that cultural citizenship would be secured and expanded in an era of expanded spending power, leisure time, and education was another question entirely. The standard policy tool was some combination of subsidy for the arts alongside some kind of popular education. This model – famously articulated by Keynes in his setting up of the Arts Council in 1945 – was increasingly restrictive. It tended to patrician elitism, failed to engage with new forms of popular culture, and could barely deal with the commercial cultural industries.

This was the context in which the 1979–86 Greater London Council "cultural industries" experiment took place, which combined a new kind of multicultural inclusion with innovative forms of local economic strategy. Ken Livingstone's GLC was "the post-1968 generation in politics"; it was "gloriously, explicitly anti-racist, anti-homophobic, anti-imperialist and anti-sexist; it was celebratory, creative and propagandistic. It loved murals, pop music, bright colours and clothes".[30] Theirs was a continuation of the urban politics of the post-'68 city, with its contestation of the top–down technocratic planning of city spaces and services in favour of the "right to the city", asserting "grassroots" control over "collective consumption" and social services.

Introduction: culture and democracy

The GLC experiment was short-lived, as much prefigurative inspiration – a "social democratic Paris Commune" – as definitive policy script.[31] Owen Hatherley suggests that "the radical economics of the Livingstone GLC attracted less attention than its brilliant propaganda and pageantry", its 1984 Festival at Country Hall "a performance of democracy and accessibility, a momentary vision of the city the London new left wanted to build".[32] Yet the cultural industries idea, which straddled the two, became one of the most influential of the GLC's "afterlives".

This radical experiment was quickly closed down by the Conservative government. Instead, as above, they embarked on the wholesale privatisation of culture, narrowing its purchase as an active site of democratic contestation and negotiation. Culture was to be a consumer economy like any other. In fact, in its exemplification of capitalism's ability to satisfy our infinite and ever-expanding desires, it became emblematic of a new kind of post-scarcity consumer society. Everything, all at once, everywhere. The world announced by Martin Amis' *Money*.

This book then seeks a return to the idea of cultural citizenship, and what this might mean in a period of social and political turbulence. How to pick up the threads of a conversation about democracy through culture and a democratic culture. We cannot return to a simple subsidy model, because this leaves the cultural industries out of the equation. The latter have grown apace in power and concentration, and the capacity of the state to regulate them has declined considerably. So too has their capacity to manage public media and other cultural systems. The public sphere itself has shattered into a thousand glass shards, blowing dangerously around the a-social media of platform capitalism. Securing social and cultural democracy at a time of stagnation, inequality, insecurity, and political volatility will not be an easy task. But first, at the very least, we have to accept this as something to which we should aspire.

The foundational approach

In seeking a way forward I turn, in this book, to the work of the Foundational Economy Collective (FEC), in whose *Manchester Capitalism* series this book appears. The group themselves are a loose collective of academics and activists, mostly in Europe, who come out of political economy and critical social science. Developing from around 2012, it is an evolving conversation, working through the damage done to social services by neoliberalism and how we might practically challenge the economic models which sustain it. In looking to reinvent a politics of the social foundations, they looked back to an older nineteenth-century municipal city building and a post-1945 state-led welfare state, recognising how neither of these were now possible. Moving forward would require a real confrontation with the damaged present as well as the reality of climate change.

The early foundational approach aligned with a broad current of work seeking to move us away from a neoliberal, and indeed neoclassical, economic framework towards a political economy grounded in social need. This chimed with the work in heterodox economics, most famously the work of Stephanie Kelton and Kate Raworth, and with a growing body of work making claims for new forms of public policy – universal basic income, universal basic services, job guarantees, public services, and so on – which prioritise social needs rather than profit-driven growth.[33] For the FEC, as with many others, these needs ought to be satisfied within our ecological limits. They are thus broadly aligned with "community" and "wellbeing", as well as "sustainable", "circular", and "post-growth" economic approaches which have all grown in appeal over the last decade.

The FEC combine this general orientation with a more robust approach derived from an historically informed political economy tradition, better able to deal with the political realities of the present. Their most recent work is concerned with the collapsing liveability of UK society. It gives a clear account of the political consensus underpinning the policy settings which have brought us to the current "quagmire", and which have proved incapable of extricating us from it.[34] Their alternative "foundational approach" is one with widely transferable basic principles and methods, but recognises that any intervention needs to be situated in context and grounded in actual practice. Rather than calling for a different "mindset" or for radical, overnight change, the FEC instead take an incremental approach to social innovation. Drawing on the work of French architects Lacaton and Vassal, they argue for "adaptive reuse which eschews rebuilding to a grand design and instead works round what exists".[35]

In their earlier work, the FEC identified the "foundational economy" as a combination of material infrastructure (such as water, roads, fibre-optics, food, and housing) and providential services (such as health, education, welfare, and public administration).[36] This is conjoined with a local, everyday economy of cafes, hairdressers, repair shops, cheap furniture, and so on, repeatedly overlooked by economic development agencies searching for high-tech, high-value industries financed by low-tax-induced inward investment. Their surveys since 2012 revealed that these "foundational" sectors accounted for between 60 and 70 per cent of local employment. The profit-driven, globally connected "transactional" economy accounted for the remaining 30 percent.

This model provided me with a basic heuristic for breaking down the "creative industries" employment aggregate, which was always more of an advocacy tool than a guide to actual intervention. Ever since the 1998 Mapping Document, it became de rigueur for all governments to aggregate the employment and "value-add" of the cultural sector so as to present a funding case under the rubric of this new growth industry. But as was widely known, the cultural sector is highly diverse in its funding, production methods, employment profile, global reach, and indeed motivation and purpose. A local library is not the same as a start-up games company; an actor-led theatre troupe not the same as a PR firm; a dance school not the same as a Hollywood-servicing CGI post-production company. Yet these were all combined under "creative industries" in a way that made little sense and provoked widespread confusion.

The FEC model, aimed at disaggregating national and regional GDP/Gross Value Added (GVA), provided a way to differentiate infrastructures like libraries and galleries, subsidised cultural services, and the everyday economies of record shops and fringe venues from transactional global corporations such as Disney, Universal Music, and Amazon.

Disaggregating the "creative industries" in this way provided the basis for a new kind of policy framework. In its early work, the FEC often ignored culture. In later work, the cultural dimension is included as part of the social foundations. Liveability is determined by the "three pillars" of disposable income, available services such as education and health, and "social infrastructure, such as parks and libraries".[37] This further suggests a new framework for cultural policy, where social infrastructure – that which makes social life possible – becomes a distinct part of basic needs.

A decade of austerity, stagnant wages, rising living costs and, of course, the Covid-19 pandemic, have led to a growing acknowledgement that states ought to provide, however incompletely and inadequately, for some basic social needs.[38] The failure of the "hidden hand" of free markets, trickle-down economics, and economic growth "lifting all boats" – as well as climate stress, cost-of-living inflation, and ballooning energy costs – has led to a "repoliticisation of needs". We can no longer rely on "market citizenship", in which higher wages (and cheap credit) would allow the purchase of such needs. The government must decide what are "essential needs", and thus it has become a political issue, one which overrides the logic of the market and justifies interventions within it. This does not just apply to "states of exception" such as the pandemic, but has also informed much "green new deal" thinking as well as other forms of state protectionism being adopted by the right.

How to identify essential needs and how best to satisfy or prioritise these in public policy is part of the "wellbeing" approach, and is of course the prime concern of the FEC. But where does culture sit with respect to essential needs? While some aspects might be conceded – parks and libraries, for example – many would argue that culture, especially in the form of art and entertainment, is a luxury. That is, something individually desired or chosen and thus to be satisfied by discretionary spending. Even if it might be accepted that some access to cultural expression might be essential, who is to decide on what is essential? This is even more pointed when it comes to cultural production – surely this is best left to the market, for who is going to say one thing is better than the other?

Though we might follow the FEC in identifying the social foundations and the place of culture within them, these questions around everyday local and large transactional global cultural activities require answering. If we cannot simply rely on the market to deliver our cultural needs, how exactly are we to organise cultural production and consumption in the contemporary world?

Reimagining the future

A core theme of this book is that one of the consequences of reducing culture to an industry has been to marginalise its contribution to important and transformative political projects. Culture-as-industry, if not dismissed as irrelevant, is deemed part of the problem. In response, I try to show what was as stake in the debates around culture and democracy which accelerated after 1945, and how the creative industries served to shut down these radical cultural politics. What, then, might the marginalisation of cultural policy and its reduction to economic benefits say about our wider ideas of citizenship, the common good, and the purpose of public policy? If there is a "void" or "hollow" at the centre of our democratic polity, what role did culture's marginalisation play in this, and what role might culture have in overcoming this destabilising democratic deficit?[39]

The absorption of the cultural sector into neoliberal policy-making, and its integration into the economic imaginary of the knowledge economy, is something I discuss in Chapters 1 and 2. This capitulation has often been characterised as the inevitable result of a "new left" or post-'68 cultural politics which carried within it the seeds of neoliberalism. The "artistic critique" of the *soixante-huitards* – the demand for meaningful, non-alienated work – resulted in the networked neoliberal capitalism of the 1980s.[40] The countercultural boomers became the yuppies and the bourgeois bohemians of the 1980s and '90s.[41] The radical cultures of the 1960s merely cleared away the old cultural ground for a virulent market-first neoliberalism freed from the neo-conservative shibboleths of flag, family, and religion.

Some dismiss radical cultural politics as a countercultural "revolution in the head" incapable of real political action. Or, as with punk rock and later rave scenes, just something you did when young and gave up in adulthood. Others charge that culture was all that was left after political defeat in the 1980s, capped by the collapse of communism and the "end of history". The cultural struggle was compensation, and diversion from the brutal reality of the defeat of the left.[42]

Little wonder that the radical cultural politics of the 1970s and early '80s dissolved into hedonism and nihilism, identity politics, and the narcissism of small differences. Recklessly attacking all the social foundations, so critics on the left and right charge, resulted in a disastrously weakened working-class culture and social institutions that no longer had any authority.[43] Everything, all the time, everywhere left us with a post-truth, post-meaning, hyper-commercial culture.[44]

While these critiques contain elements of truth, in this book I will approach the radical cultural politics that took off in the late 1950s as a crucial, unfinished, interrupted struggle over the nature of contemporary democratic society. My focus is on how the "creative industries" buried these questions under the kind of positivist acceptance of the status quo that Mark Fisher called "capitalist realism". The book tries to reopen these debates by asking what is the role of culture in our contemporary democracies, and what purpose is served by public policy for culture?

Part of the answers to these questions will be to establish culture as an essential form of democratic citizenship, but I will also suggest that without the voice of culture any attempt to go beyond the present will be hobbled.

One of the devastating consequences of the neoliberal epoch has been the inability to answer questions of value which fall outside of market mechanisms. This applies to questions of social need and the provision of care; the environment in which we live; the delivery of public services; and the functioning of culture which sustains us. Culture, though a distinct concept born of modern capitalism, was also a dissenting voice against its utilitarian reductions. Its absorption into a new kind of creative capitalism has thus been highly destructive.

In the Western tradition, since early modernity, a key function of art has been to imagine and create anew. As Francis Fukuyama famously argued, the triumph of liberal democratic capitalism meant the rule of "economic calculation, the endless solving of technical problems, environmental concerns and the satisfaction of sophisticated consumer demands". After the end of history, "there will be neither art nor philosophy, just the perpetual caretaking of the museum of human history".[45] As many contemporary critics have suggested, our culture has become circular and repetitive as our future has evaporated – "retromania".[46]

Equally, cultivation – one of culture's central traits, built into the word itself – connects past and future generations. It preserves and it hands down. Cultural economist David Throsby suggests that the Sustainable Development Goals were fully imbued with economic rationalism and had no space to accommodate culture. Little wonder, then, that they had trouble with measuring how much we owe to the future. As the members of Kim Stanley Robinson's *Ministry of the Future* quickly realised, the "future discount rates", whereby economists assess the claims of future generations on that of the present, soon dissolve into incalculability.[47]

But culture can, and must, think about the future – just as it must think about the past – and do so beyond the realms of economic calculation. The book ends by arguing that, beyond its specific contribution to the fullness of democratic citizenship, the recognition of culture's claims within public policy is itself a step beyond the neoliberal end of history. It is an essential component of our collective reimagining of the future.

Outline of this book

In Chapter 1, "Creative industries", I outline the policy context for Chris Smith's adoption of "creative industries", a folding of art and popular culture into a dynamic new knowledge economy. It solved both the problem of justifying public subsidy for the arts and used the energy of popular culture to promote a vision of meaningful jobs in a post-industrial economy. I suggest that, despite the terminology, it could never be an industrial strategy, as New Labour had neither the capacity nor the inclination to engage in such a strategy. Rather it relied on weak "factors of production" – education, skills, creativity, supportive "creative milieux" – to facilitate a "creative class" which "carried the means of production in its heads". I discuss the definitional confusion that has dogged the term since its inception but note how its emphasis on creativity cancelled out the distinct contribution of art and culture. In the meantime, actually existing cultural industries were allowed a free hand, accelerated by the new "platform capitalism", resulting in global monopolies

and concentration, and a definitive shift in power and remuneration between these companies and the creative class who
work in them.

Chapter 2, "Culture goes missing", discusses the current
situation of "polycrisis" as neoliberal capitalism gives way to a
period of uncertainty and insecurity. That we are undergoing
some sort of crisis is generally accepted – everywhere but in the
cultural sector. It has pinned its hopes on a "build back better"
recovery without questioning the neoliberal framing of the creative industries, whose basic tenets are elsewhere so contested. I
use feminist social theorist Nancy Fraser to argue that the current crisis is not just "economic" but involves the ecological,
political, and social systems on which capitalism relies, even
as it disavows and undermines them. Using the image of the
ouroboros, the serpent that eats its own tail, Fraser outlines an
approach to the current crisis of capitalism which, I argue, can
be applied to culture. I ask, if culture is part of the social system
in crisis, what does that look like? But also, what will it take for
culture to acknowledge its implication in the current crisis, and
to start to find a way out?

In Chapter 3, "Necessity or luxury?", I confront the common idea that culture is a luxury, something to be enjoyed after
the essentials have been met. Alternatively, I suggest culture is
part of the social foundations, an essential part of human life.
To make the argument I suggest that the opposition of essential
needs and inessential wants is a false one, and that we have to
expand our understanding of human need to encompass aspirations to meaning, belonging, and freedom which are fundamental. I suggest that art and culture articulate these aspirations
to meaning making and to freedom, and that as such they have
been recognised as basic human rights. I draw on the work of

Amartya Sen and Martha Nussbaum to talk about capabilities, both the right and the effective means to engage fully in art and culture. However, I suggest that this is also a collective capacity. It is crucial to our democracy and needs to be guaranteed socially and politically. But it also forms a systemic function, part of our collective ability to keep coherent and to connect the past to the future. Without such an extended connected conversation, it is impossible to reimagine a different future.

Chapter 4, "Culture and the social foundations", I outline in detail the foundational approach discussed above, and show how it can be applied to the cultural sector. I introduce both the FEC's zonal account of the economy, and the more recent concept of liveability. The zonal approach allows us to disaggregate the complex structure of the cultural sector, which extends from the local and publicly subsidised to the global and commercial. Culture is distributed across the different economic zones in ways that can provide important heuristics for cultural politics. I outline the material and service foundations of culture, those usually publicly provided, such as libraries, theatres, concert venues, and parks. There are also "overlooked" or "everyday" small-scale local economies of small book and record shops, venues in bars or cafes, indie galleries and art spaces – all those elements which make for the vibrancy of towns and cities. Finally, there is the "transactional", fully commercial sector of big cinema chains, ticketing agencies, streaming services, and the global cultural industry outfits such as Disney or Universal. Creative industries models suggest the best policy is to move as much as possible from the foundational and everyday to the commercial. We might want to start moving it back in the other direction.

In Chapter 5, "Cultural infrastructures", I build on the disaggregated, zonal schema of the economy while engaging with the recent FEC work on the social infrastructure as a crucial element of liveability. In addition to disposable household income and foundational services, the FEC see the social infrastructure – sociability, exercise, creative expression – as one of the three pillars of liveability. In a similar vein I argue for a cultural infrastructure approach, one which is both part of that social infrastructure, and which contributes its own crucial and conceptually distinct elements. As with the social infrastructure and foundational services, the cultural infrastructure has an immediate presence in the lives of households and local communities, sustained by complex systems of delivery, finance, skills, training, and research. Similar to education and communications, health, and social welfare, the cultural infrastructure provides society-wide functions without which our society could not function. And, as with these other social systems, cultural infrastructures now face serious erosion, as inequalities, budget austerity, deregulated planning, and the distortions of global platform monopolies have combined to undermine them.

I outline a rationale for cultural policy as a crucial dimension of individual autonomy and democratic citizenship. I first look at the household as a centre of cultural consumption and how the cultural infrastructure is crucial to sustaining their participation in culture as collective consumption. Then I examine the "hard" cultural infrastructure of the built environment and its utility "pipes", followed by the "soft" cultural infrastructure. I suggest that these infrastructures sustain the capacity for individual autonomy and freedom essential for any democracy, as well as connecting us to our pasts and opening up spaces for reimagining the future.

The final chapter, "Culture and economy", argues that any cultural policy must address both the small-scale local economies and the large-scale corporate cultural industries. To avoid these questions is to shrink culture to a residual "market failure" publicly subsidised sector rather than a society-wide system. I make the case for a more robust assertion of the role of state funding for culture as part of local development, and how we might reframe this social investment. This also requires strong protection for cultural jobs, both within formal employment and amongst the independent freelance sector. I discuss issues around universal basic income, but suggest, ultimately, that universal basic services, job guarantees, and social investment are the way forward.

I then address the question of the everyday local economies of small and independent businesses. These were addressed by the Greater London Council, whose "SME approach" was very influential in New Labour's adoption of cultural and creative industries. I suggest this is no longer viable, and we have to reframe these more as embedded economies within a broader commons that requires careful nurturing as both social and economic outcomes. Ideas of the commons, of co-operatives, community wealth building, and citizen platforms have become far more relevant to the cultural sector than SME (small to medium enterprise) start-up models.

The core challenge, however, is the large-scale transactional, the global platform driven behemoths that now control large parts of the world's cultural system. I describe how older cultural industry models identified in the 1980s and 1990s have been spliced with a new franchise or rentier model in accordance with wider tendencies in contemporary capitalism. I suggest ways in which we can begin to deal with these challenges, but ultimately this will require a collective effort which, at the moment, seems some way off. But recognising the problem is key.

Culture is not an industry

Throughout the book I try to follow the FEC's idea of "adaptive reuse", and seek a pragmatic starting point. As Deng Xiaoping suggested, to cross the river stone by stone requires a tentative, probing technique. But a vision of the further shore is also essential. The vision might not be some shining city on the hill but simply a knowledge that culture is essential to us, that "survival is not sufficient", and that we'll need it even in the ruins.[48]

1

Creative industries

Introduction

In 1997, Chris Smith, head of the newly established Department of Culture, Media and Sport (DCMS), prepared to get approval for his new budget. Minister of the smallest of government departments, Smith needed to convince the Treasury hard heads to reverse two decades of cuts to arts and culture. His bright new research team suggested rebranding the whole thing as "creative industries". A seemingly random decision, the replacement of "culture" by "creative" perfectly suited the moment. Culture, as coupled with "art", was inevitably seen as elitist. Creativity was democratic, modern, energetic. The cultural sector, officially recognised as an "industry", could now bellow more confidently that it, too, was economically productive.

The "creative industries" gave art and culture a powerful new policy relevance, one that seemed to open the door to political influence and resources. The "creative industries" would provide jobs to replace those lost in manufacturing and, hitched now to a new "knowledge economy", opened up exciting vistas of social mobility and meaningful work, leaving the factories behind. The core justification for art and culture was no longer as part of some social democratic citizenship (however conceived) but as a driver of post-industrial economic modernisation.

In this chapter I'll show how this came about, and the damage wrought by its failure. I argue that it was an essential part of a new kind of "soft" neoliberalism developed by ex-social democratic parties in the 1990s. They recognised the social upheavals and fragmentation caused by neoliberalism, the rise in unemployment and cuts to welfare, and sought to ameliorate this by better policies for social inclusion and mobility. Promoting creative subjects able to take advantage of the knowledge economy, providing good jobs to pay for services, was a part of that "market citizenship" which New Labour took over from the Conservatives.

It was not about "bean counters" imposing economic targets on culture. That had been going on for years. This was different. The positive embrace of culture's economic contribution, one that was one step ahead of the zeitgeist rather than hanging on its coat-tails, was a game changer. In the form of "creative industries", culture bought into a whole new imaginary – global, cosmopolitan, entrepreneurial, forward-looking – dropping its long-standing aversion to "the economy" in favour of win–win. What was good for culture was good for the economy. And vice versa. It was a complete de-politicisation of culture.

Will Davies called neoliberalism "the disenchantment of politics by economics".[1] If that is so, then the creative industries provided the affective "buy-in" to a new economic landscape in which knowledge, creativity, culture, aesthetics, and those that wielded these, would be at a premium. People talked about the "culturalisation of the economy", where aesthetics was to be as important as hide-bound calculation, "tee-shirts" as powerful as "suits".[2] The utopian appeal was real. The creative industries would provide good, well-paid, meaningful jobs driven by an increasingly educated workforce and delivered by a rapidly expanding higher education sector. The "creative class" would be the beneficiaries of a new kind of "creative economy" in which "progressives" now carried the torch of history's advance. Unlike "art", which seemed a minority pursuit, everyone had creativity, if they just looked hard enough. The "creative industries", part of a wider "creative economy", were the exciting part of a new knowledge economy which, in an era of mass higher education, could be felt as the warp and weft of a new democratic society.

But the creative industries agenda, initially carrying all before it, was to prove a damaging failure. The jobs it promised never materialised, the statistics kept afloat by adding software, or industrial design, or picking out "creatives" in other sectors to add to the agglomerate. The most successful creative places turned out to be the old successful places, London outstripping its nearest UK rival Manchester by a factor of eight. The cultural sector certainly managed to convince itself but the "bean counters" had other ideas. The contrast between extravagant claims for creative industries as part of an informatic Kondratiev wave, and the paucity of resources actually given over to its development, was stark. This was the case even before the "industry" was effectively abandoned to its fate in the Covid-19 pandemic. Despite the endless statistical *trompe l'œil* placed before it, most government economists saw art and culture as a consumer economy like any other, needing to pay its way, rather than an emergent industry behemoth requiring massive investment.

Culture is not an industry

As a concept it was incoherent. After a quarter-century it is still unable to convincingly nail down a definition for a sector whose core characteristic – creativity – was effectively ubiquitous. What was not creative? As the borders of the "creative economy" expanded to the horizon – biotech, business consulting, rocket engineering – the cultural sector tried to place itself at the creative heart. Art as R&D, culture as the groundwater of innovation. But "creativity", like the pineal gland that philosophers thought connected mind and body, was where the values of art and culture were made available to economic reason, reduced to a measurable input into the commercialisation process.

Hence the endless series of mapping documents and "hot takes" on how art and creativity relate to innovation, to regeneration, to development. Hence the infinite play of interchangeable concepts – creative, cultural, creative and cultural, digital and creative, art and createch – but never settling on a clear meaning. What other industrial sector spends half of its time trying to describe what it is? But that's because it can't ever be an industry; it is an amorphous set of activities and institutions, some commercial, some public services, some not for profit, all roped together by the statistics provided by an ever-expanding cultural consultancy sector.

The grand irony is that "creative industries" was announced at the same moment New Labour abandoned any aspirations to industrial strategy, the tools for which had anyway long been discarded by the Conservatives. So the government's creative industries strategy was mainly about the education and nurturing of "individual creativity, skill, and talent" which, as per its own definition, have the "potential for wealth and job creation through the generation and exploitation of intellectual property".[3] If, as Richard Florida claimed, the "creative class" "carried the means of production in their heads", all we had to do was provide them with a supportive milieu in which their creativity could be let free.[4]

Meanwhile, the creative industries agenda had little to say about actual cultural industries, those large-scale, global corporations which were to be joined by an emergent "platform capitalism" in a process of ever-accelerating global monopoly. The actual cultural industries – live and recorded music, films, games, books, TV and radio, newspapers and magazines, commercial theatre, and so on – were given over almost entirely to commercial operation. The system of publicly owned and regulated commercial broadcasting was effectively dismantled. The BBC, like the National Health Service , acted as a well-loved façade behind which most of its activities were commercially outsourced, its independence whittled away to almost nothing. The new digital platform companies were soon busy privatising the early internet's promise of a new global public sphere and gobbling up large chunks of the "heritage" cultural industries.

While consultants and statisticians played endlessly with definitions and mapping methods, the actually existing cultural industries took increasing control over the creative work process, the intellectual property regimes, and the employment conditions of their workers. The result has been a diminishing of the creative autonomy, remuneration, and security of cultural workers, resulting in high levels of "proletarianisation" and precarity. This was combined with the wider impact of increasing educational debt and lack of affordable housing, healthcare, and social insurance. And despite their gamble on the rhetoric of creative industries, art and culture are now more marginalised in public policy than at any time since the 1980s.

The creative industries agenda has failed on its own terms, the much-vaunted employment effects woefully small. But the real damage has been the hollowing out of the language of culture by that of economics. It sold itself to an agenda that only it really believed in. It tried to get itself to the top table of political influence but found it could only talk an econometric language, leaving its real value marginalised and degraded. How else to explain culture's treatment in the pandemic, and the funding cuts that have followed? When it makes the front pages, it is only too clear that nobody – really, nobody – has any idea any more how to make an argument in its favour.

Worse, cultural sector advocates cleave to a neoliberal economics which is now looking more redundant by the day. The knowledge economy might be storming ahead, but the robots are now eating culture's lunch. There's a purported shift to a new industrial strategy driven by the green transition and relocalising jobs, but the cultural industries are not any part of this. They are the fading memory of the glorious 1990s, an age of global optimism long gone, kept alive by development agencies and academics looking for "industry impact". It's now time to divest and seek a new social contract for art and culture.

This is the focus of this chapter. In the next chapter I will outline the new landscape in which any new vision for culture most unfold.

From impact to industry

The "creative industries" brand was never about industrial strategy, but rather a clever piece of arts advocacy that got out of hand. Its roots lay less in the radical experiment of the

Greater London Council than an arts and cultural sector that badly needed a rationale for continued government funding. The New Labour government of 1997 was committed both to funding the arts – a core element of its anti-Conservative rhetoric – and to support a buoyant popular culture, which, in the form of "Cool Britannia", seemed to give it the imprimatur of the zeitgeist. "Creative industries" allowed the new Department of Culture, Media and Sport to embrace both, wrapping art and popular culture in a dynamic new industrial sector which would reinvent a post-industrial "UK PLC" as a new "creative workshop of the world". Unfortunately, it did so while accepting Thatcher's foundational belief that the state should abandon any industrial strategy and consequently jettisoned the policy levers and capacities developed in post-war Britain.[5] Creative industries arrived at the very moment industrial policy was finally declared dead.

The creative industries idea was itself a response to a neoliberal critique of public policy for culture which began in the 1970s. Its basic thrust was that – contrary to the beliefs of older cultural conservatives – art was a consumer economy like any other. In 1976, Gough Whitlam, who had just established the Australia Council for the Arts, asked the Industrial Assistance Commission for a justification for public arts subsidy. The brutal reply was that there were no such grounds:

> [The] performing arts … provide psychological, emotional or intellectual stimulation and other forms of personal satisfaction to individuals. However, [these] … do not, of themselves, justify public assistance … There are many other activities which serve the same purpose and … could have equal claim to public assistance. These include reading and a growing number of alternatives such as cinema, foreign travel, and sporting and recreational

facilities which compete for the individual's resources ... It appears self-evident that once government assistance can be claimed for entertainment, the drain on resources would be endless.[6]

The arts, just like anything else, should be left to the individual judgement of the sovereign consumer, their choices aggregated by a market best left to do its own thing.

By the 1980s, this had become the default position of "dry" neoliberalism. According to this view, the arts did not, of themselves, justify public assistance. In a political context in which the state was deemed less efficient than the private sector, by the 1980s all public spending was expected to achieve more with less. As Ronald Reagan had it in his 1981 inaugural address, "government is not the solution to our problem, government is the problem". It was inevitable that public funding for culture would be cut, and as much of its activity as possible shifted into the private sector. In consequence, the remaining cultural organisations had to be more "business-like" in their requests for funding.

The use of economic metrics to make the case for arts and cultural funding began in the early 1980s. "Impact studies" tried to show how such funding was not just about taxpayer subsidy but "investment" which generated economic activity. John Myerscough got his fifteen minutes of fame with his use of "multiplier effects", where public subsidy was shown to create employment along with direct (tickets, interval drinks) and indirect (car parks, local restaurants) consumer spending.[7] Cultural institutions and precincts, events and festivals, even yearlong events such as Glasgow's 1990 City of Culture, could be shown to be good value for money. This argument gave a pointed quantitative edge to more diffuse claims for the role of culture in urban regeneration – attracting tourism, inward investment, and "mobile talent" to hard-up de-industrialising cities.

As New Public Management (NPM) made real inroads into public administration from the 1980s, such metrics became compulsory as part of any public funding.[8] NPM was the term given to the imposition of quasi-market indicators on public services, sending quasi-price signals to "public servants" to induce market-like, and thus more efficient, individual-rational behaviour. As has been extensively documented, this has been responsible as much as anything for the hollowing out of both the idea and practice of public service in the last forty years. These indicators were quantitative measures against which individual officers and departmental performance could be judged, and the "contract" between the public service and its customers could be deemed to have been fulfilled or not.

For the cultural sector, the challenge was one of quantification, anathema to its traditional forms of appraisal.[9] The requirement to show value for money, in terms of efficiency of spending and delivery of the implied contract with its customers, spread downward through the arts councils and local authorities to the cultural institutions, and eventually to all the artists applying for and acquitting their grants. This became ever more punitive, for what could be more gratuitous than public spending on art?

It also spawned a whole new genre of "cultural consultants", a classic example of what David Graeber famously called "bullshit jobs".[10] These new jobs began as a cottage industry, with self-taught ex-artists, cultural activists, local government officials, and academics (*mea culpa*) making it up as they went. Much of this, especially at the quantitative end, is now routinely

43

done by the "big four" accountancy firms, where so many bullshit jobs eventually end up.

This was a process in which the "social licence" of culture was shifted from its contribution to citizenship to its contribution to the economy. The 1980s saw in the new discipline of "cultural economics", which sought to provide a robust defence of public funding for culture by the application of orthodox neoclassical concepts rather than waffly hand-waving. Those coming from this discipline came not to bury the arts but to praise them, only now in the grown-up language of economics. Only in this way could they get government to take them seriously.

Cultural economists were concerned both to investigate the economics of arts organisations – what was soon to be called their "business model" – and to develop more "rational" legitimations for, and mechanisms of, public subsidy. They accepted the central premise that art was about individual satisfaction, but, they argued, it was more complex than that as there were "externalities" – those impacts or costs falling outside the economic transaction proper. Rather than negative externalities like pollution, cultural economics is mostly concerned with positive externalities, the benefits that come even though they are not formally part of the provider–consumer contract. Yes, the individual consumer gains whatever "intrinsic" satisfaction from the concert or play or book, but there are other benefits which are more difficult to measure. These might be building social cohesion, encouraging education and training, reducing crime, making hospitals better places, or simply stimulating a wider dynamic of creativity.

So began the impact taxonomy years. David Throsby identified multiple non-economic values for art and culture.

François Matarasso itemised the various social impacts of art participation. John Holden developed an intrinsic-instrumental-institutional heuristic, which folded in consumer satisfaction, various social impacts, and the upkeep of the institutions within which cultural production and consumption took place.[11] A new sub-discipline of audience development began, in which older ideas of democratic citizenship, radical pedagogies, community art, and anti-institutional avant-gardism were applied to helping publicly funded companies reach out beyond their actual audiences to a wider, more diverse demographic.[12] Finding ways to classify and measure all these non-economic impacts reached some kind of baroque pinnacle in the online "dashboard" of *Culture Counts*, a whole set of indicators and feedback loops which organisations could use to show how they were fulfilling their contracted service delivery to their real and aspirational publics, often in "real time".[13]

This proliferating apparatus of cultural value accountancy, with its apparatuses of multiple bottom lines, contingent value, and audience evaluation studies, has hollowed out our societal sense of the value of culture, replacing it with the death rattle of statistics. This now involves large amounts of unpaid labour from grant applicants while absorbing the resources of larger organisations who also splash out on exorbitant fees for a PwC or Deloitte "killer stat". But, at the time, these kinds of arguments had little traction outside the internal game of arts funding.

The idea of "creative industries" was about more than socio-economic impact. It allowed culture to take a more active role in a new economic imaginary, a knowledge economy in which creativity would be at a premium.

45

Culture-as-industry

The creative industries solved a political problem. While cultural consultants dealt with bottom lines and technical accountancy, the New Labour government was concerned with a broader political narrative in which art and culture could receive public funding without being seen as elitist.

Chris Smith – along with many Labour politicians, kicking their heels in eighteen years of opposition – made repeated visits to Australia, where Labor had been the dominant party since the 1970s. Having transformed an historical social democracy into a neoliberal polity that yet seemed to have a place for unions and welfare, it was attractive to a New Labour ready to reclaim power. The latter had accepted most of Thatcher's reforms but wanted to assert the social needs of its core constituency within them. A social safety net, education and training, pathways to inclusion, and, above all, jobs. Good wages would enable people to satisfy their social needs as a form of choice, not "standardised", "top-down" public provision but "market citizenship".[14]

Smith's 1998 book *Creative Britain* was inspired by Australian Prime Minister Paul Keating's 1994 cultural policy document *Creative Nation*.[15] "Culture creates wealth" was one of its claims, and many have seen (rightly) its imbrication of culture and economy as accelerating culture's instrumentalisation, subsuming arts organisations into standard business and marketing discourses, and promoting the rise and rise of business leaders and corporate lawyers within arts policy bodies and boards.[16] *Creative Nation* is also credited with introducing the idea of art and culture as industries, but this has been retrospectively overemphasised.[17] The modernising vision which energised *Creative Nation* came less from its promotion of any cultural industries strategy per se than its rhetorical embrace of a democratic-popular, commercial culture. It was part of a renewed, forward-looking identity for a modern multicultural Australia stepping out from its colonial heritage and seeking a new place in an exciting Asia-Pacific world.

This modernising vision animated Smith's – and New Labour's – cultural project. As their think-tank, Demos, had it, a backwards-looking, heritage-bound country needs a new identity, a "rebranding" in which culture led the way. "National success in creative industries like music, design and architecture has combined with steady economic growth to dispel much of the introversion and pessimism of recent decades. 'Cool Britannia' sets the pace in everything from food to fashion."[18]

The creative industries was so attractive because it embraced commercial, market-driven popular culture as democratic while promising meritocratic jobs for post-industrial workers now being told to go to university (drop your toolbox and pick up your laptop). Smith's cultural vision was one of meritocratic achievement: "access, excellence, and education", three words to be emblazoned across the grand portico of the arts and culture sector for the next two decades. But it was the commercial sector, the rebranded "creative industries", that were to provide the real democratic energy. As a prescient opinion piece in the *Irish Times* suggested:

> While Chris Smith's mini-revolution of placing the arts within a broader economic/industrial agenda may yet be the worst thing for the arts since Margaret Thatcher's slash 'n' burn approach in the 1980s, he is to be applauded for bringing an element of democracy to arts awareness and funding. It may only be symbolic but someone who can mention Rachel Whiteread and Massive Attack in the same sentence as Opera North is doing something half-right. The danger, though, lies in confusing price with value.[19]

47

The value articulated by Smith was that of a broad, open democratic culture, but the engine and guarantor of that cultural democracy was the market, the domain of price.

This was precisely the question that those pursuing the cultural industries approach had set out to confront in the 1970s: how to promote a democratic cultural policy in an age of the mass commercial production of that culture? Those in the GLC had concluded it would require intervention into the organisation of cultural production. This was not something New Labour would countenance – markets, not governments, were the best way to deliver democratic choice. Democracy would come from access to cultural consumer goods, but these would be produced by a new democratically expanded workforce.

Two aspects distinguished Keating and Smith's visions from that of standard conservative approaches to culture as a commercial consumer market. First was their belief in the intrinsically progressive nature of art and culture. A thriving cultural sector would naturally favour their modernising projects, becoming emblematic of them. This was a nod to the nostrums of cultural modernity, avant-garde and popular, whose rebellious strands had now been woven into the fabric of a new economic reality. It underpinned the second aspect, that democratic inclusion was to come in the form of jobs. The growth of the creative industries sector would spearhead a modern, progressive kind of nation, providing meaningful, well-paid jobs, from which creativity would flow more widely across the economy and society.

> Dubbed "post-Fordist socialism" by [Noel] Thompson, the premise of many creative industry support initiatives was that the kind of work they provided was inherently progressive, combining

demand for high skills with notions of self-expression and deter-
mination, in a workplace that was no longer hierarchical, but collaborative, flexible, even fun.[20]

Australian Labor and UK New Labour were both understand-
ably concerned with the challenges facing their traditional
working-class constituencies, many of whom had lost secure,
long-term industrial jobs. The potential for the cultural industries to provide replacement jobs had long roots, as we saw in
the last chapter. But the idea of the creative industries related to
more than just jobs in a newly expanded cultural sector – films,
or music, or graphics; it inserted culture into a much wider narrative of epochal change, of a knowledge economy in which
"creativity" was to be a privileged driver.

Neoliberalism and the new economy

This appeal to the radical popular inheritance of culture was
strengthened by a new kind of argument. No longer looking to
the post-war rise of democratic citizenship, culture's power was
part of a wider "new" or knowledge economy in which stores
of cultural knowledge, and the creativity this facilitated, were
now a direct economic asset.

Ideas of the knowledge economy began in the 1960s as science and technology-led innovation were seen as the driving
force of economic growth and modernisation. A key muta-
tion occurred in the 1970s as countercultural ideas challenged
the dominance of established science and technology institutions over knowledge and innovation. The evolution of countercultural libertarian ideas into the ethos of Silicon Valley
tech-entrepreneurialism – the "Californian Ideology" – is now

well-aired.[21] Emblematic is Ridley Scott's 1984 Super Bowl advert for Apple. Here, grey-suited IBM workers are presented as an Orwellian, Soviet bloc-like slave labour force soon to be liberated by a colourful female runner wielding a hammer. The new Macintosh – personal computing taken out of the hands of the mainframe operators – would show us why "1984 won't be like 1984".[22]

The "new" or knowledge economy underlay the wave of neoliberal reforms led by social democratic parties in the 1990s and early 2000s. In very different contexts, Paul Keating, Bill Clinton, Tony Blair, Gerhart Schröder, and others (such as Lula da Silva in Brazil) saw themselves as economic, social, and cultural modernisers of their respective parties and countries.[23] They wanted to provide social protection for their traditional supporters against the harshness of free market policies, but in the process adopted many of the key tenets of neoliberalism. In this sense, they acted as a kind of "soft shell" for the extension of neoliberalism, preparing the way for subsequent post-2008 "austerity" policies.[24] But "soft" neoliberalism did more than simply ease the social impact of market-facing reforms. It would not just extend markets, but also create new subjects, productive and governable.

If the collapse of traditional industries and communal identities across the 1980s and 1990s posed serious questions for governance and social cohesion, it also promised new productive energies. Crucial in this was the ability of the "soft" neoliberal programme to adapt and enlist the countercultural movements of the 1960s and 1970s. In this way, neoliberalism's transformative programme could also be experienced as a kind of liberation from many of the oppressive hierarchies, restricted social identities, and repressed emotions of the industrial era. The

kinds of entrepreneurial subjects and institutional frameworks
required for the creative economy demand far more than the
classic Hayekian nostrum of securing strong private property
rights, free markets, and free trade. The neoliberal programme
involved not just markets but also new subjects, and these were
thought of together as a legal-constitutional order underpinned
by shared values or, we might say, a shared culture.

This strand of neoliberalism had what Sam Binkley calls an
"emotional logic", which involved new relations to the self, to
the emotions, and to forms of sociability.

> Through the minimisation of any plausible collectivist alterna-
> tive to market autonomy, the subject of neoliberalism is one that
> is induced to take up a certain instrumental relation to her own
> capacities and aptitudes, to produce on her own accord those
> qualities of self that will enable her to compete successfully in a
> social world reimagined in the image of a market.[25]

The knowledge economy would progress out of these shared
cultural values, which "soft" neoliberal parties sought to secure.

As with neoliberalism more generally, a range of different
forces were at play in Australia, the US, the UK, Germany,
and Brazil. From the techno-libertarianism of the "Californian
Ideology" to UK pop cultures, from European post-1968 coun-
tercultures to deep-rooted Latin American popular cultural radicalism: this new "imaginary" adapted multiple cultural tropes
required for subjects in a new kind of economy – networked,
knowledge-based, entrepreneurial, "creative".

While conservatives had considered "the sixties" a major
cultural threat to capitalism – eroding family values, spreading anti-authoritarian and anti-capitalist ideas, and promoting
hedonistic consumption at the expense of productive work – its

ideas became central to a revitalised post-industrial capitalism over the 1980s and 1990s. The "revenge" of "bourgeois bohemians", the rise of the "creative class", the youthful techno-modernism of the "start-ups" – all pointed to a transformative cultural, as well as economic, imaginary.[26]

"Soft" neoliberalism – "neoliberalism 2.0" as we might call it – drew on a form of utopian promise derived from the 1960s. Rather than a sign of the decadence or affluent hedonist unravelling, these post-sixties creative subjects would give the liberal democratic West its global competitive advantage.

The counterculture expanded the conception of innovation, suggesting something more was needed than the ability to routinely "process knowledge and manipulate symbols". It needed to operate at the very edge of taken-for-granted rules. By the early 1990s, management and business literature began to promote working "outside the box", systematically courting chaos and disorder, using para-rational or intuitive knowledge, and celebrating mavericks and outsiders.[27] These new ways of working drew on the unorthodox and unpredictable practices of artists and "crazy" scientists. The newly emergent notion of "creativity" within mainstream business language was parasitic on these exemplary figures. This was not just in the "blue skies" research labs but out on the street. There was a new kind of entrepreneur, one who attracted to themselves the cultural capital previously reserved for the artist as social rebel.

In the 1980s, Joseph Schumpeter's entrepreneur had made a comeback. Schumpeter had argued back in the 1940s that capitalism (unlike socialism) was able to reinvent itself and restore its profitability via the entrepreneur who opened up new markets for new products, often at the expense of the dominant industrial corporations. Thatcher and Reagan eulogised the entrepreneur as the "self-made man", setting dynamic, "hungry" small businesses against ossified state corporatism and Fordism's "organisation man". It was an imaginary return to an older "grassroots", corner-store capitalism.

The counterculture gave a rebel colour to this figure of a middle-England, middle-American small business person, one who was more likely to be found at rock concerts and art happenings than in the local golf club. Entrepreneurs were outsiders working the edges of the system, pushing its boundaries, charting new territories, confronting hoary ways of thinking and doing. Schumpeter's vision of "creative destruction", where "disruptive" entrepreneurs overturned the existing business order, increasingly crossed over into cultural modernism, with its iconoclastic, shock-of-the-new obsession with innovation.[28] During the 1980s, entrepreneurs and artists came to occupy an adjacent space in new management literature, society's outriders and productive rebels who might glimpse the outline of the future. Marshall McLuhan had written in 1964:

> The power of the arts to anticipate future social and technological developments, by a generation and more, has long been recognised. In this century Ezra Pound called the artist "the antennae of the race". Art as radar acts as "an early alarm system," as it were, enabling us to discover social and psychic targets in lots of time to prepare to cope with them.[29]

By the 1990s, this visionary ability was becoming a resource to be harnessed to a knowledge economy that would remain competitive only if it engaged in systemic innovation. Looking enviously at the rise of the Silicon Valley tech sector in the 1990s, New Labour think-tank Demos ditched European "stakeholder capitalism", with its socially embedded markets and commitment to labour consultation, and adopted the free-wheeling start-up entrepreneurialism of the dot-com boom.[30] The creative industries idea blossomed from this transplanted imaginary.

This new "economic imaginary" became part of the everyday toolkit of arts advocates, representing as they did a creative practice now working at the cutting edge, with science and economics. Creative education, the source of our future competitiveness, now made economic good sense. Artists ran leadership training in the boardroom, and tech company execs looked to Miles Davis or David Bowie as role models.

The creative industries were at the heart of the new economy, and not just in the transferable skills that artists now displayed. For consumption itself had made a transition from standardised mass products to a "post-materialism" in which the aesthetic, symbolic, and experiential dimension provided the basis by which individual identities could be created and amended. Gough Whitlam's Industries Assistance Commission might have dismissed these as just another recreational good but, in this view, they represented a new kind of production–consumption relationship. Education, leisure, and disposable income were expanding, while the desire to acquire material stuff was quickly sated. One could consume too many fridges, but not too many films, books, CDs, or indeed "experiences". Identifying and commodifying these experiences, value created over and above any direct utility, drove a whole slew of marketing consultancies, bullshit jobs par excellence. However one looked at it, the cultural consumption sector was set to grow, and to provide a source of employment and competitive advantage for "advanced" economies.

Abraham Maslow's famous "hierarchy of needs" was invoked to argue that affluent societies had satisfied the basic needs and so could now move to "self-actualisation" through more artistic, cultural, and spiritual activities. To supply such intangible, elusive commodities required a new kind of knowledge worker. These possessed highly personalised, embodied knowledges which could not be easily transferred or codified. These knowledges were not just technical, but drew on embodied experience and a relationship to both product and consumer that was emotional and aesthetic. This "cognitive capitalism" thus involved specialised tacit knowledge, accumulated and shared within the complex ecosystems typically found in larger urban agglomerations, which were emerging as the "command and control nodes" of the global economy. This provided the connection between an older, urban, artistic Bohemia, and the new ideas around industrial districts, quarters, and hubs which formed the bedrock of the creative cities and creative class discourse.

In this way, postmodern sociologists such as Scott Lash and John Urry could write in 1994 about the coming "culturalisation of the economy", and a decade later Richard Florida about the economic necessity of attracting the creative class to one's city.[31]

The 1998 Mapping Document: squaring the circle

The rebranding of culture as the "creative industries" was purely rhetorical. There was no creative industries strategy in 1998, nor has there been one since. It certainly legitimised the arts and cultural sector, which, in the UK at least, tended to embrace it as their last best chance. The document's main pivot was to redefine the cultural sector around "creativity" and to attach it, through the notion of intellectual property, to the wider knowledge economy. As the 1998 Mapping Document had it, they are "those industries which have their origin in individual creativity, skill and talent and which have a potential for wealth and job creation through the generation and exploitation of intellectual property".[32] This is not a definition that could have much purchase in terms of an actual industrial strategy. As many critics have pointed out, the focus on the creative individual, rather than teams, companies, value chains, or ecosystems, is quite useless as an analytical frame. So, too, most people employed in the cultural sector are paid in wages or fees, and if they do generate intellectual property rights (IPR) they rarely get to own them. Between the talented creative workers and the owners of the IPR falls the shadow.

But the substitution of "culture" with "creative" opened a Pandora's box of definitional and taxonomic nightmares which remain at large to this day. What is not creative, and what is distinctive about culture beyond creativity? So began a two-way flow. First, an expansion of creativity out of art, out of culture, across the full breadth of the economy – a democratisation of creative productivity. Then, a countervailing attempt to assign a distinct and privileged space for art and culture within this, a special "cultural creativity" by which the sector could remain in command of this creativity agenda and not be washed away into a generic "creative economy".

The definition came with lists of creative industries, all fairly standard except for "software"; not "video games" or "leisure software", but software per se. This has been disputed ever since. For while software is undoubtedly creative (manipulating symbols and creating novel products), so too are those working in, say, financial services or biotech. Software (and hardware, which is always ruled outside the creative industries) has certainly transformed the cultural sector, but it has transformed financial services, healthcare, and education as well.

Software made the dot.com tech–entrepreneur connection, but, more to the point, in the immediate context of bargaining with the Treasury, it almost doubled the total employment figures. This added a premium to its advocacy value that has been hard to relinquish, as software engineering was also one of the fastest-growing occupations. It's the hidden motor behind the repeated claims for this being a rapidly expanding sector of a future "creative economy". Strip out software and industrial design (also added), and your employment figures drop by well over half.

Where to draw a line around creativity? As these lists proliferated across the globe, picked up by states, city governments, and consultancies, as well as the big international agencies, all sorts of creative activities were tacked on. Industrial design, PR and business consulting, biotech, toys, furniture and interiors, glassware and ceramics, footwear manufacture, and fashion retail. All of these could conceivably be brought under the DCMS' definition. As could health, education, and financial services, though to do that would have given the game away – that this was always about art and culture.

The boundaries fluctuated again when cultural occupations were added to industry employment figures. That is, "creatives" employed outside the creative industries proper, or, in current parlance, "embedded". So rather than just those employed in specific creative industries – music or publishing, for example – there are many creative occupations listed outside these, like musicians on a cruise ship (transport) or music teachers (education). Adding these to total employment aggregates increases the figure by a third, while seemingly testifying to the unstoppable seepage of creativity into the wider economy. But what is a "creative occupation"? Music teachers, graphic designers, and other cultural professionals are one thing, but counting as part of total "creative employment" a database engineer in a mining company, or an industrial systems designer, is something else entirely.

This was the problem with the notion of "creative economy", which increasingly served as an alternative name for the creative industries. For John Howkins, who popularised the term, the creative industries are just part of a wider "creative economy" driven by individual creativity and the commercialisation of knowledge through IPR – patents, copyright, trademarks, and so on. NESTA, which had systematically picked through all the various occupational categories in search of creatives, defined a creative occupation as: "a role within the creative process that brings cognitive skills to bear about differentiation to yield either novel or significantly enhanced products whose final form is not fully specified in advance".[33] This shows clearly how "creativity" did not just sound "sexier" than culture, but was the essential conduit whereby culture was connected to economic productivity. It had been a long-standing argument, from avant-garde and community arts alike, that creativity should be part of everyday life. NESTA's formulation spells out how this democratisation of creativity is in fact about its channelling into economic productivity and innovation. It was through its reduction to creativity that culture could be formally and systemically absorbed by the economy. But this is also the point at which it threatened to disappear. For in extending creativity beyond culture and redefining it in economics-friendly terms as the "cognitive skills" to yield "novel products", it dislodged creativity from its privileged position in relation to art and culture.

Trying to relocate art and culture within this amorphous creative economy became a new academic and consultancy industry. Older cultural economists envisaged art as "R&D", the "core"

of creativity which became more diluted as it moved to the commercial creative industries, flowing on eventually into the sea of
the creative economy. But was this not art-elitism by the back
door? Why was "art" the privileged font of creativity? Indeed,
many East Asian countries pushed the boundaries beyond software into biotech and all forms of business consulting. Agencies
such as United Nations Conference on Trade and Development
(UNCTAD) counted the mass manufacture of glassware, ceramics, and furniture. One of Shanghai's first creative industries
awards went to a new, locally designed Porsche.

The proliferation of incoherent definitions and statistical
taxonomies is the most salient characteristic of the creative
industries/creative economy. Art and culture, cultural industries, creative industries, cultural creative industries, creative
economy, creative and digital – pick any website and you will
see all of these terms used interchangeably, often within one
sentence. I've been to many CCI conferences over the years,
and they spend hours discussing just what creative industries or
creative economy *really* is, and where art and culture are located.
This is usually presided over by some statistical PPT where even
a cursory inspection reveals multiple fractal confusions. Attend
a dairy or wine or car industry conference, and there will be all
sorts of conflicts over organics and electrics, government regulations, and new markets. They will not spend three days talking
about what the dairy industry is, or cleverly counting leather-
derivative producers and pâtissiers as embedded dairy farmers.
Or be in a position such as at a recent creative economy conference in India during which rocket engineers were discussed in
the same category as rural village weaving co-ops.

The point of the Mapping Document had been to strengthen
the hand of arts and culture by establishing the economic

gravitas of a sector which had been previously unacknowledged or ignored. It was a tool instantly replicated across the globe as this new industrial sector sought to prove its economic relevance. But once the attention was grabbed, what then to do with it? What kind of industry is the creative industries?

Unlike film or music or games, which people understand as "industries" even if they don't know quite how they work, creative industries is a second-order industry. It is based on the grouping together and redesignation of a vast range of different activities within a statistical taxonomy. Not immediately visible or easily imagined, the creative industries is unified by an abstraction, the outcome of conceptual work performed by consultants, technocrats, and statisticians who have the prosthetic knowledge devices required to aggregate its economic worth.

This is not analytical knowledge, such as with supply chains: how chocolate is made from cocoa beans, through what hands the commodities pass, under what regulations, and how the benefits from the enormous wealth are divided. This is not what creative industries mapping does. Rather, it is an advocacy tool, aggregating employment and associated value from a transversal section of a vastly complex set of socioeconomic practices on the basis of an abstracted "creativity". It's the perfect industry for an age of "derivatives", patterns of value identified second-order, far away from immediate producers and consumers, of its immediate use or exchange value! The perfect industry, as well, for an age of PR and marketing, the huge increase of which it gratefully adds to the employment figures.

As we briefly highlighted in the last chapter, culture is a sphere of social practice that had become progressively separated out from other areas (such as religion, the economy, politics, and administration, but also health and education) since early modernity. The attempt to shoehorn the totality of this sphere into the narrow frame of "economy", and an even narrower one of "industry", was always going to end in incoherence. Most ironically, however, it failed to deal with those parts of culture which actually were industries.

Creative labour as industrial strategy

Thatcher and the Conservatives abolished industrial strategy. The idea that the state should somehow direct investment decisions in industry was, in their view, a project of post-war socialism; consequently, its apparatuses were dismantled. Blair's famous address to the Economic Club of Chicago in April 1999, in which he celebrated economic globalisation as foundational for a new international community, set a seal on New Labour's acceptance of this. The creative industries might now have official state sanction, but the available developmental levers were few. As good supply-siders, New Labour's focus was on assembling the right "factors of production" – land, labour, capital – and letting the market do its work.[34]

A great attraction of the creative industries, and creative economy, was that the dominant factor was a creative labour engaged in immaterial production. Land – "creative space" – was certainly required, but, outside certain technical facilities, it was mainly relational, about providing creatives with the aesthetic-functional bare bones of spaces of encounter, or, in other words, a "creative milieu".[35] As for capital, most crucial was the social and cultural capital possessed by creative labour itself. As Richard Florida had it: "If workers control the means of production today that is because it is inside their heads; they are the means of production".[36]

Chris Smith's "access, excellence, education" was his industrial strategy. If creatives possessed the means of production "inside their heads", then it was crucial that governments help put it there. In a knowledge economy, education was everything, and it was the basis of the meritocratic democracy they strove to create. As Bill Clinton had it, "you gotta learn to earn".[37] This was a seismic shift of social democratic parties away from the industrial working class towards a new "knowledge class" or "professional-managerial class" or, more broadly, "intellectual workers". This class or "class fraction" appeared on its way to social dominance in the corporate capitalism of the 1950s and 1960s, the background to C. Wright Mills' "cultural apparatus".[38] The older social democratic parties, devastated by the defeats of the labour movement and the collapse of the global alternative in 1989–92, had become dominated by the professional-managerial class. They were strongly attached to the public service sector and civil society organisations – hence Thomas Piketty's term "Brahmins". The creative class could be seen as its vanguard body.[39]

A creative industrial strategy would focus on building knowledge through education and training, and then creating the context in which these creative means of production could be best put to work. This context was cultural, a set of values that would nurture new kinds of subjects. The creative economy required its participants to adopt what Michel Foucault had called new "technologies of the self", the means "to produce on her own accord those qualities of self that will enable her to compete successfully in a social world reimagined in the image of a market".[40] This "entrepreneurship of the self" was a central part of the "creativity dispositif" or apparatus, in which the artistic promise of meaningful, self-directed, non-alienated work became hitched to the new economy.[41]

Yet, despite the emphasis on "individual talent" and entre-preneurship, the "means of production" were actually shared. The cultural resources on which the creative economy drew were held in common, and they were often embedded in par-ticular locales. This was recognised through the application of economic-geographical concepts of "industrial districts" or "clusters", the competitive strength of which came from the "untraded externalities" of common tacit knowledge accessible only by being there. These creative clusters, or creative milieux, facilitated a complex, situated division of labour, which gener-ated accumulated knowledge in a virtuous circle often extend-ing across whole districts and cities.

Creative industry strategies thus combined the promotion of creative individuals within a competitive-collaborative, highly networked creative milieu. This gave rise to a small and micro-business, or "start-up", economy, in which a set of actors and business entities operate in a fluid, permeable zone between formal, legally defined businesses, and completely open social networks. It is a zone of temporary project-based work, some-where between competition and collaboration, between "pure" market transactions and collaborative "civil society". It operates, the story went, as a kind of "ecosystem" not amenable to either top-down state planning or corporate control. These ecosystems embody the "soft knowledge" that is, for New Labour economist Will Hutton, the gift of the counterculture to the modern econ-omy, that bundle "of less tangible production inputs involving leadership, communication, emotional intelligence, the disposi-tion to innovate, and the creation of social capital that harnesses hard knowledge and permits its effective embodiment in goods and services and – crucially – its customisation. Their interaction and combination are at the heart of the knowledge economy".[42]

For Hutton, as for Chris Smith, it represents a new, post-1968 modernity, and one that sets off a modern, enlightened liberal country from authoritarian dictatorships such as China, where heavy industry might be able to be force-marched, but a creative economy would be unable to develop.

> So here is the mechanism, plural public institutions; and here is a consequence, human happiness. Enlightenment institutions need Enlightenment people to breathe life into them; modernity has to be won by real people who are prepared to imagine a life that they themselves want to make and are prepared to act on that concept, leaving behind the universe in which preferences are inherited and fixed … [T]his involves a mental shift from the traditional to the modern.[43]

Creative industries, then, demanded new kinds of cities (or, at least, zones therein), which encouraged creative milieux, new kinds of industrial organisation (SME/start-up ecosystems), and new kinds of subjects able to autonomously create and innovate. This "creativity bundle" provided a highly exportable "fast policy" template for the creative economy. It was cheap, requiring a combination of ex-industrial buildings and a nucleus of creative labour with the required educational and cultural capital. Provided with Western know-how – mapping documents, entrepreneurship, social media skills, and so on – these creative hubs could act as catalysts for a wider creative economy. These were benign economies, because their growth both relied on, and in turn promoted, the education, skills, and social capital required for "sustainable development". They were also nicely tailored to the UK's soft power project, in which the promotion of creativity would help build modern liberal democracies, of the kind exemplified by the mother country.

The creativity bundle has benefited arts and culture. Indeed, the biggest beneficiary of New Labour's increased cultural budget – as well as the new National Lottery – was art and culture.[44] Cultural infrastructure was enhanced, with large-scale galleries, museums, and venues complemented by many smaller "creative hubs". These often provided the social and cultural services, as well as the sense of citizenship and community, so often absent elsewhere in the city. Quite often they were inventive, generous, open spaces which had reinvented the idea of the community arts centre for the twenty-first century, all wrapped up for their funders in the language of creative economy. Across the globe, arts spaces and creative hubs sprang up in cities previously given over to industry and commerce, providing glimpses of a different creative modernity associated with New York, London, or Paris, but also trying out a new experimental kind of local modernity. All power to them.

These kinds of spaces featured heavily in the many hundreds of creative industry strategies produced in the UK, and under the auspices of agencies such as the British Council. But the creativity bundle is not an industrial strategy. At best, it is a supply-side charter for an educated creative workforce; at worst, a charter for post-industrial real estate development.

To see an industrial strategy, one would have to look at China or South Korea. These two countries have applied to the cultural industries the resources of the "developmental state".[45] This refers to a state-directed (if not always state-owned) process of rapid industrialisation which stood outside the "Washington Consensus" promoted by the World Bank, IMF, and World Trade Organization (WTO), and celebrated by Tony Blair's Chicago speech. After flirting with the creativity bundle – which in China quickly became about real estate and new forms of urban consumption – both China and South Korea applied their analytical research resources to a thorough investigation of the different non-generic branches (music, films, games, theatre) of the cultural industries. Then they used their capacities for economic mobilisation to intervene in the cultural "value chain". What were the markets, and where were the barriers and possibilities? What needed to be done to capture some of their value?

This could be very heavy-handed and clunky at first, but the sights were set on rapid growth and strategic control over parts of the national, then, eventually, global value chain. The results might be considered tediously formulaic (China) or irredeemably kitsch (K-Pop), but economically they were very real. This is not to endorse such an industrial approach. It was primarily driven by economic motives, though with the attraction of soft power too. In fact, certain parts of art and culture have been cordoned off from these purely commercial operations on the basis of their cultural importance to these countries' identity or political regimes. Investment in various forms of creative education (design, film, art, games, and so on) is taken seriously (contrasting with the progressive cutting of resources for this in the UK and Australia), but this is not considered only as an industrial strategy.

The US has its own strategy, built around its position as dominant global incumbent. It is a cultural industries powerhouse, and its leading global position is not contested. Indeed, with the rise of the platform companies, its position has been strengthened over the last decade or so. Its strategy is not about putting twenty creatives in an old factory but rather ensuring that IPR legislation is built into all international and bilateral trade treaties, and rigorously enforced through its considerable means as global hegemon.

Creative industries

When the UK, EU, or Australia do get involved at this level, it occurs in specific industries, often in close consultation with big industry players. These latter have privileged access to governments, who play hardball in pursuit of whatever legislative or regulatory measures they deem necessary. These have very little to do with the "creative industries" strategies regularly produced by an army of consultants and academics.

Falls the shadow

John Howkins, in *The Creative Economy*, suggested that in addition to the three classical "factors of production" there is now a fourth – knowledge.[46] This is a long-standing claim of the knowledge economy, and one that sees knowledge workers, the professional-managerial class, as set to be dominant within it. But, as Thomas Piketty and others have noted, part of the neoliberal revolution of the early 1980s was the assertion of the rights of ownership over those of managers.[47] "Shareholder value", for example, put return on investment before the needs or core purpose of the corporation, as determined professionally by managers. This was part of a shift away from an older corporate management style towards one based on a range of economic indicators, linked to new forms of finance.[48] Financial managers in turn began to command salary packages way above other forms of professional management.

In this context, Piketty pointed to a divergence between "Brahmins" and "Merchants", with the latter's dominance drawn from their links to corporate and financial power. Despite the growth of the public sector, and the accompanying rise of the professional-managerial class, the ongoing ability of the owners of capital to assert their interests against the autonomous knowledge of the professional-managerial class remains. According to one recent estimate, at least a third of this group is fully integrated into the private sector; another third could be classed as "Brahmins" in the public sector; and another third is becoming increasingly "proletarianised", especially concentrated in public services such as education, health, transport, and, of course, culture.[49] Underlying this is not just the decline in public sector funding, but also the ongoing reduction of professional autonomy through new managerial techniques linked to new forms of digital technology, with many previously professional-managerial class functions routinised, outsourced, or simply abolished.[50]

Something akin to this has been happening for some time in the cultural industries. The autonomy of creative labour, central to its appeal, has been eroded. There are some very well-paid creatives, of course, but these are in decline as a proportion of the whole. Salaried workers have reduced in numbers, as increasingly precarious project work becomes the norm. This is the other side to the growing monopoly exercised by the large platform companies and their complex intersection with "heritage" cultural industries in film, music, publishing, and the like.

While large well-funded international agencies compiled statistics of trade, employment, GVA, GDP, and so on, few of them cared to examine how these industries work on the ground. Much of culture-as-industry was predicated on the rise and rise of small grassroots businesses and individual artist-entrepreneurs, the "T-shirts" taking revenge on the "suits". The opposite happened. Though, as we are frequently told, technology has allowed more people than ever to be creative – do

music, films, books, games – the fruits of this labour are con-
trolled by fewer and fewer people. As a recent book opened:

> Three massive conglomerates own the three record labels and
> three music publishers that control most of the world's music.
> They designed the streaming industry, dominated by Spotify,
> which itself is (or was) partly owned by those same three labels.
> When Disney swallowed 21st century Fox, a single company
> assumed control of 35 percent of the US box office. Google and
> Facebook have a lock on the digital ads that are wrapped around
> music, videos, and news online. Google, along with Apple, is the
> gatekeeper of everything mobile, giving it a massive cut on games,
> books, music, and movies. Via YouTube, it controls video stream-
> ing … Amazon has an iron grip on book, ebook, and audio- book
> sales, and dominates ebook and audiobook production. The only
> publisher that might be able to hold its own is Penguin Random
> House, and then only by gulping down as many other big pub-
> lishers as it possibly can.[51]

And so on, through radio, live music, artists' agents, games,
apps, devices – the whole ecosystem has been captured by huge
corporations prioritising above all else the reduction of costs
and the maximisation of profits. "Ecosystem" has a benign
ring to it, but a corporation is more like "an immortal colony
organism that treats human beings as inconvenient gut flora.
It doesn't have a personality and it doesn't have ethics. Its sole
imperative is to do whatever it can get away with to extract
maximum economic value from humans and the planet".[52] This
growing commercialisation and concentration, exacerbated by
the rise of digital platforms, is based on a robust assertion of
IPR. As it turned out, the creative class did not own the means
of production, just a very sophisticated toolbox. Though the
cultural sector abounds in freelancers and micro-businesses,

often accounting for over 90 per cent of firms in the sector, these work within a framework set by the owners of IPR.

Herman Schwartz calls this new digital economy a franchise model, in which the older integrated corporation of Fordism now outsources much of its work to independent companies.[53] There's a tripartite division of a core company, a periphery of skilled supplier companies, and an outer circle of routine, semi-skilled production. What keeps them all dependent on the core company is control of IPR at multiple levels, from branding, to products, to specific ways of managing work and data. Similar processes are visible in film, games, music, and publishing, with extremely complex divisions of labour stretching from textured post-industrial offices in Manhattan to CGI render sheds full of over-qualified graduates in East Asia.

In short, the "talented individual" celebrated by the Mapping Document – indeed, whole creative milieux – has been definitively separated from the IPR to the products they help produce. To this challenge, those advocating the creative industries simply have no answer. This model – the default settings of creative labour, equipped with the requisite skills and entrepreneurial attitude, encouraged into start-ups which can then be "scaled up", bringing significant local employment benefits – has atrophied.

There has been much debate over the nature of the new "digital capitalism". It undoubtedly lends itself to concentration and monopoly by the nature of its use of IPR. It accumulates rights over protocols, platforms, algorithms, data, and technologies, as well as copyright. These accumulated proprietary rights over the vast amount of data which flows from them mean that breaking into this monopoly is almost impossible. The incumbents thus extract huge monopoly rent while seeing off the challengers. Some critics have called this digital or neo-feudalism.[54] The scenario is now very far from "free market competition", and most workers and consumers are in the position of "serfs", while the billionaire class lords it over the state. Others suggest that this is capitalism as usual, which has always used rent, monopoly, and violent extraction whenever necessary.[55] Whichever way we take it (I'm inclined to the latter view), we certainly have a new kind of dominant economic model based around monopoly and rent, which is central to our current economic stagnation and the erosion of democratic forms.[56]

This "secular stagnation" has resulted in the atrophy of the sense of future promised by the knowledge economy, and in which the creative industries were to be central protagonists. However we view it, the creative class have been pushed to the margins of the cultural commons, their claims to possess the means of production in freefall.

Conclusion

Advocates embraced culture-as-industry at precisely the moment governments had more or less abandoned industry policy.[57] Governments facilitated; they opened doors to capital investment and market access. They did skills and training. Investment came from a deregulated system of global finance that had become dominant by the turn of the millennium, and (in the name of shareholder value) imposed short-term, high-return conditions on its recipients. As for policy, the public service that once directed industrial investment was long gone. The relationship between government and the private sector now increasingly took the form of "political capitalism" in which connections with government were key.[58] In these circumstances, large-scale media and publishing, the big tech corporations, and the more commercial end of entertainment stood to benefit – as did commercial sport – but not the ramshackle ecosystem known as culture or the creative industries. The exception has been cultural infrastructure – galleries, museums, and various performance venues – the economic benefits of which mostly flow to large, well-connected construction companies.[59]

At the same time, as governments, advocacy groups, academics, and international agencies have been talking up the glamour of the creative industries, upstairs, in Dorian Gray's attic, "actually existing" creative industries looked very different. Studies of creative labour have been around for nearly two decades, stressing low pay, lack of pensions or health insurance, no paid holidays, precarity, self-exploitation and, indeed, exploitation. All the while, we followed the cheerleaders who told us how great this work was and how we will, eventually, make it. The pandemic merely stripped away the last illusions.

This sits alongside another piece of common knowledge: that the "creative city" benefits real estate and hospitality, development capital, and city marketing rather than the creatives themselves. The quaint eighteenth-century-derived word "gentrification" does not do this justice. Initially, the word alluded to the replacement of older working-class communities by a new kind of adventurous, culture-consuming middle class, installing galleries and wine bars in a similar fashion to those country houses involving the demolition of whole villages "for the view". Nowadays, the artists – those "stormtroopers of gentrification" – are barely needed. Huge flows of surplus capital circulate the globe in search of quick returns, enabled by an array of human and non-human actors able to identify spaces and broker deals. Letting artists go in for a bit to spruce the place up is no longer so necessary.

In Grant Gee's 2007 documentary on Joy Division, Tony Wilson, legendary manager of Factory Records, had eulogised a 'shiny, revolutionary Manchester' built on a "a bunch of groups" which had reversed its post-industrial decline. In fact, it was mostly their managers who had started to invest in underappreciated real estate in the 1980s. But not so much these days. The big players are now the universities, the global development funds, and Abu Dhabi. The hospitality chains can have the once-funky Northern Quarter, but the big returns go to those able to build the skyscrapers and bijoux apartments that surround the city centre.[60]

The creative industries, in which Manchester takes great pride in being the biggest "cluster" outside London, start to lose their shine on closer inspection.[61] A recent study found the creative industries in Greater Manchester accounted for 4 per cent of all employment. But, as in 1998, "IT, Software, and Computer Services" – basically, digital business-to-business services – accounted for almost half of this. So, after all the sound and fury, the cultural sector accounts for 2 per cent of total employment. Over a quarter of this is made up by "Film, TV, Radio, and Photography" (16.1%) and "Advertising and Marketing" (12.5%). The six remaining sub-groups (out of nine) account for only a quarter of the total creative industries employment. That is, architecture, design, publishing, museums and galleries, crafts, music, and performing arts account for roughly 1 per cent of all employment in Manchester.

This employment is highly concentrated in Manchester city centre, with concentrations in Media City in Salford (the BBC relocated some of its operations there), and of IT firms in Cheshire, along with rich footballers and their WAGS. Just thirteen of Manchester's 376 neighbourhoods accounted for over half of the city-region's total creative industries employment. Many of the outlying areas barely record any creative employment, and some have no creative industries employment at all. As the report notes, "the CIs are providing good and (generally) higher paying jobs to some, but few opportunities for others".[62] 85 per cent of creative industries businesses employ fewer than five workers, with only twenty workplaces employing more than 250 workers. This concentration is mirrored at the national level, with London having eight times the jobs as Manchester.

This is not the creative industries revolution. Was it worth the economic reduction of a whole sector of social experience for a 1 per cent employment figure? The statistical bait-and-switch is revealed as a prime example of Harry Frankfurt's *Bullshit*, "speech intended to persuade without regard for truth. The liar cares about the truth and attempts to hide it; the bullshitter doesn't care if what they say is true or false".[63] The complete indifference to how things really go down in the creative industries, and the abuse of statistical data to "persuade without regard for the truth", more or less sums up twenty-five years of CCI policy. And in the end, bullshitters believe their own bullshit.

Despite this clear evidence as to the paucity of economic claims for the sector, Manchester's recent industrial strategy singled out the creative industries as one of the "keys to future prosperity":

> Manchester also has a vibrant grassroots cultural scene; contin-
> ued support of this is required to ensure the sector continues to
> deliver its positive economic and social impact ... Culture, media
> and sports was the most referenced sector by young people ...
> when they were asked to name their dream job and to name the
> available jobs in the city.[64]

74

Creative industries

The strategy proposes a new "international hub" in which the Greater Manchester Cultural Skill Consortium aims "to create opportunities for people to develop skills in the arts and culture sector and to help improve diversity". It was called Factory, but in a deal which will help "service the loan" the naming rights were sold to the insurance company Aviva. A final demonstration of the victory of FIRE over "creative industries".[65]

2

Culture goes missing

A recent consultancy tender, taken almost at random, prepared by various EU and Turkish ministries for industry and technology, foreign affairs, and finance, suggested that:

> The creative economy encompasses … culture economy and creative industries. Creative industries (film, TV, Digital media/game AI, fashion, design, and architecture) mostly build on the culture economy (includes the traditional cultural sector, Patrimony, Heritage, Crafts, Cultural practices).

What happens when a whole sector of human experience is reduced to an industrial sector, set to be managed by various financial, technology, and industrial ministries?

In the last chapter, I tried to show the consequences of reframing culture as industry. Responding to the undoing of post-war social citizenship, the privatisation of cultural production and consumption, the decline of the industrial working class, and the embrace of a "knowledge economy", creative industries held out the promise of good work, economic modernisation, urban renewal, social cohesion, and emancipated, productive subjects. The creative industries began as an argument for the continued state funding of culture, presented via econometric statistics that hid the paucity of its claims and the extractive realities of "actually existing cultural industries". It resulted in the hollowing out of the language of culture and an embrace of what Mark Fisher called a "business ontology", leaving it unable to grasp the extent of, or the reasons for, culture's radical marginalisation in public policy.[1]

In this chapter we pan out to look at the wider crisis of neo-liberal capitalism, in which the undermining of the post-war consensus has resulted in widespread inequality and precarity, leading to a deep sense of social disintegration. This has occurred within a wider crisis in the trade and finance system, in geopolitics, and, standing over both, the accelerating climate emergency. However this crisis ends, it is clear we are not going back to the old system. We are in an interregnum. Yet mainstream cultural policy and advocacy remain stuck within the creative industries paradigm, emerging from the pandemic with a "build back better" mindset.[2] To attend a creative industries conference is to encounter a Jurassic Park of neoliberalism, where concepts and imaginaries long since dead in the real world are there, roaming free.

In what follows I will look at how culture is being left out of the new transformative agendas that have emerged in the last decade. Attention is being paid to all those aspects of social life ignored or eroded by the GDP-centric growth models of the last forty years. Yet somehow culture is barely mentioned. I use Nancy Fraser's account of capitalism as a social, rather than just an economic, system, which relies on a range of environmental, political, and social resources which it constantly disavows and undermines. The current crisis is as much about these support systems breaking down as it is "purely" economic disfunctions.

Culture is not an industry

I suggest that culture can be seen as part of these support systems and that it, too, is part of the crisis. However, unless it understands itself as part of the social rather than an industry, it will remain part of the problem rather than the solution.

Where's culture?

Culture is part of this systemic crisis. It is not its unique cause, nor can it be its unique salve, but it is crucial to its overcoming in important ways. What is disturbing, however, is that it is largely absent from the visions being proposed as a way out of the interregnum. Partly, this is a strategic failure by the cultural sector. The creative economy development paradigm may have brought some benefits. Those driving these policies tended to do so in the service of "culture", happy with new levels of government attention and convinced they were doing so in the service of culture. The economic arguments, they suggest, were a mere Trojan Horse to smuggle in culture to the mainstream. It's failed dismally.

Globally, cultural policy is in a very bad place. Despite twenty years of creative economy, culture is marginalised in mainstream development discourse. Whatever the cultural sector thinks about the ever more detailed compendia of metrics now available, mainstream economic, social, and environmental policy makers do not take it seriously. The failure of culture to get its own goal in the 2015 Sustainable Development Goals (SDGs) is telling. So, too, was the failure of the UN's new strategic document *Our Common Agenda*, which set out to restore the "social compact" but failed even to mention culture.[3] One of the most common complaints in the pandemic was how culture was ignored, an ironic backdrop to its claims to be a cutting-edge economic sector.[4]

There is much truth in these charges, and we will address some of them in what follows. Culture-as-industry avoids all these questions. Here I want to simply state that culture as a sphere of shared meaning, embodied in practices, rituals, and particular products, is as much part of our social life together as bodily sustenance, care and nurture, learning and adapting, exchanging and accumulating. A focus on culture does not necessarily entail a compensation for a failure of politics, but can be a site on which that politics can be engaged.

Nor do we fix culture by a return to some prior state – of self-contained local communities or art untainted by commerce. I would follow Mark Fisher and seek to build on what I consider to be the real gains, both of capitalist modernity, but also of the new left and the 1960s counterculture. These have been repurposed and co-opted, often willingly and easily. But the project of "popular modernism" – of a folding together of art and popular culture in a future-oriented project of political and cultural transformation – remains to be reclaimed.[17] As does Fisher's other idea of "luxury communism", that the pleasures and spiritual possibilities of our modern culture can only be expanded and deepened outside capitalism, in some other possible world. Creative imagination and social solidarity are not opposed.[18]

The full realisation of the idea of culture, unlocking what it promised but doing so in full recognition of its limits, and the limits of the creatives and intellectuals invested in it, can, I will argue, provide a crucial beacon through the interregnum.

Culture was a highly visible protagonist in the modernising thrust of the post-war era, as it was in the rise of a post-industrial period that reframed this modernity in terms of knowledge, innovation, and creativity. As we leave one era and enter an uncertain landscape, culture is absent – or worse. Most of the transformative post-neoliberal agendas we discuss below either ignore culture or see it as part of the problem. This is problematic for culture, but it is also problematic for these transformative agendas. Without due consideration of the sphere of our common life represented by culture, these transformative agendas will be hobbled.

Crisis, but what kind of crisis?

Neoliberalism, a distinct phase of global capitalism that emerged in the early 1980s, is in crisis. The economic, political, and social solutions it brought to the prior crisis of Fordist social democracy in the 1970s no longer work. That much might be broadly agreed. It has become ever clearer since the 2008–10 global financial crisis. Stagnant growth, stalled wages, growing inequality, cost-of-living increases, rising indebtedness, increasing precarity of employment, and the erosion of public services are the stuff of the nightly news. This is accompanied by widespread disaffection and disconnection from the political process, resulting in alternating moments of political effervescence (often as anti-politics) and resigned passivity. This in the face of a growing perception of the deepening hold of powerful elites over the workings of government, in the form of lobbying, political finance, corruption, cronyism, the public–private "revolving door", and a pervasive cynicism towards technocratic political expertise. Standing behind these are growing geopolitical tensions, as the global settlement promised at the 1990 "end of history" unravels, alongside the accelerating climatic and ecological emergencies which threaten, like a nuclear exchange but slower, to end life on earth as we know it.

Few would deny a sense of crisis, even if its definitional outline might be debated: "a time of intense difficulty or danger"; "a time when a difficult or important decision must be made"; "the turning point of a disease when an important change takes place, indicating either recovery or death". Are we at a moment of serious, but passing, danger, or a systemic, life-or-death crisis?

For many economists, we are in a transition from one kind of industrial-technological system to another, from the third to the fourth industrial revolution – one led by AI, big data, mass customisation, automation, and so on. History tells us there will be suffering and pain, writes leading global economist Branco Milanović, but technology will ultimately come up with an answer.[19] There is no viable alternative to capitalism, but such technological solutions, Milanović concedes, do need more leadership from the state and a new social compact. Proponents of the "green transition" also see an enhanced role for the state and "ethical" private sector investment in moving us out of fossil fuel dependence towards renewables. However, to facilitate this transition there is a need to move away from the market-first, narrowly growth-driven ideology of neoliberalism and build in new social guarantees.

As a consequence, there are calls for a new "wellbeing economy", whereby we value things other than GDP, and put human needs at the centre of our economy. Robert Kennedy's 1968 remarks at the University of Kansas are paradigmatic:

> [T]he gross national product does not allow for the health of our children, the quality of their education or the joy of their play. It does not include the beauty of our poetry or the strength of our marriages, the intelligence of our public debate or the integrity of our public officials. It measures neither our wit nor our

courage, neither our wisdom nor our learning, neither our compassion nor our devotion to our country, it measures everything in short, except that which makes life worthwhile.[20]

The "wellbeing economy" takes aim at this narrow frame and seeks to fold in a wider set of values and metrics. Though often lurching close to "motherhood and apple pie", at its best it expresses the widespread concern to "re-embed" all those aspects of our lives together which seemed to be external to the core preoccupations of the neoliberal economy.[21]

The question, then, is how to think of the economy in ways that will allow us to value those things which market-first neoliberalism could not. Bestselling author Kate Raworth promotes "doughnut economics", creating a floor for our essential social needs within the ecological limits set by our finite planetary resources.[22] The "doughnut" is the sweet spot between floor and ceiling. Her high-level enumeration of what constitutes the "social foundation" closely follows the United Nations' seventeen SDGs, which include access to basic infrastructures (water, energy), services (education, health), employment, and social rights, and links to ecological sustainability and climate action.[23]

The 1990s nostrum that free markets, trade, and manufacturing would result in global development is more or less dead. The emphasis on the provision of basic infrastructure and human services, rather than exports and industry, marks a new trend in developmental thinking.[24] The United Nations is working with the OECD and World Bank to mobilise the global financial sector to provide investment capital for the social infrastructure required to attain the SDGs – capital that many states find difficult to access. [25] This focus can also be found in the recent report by a senior KPMG director who, recalculating the 1972 *Limits to Growth* report, sees global investment in social infrastructure (especially health and education) as the only viable way out of economic and climate breakdown.[26]

The shift of focus from growing GDP and expanding "free" consumer markets towards providing for basic social needs has been accelerating over the last decade, and more so during the pandemic. Hence, there has been talk of FDR's New Deal , William Beveridge and the 1945 welfare state, and Australia's "reconstruction" under the Labor governments of the 1940s. However, the social democratic focus on social welfare is now combined with the need for climate action, a convergence made explicit in the various "green new deals" across the US, the EU, and China.[27]

There is, therefore, a new, positive emphasis on state action. Rather than a small state "getting out of the way" of markets, the state now returns as guarantor of social cohesion and well-being. This was certainly boosted by the pandemic, but the role of the state has been growing in visibility since the global financial crisis. For some, this new role involves the state as leading the economy out of neoliberalism's "secular stagnation", having a unique capacity to act in an "entrepreneurial" fashion, launching a transformative mission as outlined by Mariana Mazzucato.[28] This mission involves technological innovation, but also a massive reinvestment in social infrastructure.[29]

In light of the new positive responsibilities given to the state, others have affirmed the state's unique fiscal and monetary capacity. Though always tacitly assumed, the state's role as "guarantor of last resort" resurfaced with a vengeance in the global financial crisis, its sovereign capacities elaborated by heterodox economists, varieties of Keynesianism, and the work around Modern Monetary Theory (MMT).[30] The economic success of China's state-led development, both domestically and as a counter-model globally, has also been important.[31] The state is definitely back, though its emergent democratic or authoritarian complexion remains ambiguous.[32]

These are now mainstream political programmes, accompanied by very real anxieties around the need for difficult and important decisions. The implications of such a seismic shift away from neoliberal orthodoxies has important consequences for thinking about culture. The aftershock was picked up by UNESCO, as the leading international agency concerned with culture. At the end of 2022, its Mondiacult conference declaration evoked a world

> marked by multiple, protracted and multidimensional crises – linked in particular to the dramatic consequences of climate change and biodiversity loss, armed conflicts, natural hazards, uncontrolled urbanisation, unsustainable development patterns, as well as the erosion of democratic societies – which lead in particular to an increase in poverty, inequalities in the exercise of rights and a growing divide in access to digital technologies.[33]

The draft declaration then suggested that this situation calls "more than ever, for reinvesting in the transformative role of culture in public policies, for the full exercise of fundamental human rights". This is a significant break with creative economy rhetoric. But what can this new line mean after at least two decades during which culture's primary justification has been the economic and social contribution of the creative industries to "sustainable economic development"?

A similar question might be posed more generally. The reframing of the economy around wellbeing and sustainability, and towards a just, green transition, tends to downplay both the systemic nature of these crises and the effects of forty years of neoliberalism on our collective ability to make serious political decisions. The agency of change seems to come from the same political and socioeconomic system that got us into this position in the first place. Can we flip the policy settings just like that? On the contrary, the multiple "wicked" problems and the "poly-crises" that beset us may not be just an unfortunate confluence of different political, social, economic, ecological, and geopolitical issues, but seen as systemic, deriving from neoliberalism and, more fundamentally, from capitalism.[34]

Systemic crisis

This systemic view does not use capitalism as an easy, all-purpose "master-signifier", or as a huge, unstoppable mechanism which justifies inaction through despair, encouraging us to postpone doing anything until the "big day of revolution".[35] It provides a real historical insight into the concrete interests served by the neoliberal revolution, and which need to be confronted if we are to go beyond it. It is tempting, as we shall see, to just add culture to a "wellbeing" economy, or the "doughnut" or even "foundational economy". But first we need to explore more systematically how culture came to be caught in the neoliberal frame, and with what consequences.

The post-1945 settlement, which resolved the geopolitical struggle, class conflict, and economic contractions of the inter-war years, was a compromise between a reforming political class and a powerful, politically organised labour movement. It brought into being, in the West and in some newly independent countries, an electoral democracy underpinned by a strong social capacity, with a welfare state that guaranteed a basic but expanding sense of social citizenship. This, within a geopolitical

89

order overseen by the United States, including a Cold War stand-off with its weaker communist rival.

The neoliberal revolution effectively tore up this settlement as it ran into crisis in the 1970s. It destroyed or severely weakened the labour movement and dissolved its industrial base via outsourcing and automation. It wound back many of the constraints on owners of wealth and capital while removing the various social safety nets which had been created to contain the worst excesses of capitalism. So, too, globalisation under the auspices of the US as "unipolar hegemon" became increasingly chaotic as Bretton Woods was abolished and finance deregulated. The rapid global economic development so unleashed created highly complex supply chains and divisions of labour, phenomenal economic growth in some previously "developing" countries (especially China), as well as accelerating inequalities both within and between nations. In the face of this new global financialised economic system, nation states lost much of their sovereignty, "markets" trumping "citizens" as the prime rule-givers for increasingly technocratic governments.[36] This rapid growth, finally, produced both an accelerated climate crisis (more than half of all historic carbon emissions have been since 1990) and the astonishing emergence of China as a perceived challenger to the United States' hegemon status.

The systemic crisis of neoliberalism is not just economic or even environmental. It is a political crisis because of the huge loss of agency, as governments and elites seem to rule for themselves in a corrupt manner, and society is no longer coherently connected to established political parties. It is also a social crisis, as neoliberalism removed the social protections and guarantees around work which had been established (for some) after 1945 precisely to address the class struggles underpinning the prior interwar crisis. These protections were also constraints on the excesses of capital and formed part of what sociologist Wolfgang Streeck calls "system integration", one which is clearly now inoperative. "What", he asked, "keeps an entropic, disorderly, stalemated, post-capitalist interregnum society going?"[37]

The collapse of secure employment and social protections consequent on early neoliberal reforms placed enormous strain on the social fabric. The ideologies and values promoted by "hard" neoliberals such as Reagan and Thatcher – nation, family, tradition, duty – were meant to be foundational of the constituted social order on which markets must rely (as Hayek had argued[38]). These proved inadequate. The 1980s and 1990s saw heightened social tensions, which came out as problems of social "cohesion" and "exclusion" – crime, long-term unemployment, decaying social fabric, and so on – rather than any direct political challenge. The erosion of civil society and community engagement was famously described by Robert Putnam in 1995 as "bowling alone", a condition that has only got worse in the internet era.[39]

As we suggested in the previous chapter, the new "third way" social democrats sought to protect a basic welfare provision (often tied to injunctions to seek employment as in "workfare") and address social cohesion while accepting the neoliberal economic model. The new social compact would be based on a social safety net, with pathways to employment through education and training (including childcare and other support), leading to a meritocracy of achievement and increased choice in the form of market citizenship.

As Anthony Giddens, one of Tony Blair's gurus suggested, this model required the self to be a "reflexive project" whose aim is self-actualisation, finding our "authentic self", a fulfilment which "is in some part a moral phenomenon, because it means fostering a sense that one is 'good,' a 'worthy person'". For the middle classes, this search for meaning and "worth" became a substitute for the old shared public traditions which had been disenchanted by neoliberalism.[40] We suggested in the last chapter how the creative industries had become part of this project.

The sense of crisis has come from the collapse of this project after the global financial crisis, not just for the working class – for whom it barely made sense – but also the professional middle class, especially its younger cohorts.[41] Debt, precarious work, fragmented careers, difficulty in accumulating the assets their parents took for granted, the devaluation of the educational capital that was to be the key to meritocratic advance – this has been the stuff of academic literature and popular culture since the millennium.[42] We can no longer rely on the state and public services, and must look to our own resources.

As Martin Wolf, associate editor of the *Financial Times* for many decades, and doyen of the global economic commentariat, writes:

> The insecurity that laissez-faire capitalism generates for the great majority who own few assets and are unable to insure or protect themselves against such obvious misfortunes as the unexpected loss of a job or incapacitating illness, is ultimately incompatible with democracy. That is what Western countries had learned by the early to mid-twentieth century. It is what they have learned again over the last four decades. Only autocracy, plutocracy, or some combination of the two is likely to thrive in an economy that generates such insecurity and a polity that shows such indifference.[43]

This generalisation of ontological insecurity, where one is forced back on one's own resources of family and friends, and the transmutation of professional strategic networking into a more desperate, improvisatory "hustle", has been called the "Brazilianisation of the world":

> growing inequality, oligarchy, the privatisation of wealth and social space, and a declining middle class ... the development of gentrified city centres and the excluded pushed to the periphery. In political terms ... patrimonialism, clientelism, and corruption. Rather than see these as aberrations, we should understand them as the normal state of politics.[44]

For Wolfgang Streeck, in a "world without system integration, social integration has to carry the entire burden of integration", and "the de-socialised capitalism of the interregnum hinges on the improvised performances of structurally self-centred, socially disorganised and politically disempowered individuals".[45] Crucial here is the loss of political agency which comes with the failure to envisage a viable exit from the present, what Mark Fisher called the "slow cancellation of the future", a "deflation of expectations".[46] The confident project of postwar modernity has evaporated despite its victory over its global rivals. We have come out of the period of neoliberal globalisation and technocratic politics announced by the "end of history" in 1990, but the end of the end of history has brought no new vision, no coherent political project.[47] As Slavoj Žižek said, we have woken up but only to the "desert of the real".[48]

The collapse of "system integration" and the impending sense of a capitalist crisis has not come about through an external challenge – the labour movement, communism, fascism, or, say, religious fundamentalism; rather, it is entirely endogenous. Classical Marxism saw the working class in systemic contradiction with capital, which meant that their struggle was a motor of historical progress. Socialism would take hold of the progressive elements in capitalism and push them to a higher civilisational level, in a process Marx called *aufheben*. However, as Göran Therborn suggested, though there are many groups and interests opposed to capitalism, none can be said to be structural or dialectal antagonists.[49] A purely endogenous crisis means that there is no obvious "inheritor", no systemic vision ready to replace it. There is, then, a real prospect that the end of capitalism comes with a wider civilisational collapse. Perhaps the only systemic antagonist is the planetary environment itself – no longer *Gaia* but *Solaris* – which is an equally scary prospect.[50]

It is this lack of a clear future, an ontological insecurity with no collective sense of political agency or project, that marks this interregnum.

The systemic failure of capitalism was classically framed as an internal economic contradiction – falling rates of profits, crisis of over-accumulation, and so on. But, as Nancy Fraser has argued, capitalism is a social, not just an economic, system. It has always relied for its functioning on "extra-economic" support, coordination, and legitimation systems which, nonetheless, it continually eats away at in search of profit.[51] Its crisis of profitability in the 1970s saw it undermine the state's capacity to coordinate the complex system of finance, prevent short-term excesses through regulation, coordinate private investment, and so on. So, too, it has relied on access to "free" natural resources (coal, oil, guano, lithium) and on nature as a waste dump without taking responsibility for their replenishment or negative consequences. Most crucially, though, it needs a labour force that is nurtured, socialised, educated, fed, and watered; it has repeatedly failed to ensure the sustainability of the social system required to provide these services.

This failure to ensure the basic social reproduction needs has been central to the working-class political challenge to capitalism, after industrialisation removed the population from the land, separating it from access to the means of sustenance, and thus forced them to sell their labour. The sociologist Karl Polanyi outlined the process in which the "social" reacted against its systemic erosion by the capitalism it served, resulting in the violent reactions and conflicts of the interwar years, and providing the salutary lesson for the introduction of a welfare state after 1945.[52] Yet this settlement in turn ran into crisis, neoliberalism dismantling, yet again, those protections. It is this self-destructive process that Nancy Fraser calls "cannibal capitalism", the sign of which is the *ouroboros* – the serpent that eats its own tail.

Whether we see the current conjuncture as a dangerous moment requiring difficult decisions, or as a systemic life or death crisis – not a trivial difference – it is the erosion of the "extra-economic" aspects of the system that stand out. It is for the failure of state capacity, the dysfunctions of democracy, the catastrophic impact on the environment, and the erosion of our social foundations that neoliberalism stands accused, and the urgent rectification of these that point a way forward.

Culture under neoliberalism

Where is culture in this crisis? We have charted the move from culture as part of social citizenship to culture as consumer service industry. This is part of a wider shift to a market citizenship in which the social foundations – health, welfare, education, and basic infrastructural provision – have been commodified, privatised, and outsourced.

95

Culture is not an industry

If one clear dynamic of the present crisis is the reassertion of the social foundations, how are we to reimagine culture alongside these? If we adopt Nancy Fraser's notion of capitalism as a social, not just economic, system, then we must view culture as a component of that social system. While the rise of commercial culture is presented as simply an ever-expanding, post-scarcity consumer economy, this hides the hollowing out of its systemic function within the social system. As we suggested in the Introduction, "culture" is not an eternal category (and nor is "the social") but emerged in the eighteenth century as other parts of the economy and society were reconfigured around an emergent industrial capitalism. This does not mean that culture is somehow "capitalist", just as the parallel emergence of a domestic sphere does not mean that "care and nurture" are capitalist. They are human needs reconfigured in order to serve the needs of capitalism, but which are not reducible to them. Fraser's core contention is that capitalism disavows and disrupts – cannibalises – the social resources on which it relies for its functioning. In this way, they can be sites of resistance to, and emancipation from, capitalism. We might see culture in this way too.

Raymond Williams suggested in his 1976 *Keywords* that "culture" had three broad meanings. First, a general process of intellectual, spiritual, and aesthetic development; second, a particular "way of life" (a people, a period, a group, or humanity in general); third, works and practices of intellectual and especially artistic activity. Since the 1980s at least, these last two have been run together. Already by the 1950s, "culture" had come "to signify not only the cultural industries and state cultural apparatuses but the forms of working-class subsistence and consumption, both the goods and services supplied by the

welfare state or purchased on the market, and the time of leisure and social reproduction outside the working day".[53]

The expansion of the production of culture ("specific products") and its intersection with the mixed economy of Williams'
"way of life" formed the background to post-war cultural politics, which sought to address culture through social citizenship.
Cultural consumption expanded beyond both an elite "arts and
letters" and older "folk" and traditional working-class cultures
and became intertwined with a mixed economy of "everyday
life".[54] As the emergent discipline of cultural studies argued,
this culture inevitably became a site of complex political
contestation.

Post-1968, countercultural politics focused heavily on cultures of everyday life, the collective consumption of public services, including urban space, and leisure and cultural facilities.
They challenged the cultural embedding of class, gender, race,
and sexuality in the "naturalised" language and structures of
everyday life. Culture also articulated a set of aspirations to a
different kind of self, of work, of a world which seemingly could
not be accommodated by the grey conformism of industrial
capitalism (or, indeed, communism). As education, leisure, and
spending power increased, the lines between culture as specific
products (cultural industries, state cultural apparatus) and as a
"whole way of life" became far more fluid. This, coupled with
new technologies, transformed cultural production and consumption, blurring lines of "high" and "popular", and opening up new pathways to creative expression for those previously
excluded from them.

However, since the late 1970s, each of these became recon-
tested and subtly transformed. We have the escalation of
the "culture wars", in which the political demands of the

counterculture have been met with vociferous opposition from the right, which sees it as singularly destructive of the traditional social fabric. So, too, the new urban cultures, and the aspirations to new kinds of life, work, and world, fed into the gentrification unleashed by the "creative city" and the aspirational promise of the creative industries. The new possibilities for cultural production and consumption stimulated a huge wave of commodification. Think of the way cultural products – hardware, software, "content" – now infuse the space of the household, the centrality of cultural consumption to our sense of self and social identity. Think, also, of the addition of "aesthetic" and symbolic values to even the most mundane household objects (fridges, scissors, lemon squeezers). And all of this organised through the kinds of monopoly cultural industries we outlined in the last chapter.

It can often seem as if the expansion of cultural production and consumption has been a singular, inevitable process of post-scarcity culture. *Everything, all at once, everywhere*, leading to a glut, and the ironic, disenchanted decadence of "postmodernism". But it came through a series of political choices. Which is to say that if post-war culture became an increasingly crucial site for the extension of social citizenship, this project has suffered a setback as significant as those for its other "foundational" dimensions – welfare, health, education, and so on. Though this process is often condemned in a general way as a "commodification of culture", it has systemic implications which are often overlooked.

As with other foundational services, the problem is not just that cultural commodities need to be paid for (thus excluding those who can't pay) but also that their individualised consumption disrupts the wider collective sense of public provision and citizenship. As Will Davies suggests, "The economy is cultural ... markets, property rights, work and consumption produce distinctive identities and affects, not as side-effects ... but as integral components of how they operate".[55]

This is echoed in Thatcher's 1981 statement about turning back "collectivist society": "If you change the approach you really are after the heart and soul of the nation. Economics are the method; the object is to change the heart and soul".[56] Here, culture ("heart and soul") is being used in a systemic manner to refer to the values which underpin the nation as a whole, and which constitute individual behaviour, identity, and affect. The refusal to consider art or culture as anything other than discretionary consumer choice is not just neoliberal economic dogma but part of its *cultural* project.

In fact, the emergence of an expanded sphere of cultural consumption, and the infusion of aesthetic and symbolic meanings across broad swathes of the new post-Fordist consumer economy, became exemplary for neoliberalism. Shopping as a distinct leisure and cultural activity illustrated the unique ability of the market to respond to people's innermost desires. The mall figured the expansion of choice as an emancipatory moment, the apotheosis of the "citizen consumer".[57] Where the cultural economy led, other services followed.

This is not to downplay the very real commercial opportunities which this new cultural consumption represented. We saw how from the 1980s there was a global reconfiguration of communications in which technologies, markets, regulations, and intellectual property rights opened a new space for profitable investment in which state provision (from broadcasting to the arts) was rolled back. Thatcher's promotion of commercial TV invoked both commercial and ideological reasons. This is clear in Dominic Sandbrook's work, where the explosion of the cultural industries (or his highly edited version of them) is exemplary of the Thatcherite remaking of Britain.[58] Hence her punitive attack on the arts.

New Labour's project of market citizenship responded to the social disruptions of Thatcher's neoliberal reforms and attempted to relaunch the left as a meritocratic knowledge society – Blair's "education, education, education". The creative industries saw the mobilisation of new creative subjects become exemplary for this project.

Cannibalised culture

What are the systemic effects of this reduction of culture to a consumer economy?

Most salient is cultural production. The idea that "talented individuals" with the means of production "inside their heads" would therefore get to control the new creative industries proved utterly illusory. The commercialisation and globalisation of cultural production has given rise to unprecedented levels of concentration and monopoly, in which barriers to entry are increasing by the day, just as the penetration of "social media" into the intimate lifeworld of the individual user is now the stuff of popular dystopia. This has impacted on cultural labour, whose creative autonomy and sense of meaningful employment has been significantly eroded. Creative labour studies show of course a complex and uneven picture – there are winners as well as losers, but far more of the latter than the former.[59]

Cannibalistically, the search for profit and control has come with a failure to ensure the sustainability of the very sources of creativity on which they depend. Not only the erosion of creative autonomy and time resources required for creation, but also subjection to increased competition for jobs, reduced fees and wages, stringent KPIs, restraint orders on working for competitors, self-funded skills upgrades – plus the usual freelancer issues of holidays, insurance, pensions, maternity leave, and so on. This is the other side to a long-term reduction in public investment in culture, which includes the cutting back or abolition of creative discipline programmes and departments, lack of affordable inner-city space, and the increase in educational debt. So, too, the absorption of self and social life into the injunction to be "always on" – the "sacrificial labour" in which the desire for a meaningful career eats away at your actual life. In short, the creative industries rely now on a "social factory" of creative workers' own networks, free time, and emotional resources. Just as with the natural world or the care required for social reproduction, the shared cultural "commons" are also being hollowed out.[60]

The other side to this is cultural consumption, which is less discussed. If we accept that there has been a general social disintegration, as the neoliberal state has withdrawn from and undermined key areas of the social foundations, what does culture look like from this perspective?

There has been a reduction in public spaces and accessible venues as much of cultural life has been commodified. This has implications for the kind of culture that gets produced, just as much as the domination of production by large corporations does. The idea of "communal luxury", which Kristin Ross took from the Paris Commune, makes it clear that the forms of consumption are as essential as any particular content. Collective consumption and public spaces have been systemically rolled back under neoliberalism, every nook and cranny subject to commercialisation and surveillance (which now intertwine).[61] The constriction of communal, popular pleasure to that which fits the format of a massively commercialised culture industry has inflicted deep and lasting damage on our sense of culture in common.

What does culture look like in the individualised "hustle society" of ontological insecurity, when each of us mostly looks to our own networks? Primarily, a systemic individuation of consumption, which takes us beyond diversity into a radical fragmentation of the public sphere. The logic of niche marketing sets up a series of individual rabbit holes which takes us far from any notion of a "common culture". This is exacerbated by the way digital platforms use algorithms to lock us into prior choices. The fragmentation of viewing habits, from mass television audiences to multiple screens (and multiple screens on those screens) in just one household, moves the sense of liberation from two or three available channels that all must watch into a space of distracted torpor.[62]

"Everything, all the time, everywhere" is how Stuart Jeffries describes this, as he charts the massive expansion of cultural consumption.[63] The apotheosis of consumer culture has not ushered in an age of proliferating invention and expression, but rather a widespread cynicism, weariness, "retromania", nostalgia, and stasis.

Though presented as the inevitability of "choice", contemporary culture derives from the core principle of capitalism. This is, that a small group of owners of capital get to make the decisions about the allocation and distribution of investment in our society, and this is organised exclusively under the impulse of profitability.

Culture goes missing

Until quite recently, culture was not an important site of profit. The cultural commodity goes back to Gutenberg, slowly expanding as new or more efficient technologies allowed reproduction at scale. The addition of steam power to the printing press; train, ship, and telegraph communications enhancing the circulation of news media, etchings, lithographs, and photography; and then the surge of technologies at the turn of the nineteenth century. Recorded film and music, together with broadcast sound and images introduced new commercial opportunities, and formed the backdrop for multiple debates on how these might work in a democracy. Jurgen Habermas' seminal work on the public sphere was deeply concerned with its ongoing privatisation in the 1950s and 60s.[64] Art had been classed by Marx as "unproductive labour". The pianist, Marx suggested, was paid for out of society's surplus; it did not itself generate returns to capital (unlike the piano maker). With reproduction at scale, culture could become "productive labour", its integration into fully capitalist firms increasing throughout the twentieth century.[65]

What we witnessed from the 1980s onwards was the rapid, enormously consequential withdrawal of the state from the cultural commodity market at a moment of enormous technological change – satellites, fibre-optics, telecoms and computing, pixels and MP3s, and the internet. Effectively, a combination of powerful commercial interests and an ideological project resulted in a huge, system-wide privatisation of the sphere of communications and culture. *Ouroboros.*

In politics, the obvious example is the collapse of the "fourth estate", which had emerged in a semi-commercial, semi-regulated space in the eighteenth century. The rapid destruction of that space, both its impact on the "business model" of journalism and the quality of public debate and exchange which rested upon this, is well known. What is astonishing is how the rise of a new digital public sphere has been entirely given over to a group of libertarians and sociopaths in northern California. The commercial system of the platform economy had become, by the early twenty-first century, the dominant economic, political, and ideological form of neoliberalism, and, indeed, US global hegemony. A key test over the next decades will be how far the reassertion of state and social power will curtail their operations.[66]

So, too, education, running very close to culture (as we will see), has been increasingly privatised and subjected to commercial imperatives, with vice-chancellors hell-bent on selling most of their systems and content to the platform companies. How an educational sphere central to the functioning of a modern industrial and democratic society could be given over almost entirely to commerce will be one of the lasting conundrums for future historians, picking over the debris of the interregnum.

Adam Smith, who codified the separation of "the economy" as a realm distinct from the rest of society, was famously concerned about how society would then hold together. Hence his "theory of moral sentiments" through which a society of (rightly) self-seeking individuals could yet find harmony in common feeling. He turned to the recently invented science of aesthetics, which was precisely concerned about how emotions stirred through the appreciation of sensuous beauty might do what rational self-interest could not.[67] Smith saw the string quartet as exemplary of how art allows us "imaginative sympathy" with other minds, thus allowing harmony to emerge. The simultaneous emergence of industrial capitalism and aesthetics – and, later, German Romanticism – has long been acknowledged. Terry Eagleton dismisses this conjunction as pure ideology:

> in an age when the arts were increasingly marginal, mere commodities on the market, they could claim morally privileged status. They were now the paragon of imaginative sympathy, and what could be more precious than that, not least in the brutal early decades of industrialisation?[68]

Art, suggests Eagleton, presented itself as a solution when in fact it was a symptom. There is some truth in this, and we will discuss this more in the next chapter. But ultimately this art-as-ideology critique has been damaging for the radical politics of art and culture, one which acknowledges their progressive function in the face of industrial capitalism.[69] This is a point made by Pierre Bourdieu, frequently ignored by his later disciples.[70]

Eagleton charts a particular configuration of art at a moment of an emerging industrial capitalism, just as the creation of a domestic sphere of unpaid female labour was a particular configuration of social reproduction. Securing the material requirements for that social reproduction was a definite site of struggle (wages, cheap food and clothing, drinkable water, liveable accommodation, and so on, often via the labour movement) but so too was that early feminist struggle to secure emancipation from gendered division of labour, and of the public and private spheres. One might say similar things about art and culture. Their specific outlines were configured by capitalism as a social system, but they nevertheless expressed fundamental essentials for human life.

It is for this reason that dismissing the "artistic critique of capitalism" as simply a stratagem of the professional-managerial

class completely misses the long investment of the workers'
movement (and feminism) in art and culture. As in the famous
poem by James Oppenheim, "Bread and Roses":

> Our lives shall not be sweated from birth until life closes;
> Hearts starve as well as bodies; give us bread, but give us roses.
> As we go marching, marching, unnumbered women dead
> Go crying through our singing their ancient call for bread.
> Small art and love and beauty their drudging spirits knew.
> Yes, it is bread we fight for, but we fight for roses too.[71]

This systemic approach recalls Raymond Williams' first, and
often overlooked, definition of culture as "a general process
of intellectual, spiritual, and aesthetic development". Evoking
ideas of progress, enlightenment, and modernism, this has more
recently been dismissed as a mask for destructive, extractive ide-
als, and irretrievably linked to colonialism and capitalism. This
is not necessarily so, as I will argue. We need to reclaim and
reconfigure such a notion, rather than reject it out of hand. For
the faltering of our collective sense of an intellectual, spiritual,
and aesthetic development has coincided with a widespread disappearance of a future, and is part of that ontological insecurity which pervades the present moment.

3

Necessity or luxury?

The last two chapters have outlined the consequences of treating culture as an industry, arguing that it is as essential to the social foundations as health, education, welfare, and infrastructure. I also suggested that while culture is part of the systemic crisis of the present it has been routinely ignored as an active agent of change. Culture has gone missing at the moment it is most needed. To explain this absence, I pointed to language of "industry", to culture's framing as a desire-driven consumer society, to the cultural sector's own confusions as to its public status and function, and to the association of creativity and culture with a post-1968 professional "creative" class, to name just a few.

But how is culture part of the social foundations? We might acknowledge culture as important for individuals and communities, that it should not necessarily be seen as an industrial sector or economic engine. Yet for those looking to go beyond GDP-centric growth, seeking out a new wellbeing-based society focused on securing the social foundations, is culture really that foundational? In a cost-of-living crisis, when poverty, insecurity, and inequality are rampant, is it not best to secure our needs first before we turn to the good things in life? Health, education, housing, transport, food, energy, water, basic communication systems – should these not be fixed before we get to culture?[1]

In what follows I make an argument for the centrality of culture in overcoming the present crisis, and in the following chapters sketch out what such an agenda might look like. We need to acknowledge the "legitimation crisis" to which culture-as-industry was a response – art associated with elitism and patrician subsidy, the growth of the culture industries, and the transformation of popular culture in from the 1960s. I'll discuss the practical policy implications later. Here, I try to ground culture in the social foundations from an historical-philosophical perspective, presenting the grounds on which we can build a transformative vision for culture.

I start with the issue of essential needs, separate from inessential wants, suggesting this opposition – in which art and culture are clearly on the side of the latter – is not sustainable. Needs and wants are largely inseparable and they are historically mutable. But above all, our needs involve social and psychological elements which are as essential to any account of the good society as are the material basics. I then discuss another version of this opposition, that between necessity and freedom, with the former ontologically prior to the latter. To counter this, I argue that freedom is as foundational to humans as satisfying material needs, and that art and culture provide a crucial site though which this freedom is articulated. The freedom it articulates is the necessity of deciding what one ought to do, the symbolic means through which these questions are addressed.

The chapter then argues that while art and culture can be seen as essential to the good life, this cannot be restricted to the individual's own consumption of this culture. The ability to enjoy culture is a social one, dependent on a wider educational and cultural infrastructure. Culture, in both its individual trajectory and its social guarantee, is thus essential to the development of individual capabilities, as in the work of Amartya Sen and Martha Nussbaum, and thus an essential part of democratic citizenship, a fundamental human right.

Finally, if the ability to fully participate in culture is essential to human flourishing, part of democratic citizenship, it also has a systemic social function of, as Eno says, "keeping us coherent". I return to Raymond Williams to discuss the ways in which culture is an ongoing conversation between past, present, and future, and how this conversation has been reduced to postmodern flattening and market agnosticism. A renewed culture cannot be understood just as individual flourishing but is also part of a collective historical and political project without which any concept of a viable human future is unthinkable.

Needs and wants

In seeking to outline a practical programme for the social foundations, Anna Coote and Andrew Percy attempt to define clearly identifiable and limited essential needs. Arguing for universal basic services, they suggest that "human needs are universal across time and space", and are distinct from "wants". Needs, they argue, are indispensable for life and are satiable. Wants are not indispensable, and, unlike needs, "they vary infinitely and can multiply exponentially".[2] On the contrary, I would argue, needs are neither absolute nor fixed. We can't set the benchmark for need at some physiological level of "bare life", for, as King Lear had it,

> Our basest beggars
> Are in the poorest thing superfluous.
> Allow not nature more than nature needs,
> Man's life is cheap as beast's.[3]

Nor can we separate need from want in such a categorical manner. As two well-known materialists argued:

> Life involves before anything else eating and drinking, a habitation, clothing and many other things. The first historical act is thus the means to satisfy those needs, the production of material life itself .... The second point is that the satisfaction of the first need ... leads to new needs.[4]

Coote and Percy list a series of "needs" which might have a universal, anthropological basis (water, food, clothing, and shelter) but these are now clearly understood in terms of historical expectations. We do need water, but plumbing is a very recent "need". They also admit of new needs, such as motor transport and the internet.[5] Needs such as "education" are historically specific, ranging from the anthropological requirement that infants adopt taught rather than instinctive behaviour, to a complex system of high schools, universities, and lifelong learning.

The focus on the provision of basic needs and the reproduction of material life provides a seemingly firmer basis for social policy. Utilities, housing, education, health, and transport evoke a material, even physiological, reality. Setting needs against wants is also a way of delineating socially agreed and limited essential provision from the unlimited expansion of "free", individual consumer desire. But needs expand as they are satisfied and this does not turn them into non-essential "wants". Coote and Percy's' list of needs includes shelter, secure and non-threatening work, education, healthcare, security in childhood, significant primary relationships, physical and economic security, and a safe environment. But it makes little sense to talk about "sufficiency" here in the same way you might with food or water. What does it mean to have sufficient health, education, or security?

The FEC, as with others who work on indexes of poverty, recognise that changing needs are based on shifting social expectations. Nail bars, cafes, and annual holidays are now seen as "everyday" essentials. In the pandemic, the FEC distinguished more sharply between the "real" basics – those things you cannot do without – and the "everyday" leisure economy items (including cultural consumption), which people can do without, even if life is not so pleasant.

> But the present crisis underscores the importance of [a] narrower focus because it demonstrates the importance of the foundational as that part of the economy which cannot be shut down. And the list of essential workers in each national economy provides a common sense and practical definition of what counts as foundational.[6]

This is too restrictive. Without water, one dies in nine days, yet one can live for years without human touch. Is the latter a luxury? Of course, the removal of water, food, electricity, or shelter makes life incredibly difficult very quickly, and it would take some time (childcare issues aside) for the closure of schools, or general health and social services, to register an impact. But we all accept these things as part of the social foundations. "Essential worker" is also a contested term, as those aspects of life that had to be suspended for pandemic health reasons (unlike food, energy, and water supplies) cannot be described as "inessential" or secondary. Are teachers not essential workers because they had to stay home? Are cancer check-ups "non-essential" because they are more immediately deferrable in light of Covid-19 emergencies? Identifying the social foundations is surely not just about "bare life" or the immediacy of need, but also relates to the whole system required for the social reproduction of life. These have different temporalities of impact, if absent or removed, but that should not be used to establish a hierarchy.

Social scientist Göran Therborn makes the distinction between "vital" and "resource" inequalities. The former refers to those directly affecting "health and death", the latter concerning access to education, "social capital", and income.[7] Therborn argues it is too narrowing to confine the "real" foundations to "vital" needs, as these social resources are also essential.[8] More recently, this expanded perspective of need has been adopted by the FEC in its concept of "liveability", where, in addition to disposable income and foundational services, they add the social infrastructure, of "sociability, physical exercise and creative expression".[9]

Frankfurt School philosopher Theodore Adorno suggested that the very quality of need changes as immediate deprivation is assuaged: "If production were unconditionally reoriented to the satisfaction of needs, even and especially those produced by capitalism, then needs themselves would be decisively changed … If [deprivation] disappears the relation between need and satisfaction changes".[10] In these circumstances, the social basics expand to encompass far more than bare life and to respond to the reality of wants. Otherwise, the vision of the good life becomes reductive and utilitarian.

The utilitarian definition of the good life as the satisfaction of the material needs required to reproduce life underpinned (for good reason, considering the grinding poverty of much of the population) many of the aspirations of both liberal democratic and historic communist regimes. But, as Hannah Arendt forcefully argued, the basic reproduction of life – labour – is always a means, and it does not supply an end or purpose to that life.[11] The core thrust of those critiquing GDP-focused growth is not just the failure to capture significant social inequalities in the distribution of such growth. They point to the inability of GDP to adequately describe "human development", "flourishing", "quality of life", the "good life", "wellbeing", and so on. As Tim Jackson suggests: "Beyond these material needs, prosperity is as much about social and psychological functioning – identity, affiliation, participation, creativity and experience – as it is about material stuff".[12]

In his account of vital and resource inequalities referred to above, Göran Therborn also adds "existential inequality", disparities of "recognition and respect". The social foundations, then, must include the basic human desire for recognition, respect, purpose, and meaning derived from the social world in which we live. Society's provision of these is as essential to its social integration as the vital material basics.[13]

A lack of social recognition and respect, of a sense of affiliation and belonging, meaning and purpose, contributes to the deep ontological insecurity of contemporary capitalism. This insecurity is differentially distributed. The issues of "wellbeing" faced by the professional managerial class might revolve around changing lifestyles and consumption habits, or allowing spirituality into one's life. It can often involve rather smug, moralistic calls for us to abandon our consumerist lifestyles while ignoring the constrained material circumstances out of which these "life-styles" are constructed. We can't give up the car if we are forced to live in the suburbs or eat healthy food when we can't afford to fix the cooker. The "proletarian ecosystem" is one of insecure wage-dependency, being a step away from penury, negotiating a world that is mostly beyond your control.[14]

To fix this requires a systemic redistribution not just of income and basic services, but also of job security, social infra-structure, and a sense of democratic voice – "taking back control". Ultimately, the provision of material basics is inseparable from granting respect and recognition to everyone, and the sense of control over one's life that goes with this. There should be no opposition between the demands of "redistribution" and "recognition".[15] The accordance of respect and recogni-tion means allowing the working class to pursue aspirations of "identity, affiliation, participation, creativity, and experience" just as much as the professional-managerial class. To fail to see this is to radically misunderstand the explosions of working-class "populism" in Brexit, Trump, Bolsonaro, and the "gilets jaunes".

The need for "identity, affiliation, participation, creativity, and experience", for respect and recognition, is – or should be – embedded in the social foundations alongside basic material needs. If we narrow our vision of social transformation to basic material needs, we not only diminish that vision but also hobble our ability to mobilise the energies required to achieve it.

As I argued in the Introduction, the post-war period saw new forms of cultural production and consumption reaching into the heart of traditional ways of life, giving rise to new kinds of aspirations, identities, and demands. The idea of culture became a contested site in which these complex and expanding needs and wants were negotiated. Crucial here was the ability of culture to articulate a growing opposition to the reduction of social life to the efficient administration of material needs. This discontent built on a long history of anti-materialism, of both conservative and radical varieties. The distinct, separate realm of culture (*kultur*) that emerged in the eighteenth century, and which was represented above all in the category of art, was opposed to the rationalist materialism of modern industrial society. This "artistic critique", as it was dubbed recently, had a complex and ambivalent relationship with the "social critique" (inequality, material deprivation, injustice) as exemplified by the growing labour movement.[16] But they were not opposed camps, despite retrospective attempts to make this so. Rather, they were intertwined in complex ways, as one might expect from such an alliance of workers and intellectuals.

This "artistic critique" of capitalism came into its own in the 1960s, differently informing the new left, "1968", and the counterculture. This radical redefinition of left politics is not to be dismissed simply as an outgrowth of the professional-managerial class. The discontent and aspirations articulated in this post-1960s "artistic critique" had become widespread, even mainstream, by the 1980s. Those leading these new political and social movements were not intrinsically opposed to the working-class movement nor an inevitable step on the slippery slope to postmodern consumerism, third way neoliberalism, or West Coast tech libertarianism.[17] In fact, they always had a close connection to the welfare state, making their claims within the umbrella of social citizenship.[18]

If many in the ecology and de-growth camps take a typically "professional-managerial class" moralising stance to the "bad" consumption habits of the working class, their critics often seem to think that the working classes are only interested in material security, which in my view is equally patronising. They both ignore the extent to which a new "creative economy" was tied up with the diminishing of the welfare state and the rerouting of radical wants and desires into individualised consumption.

Just as we might accord needs that go beyond the purely material to the working class, we might also reclaim want and desire for a more radical agenda.

Necessity and freedom

The "realm of necessity" and the "realm of freedom" are both essential parts of our lives in common. We cannot think one without the other. Culture straddles these two realms – it is a basic need, present in the darkest recesses of material deprivation, but part of the need it satisfies is a freedom over and above that necessity.

In a John Peel lecture of 2015, musician Brian Eno framed art as oppositional to "GDP" and "industry", suggesting the paradox that art is something basic, essential, and necessary to human beings, but also beyond "necessity". His definition of art is "everything that you don't have to do".

> Now what I mean by that is that there are certain things you have to do to stay alive. You have to eat, for example. But you don't have to invent Baked Alaskas or sausage rolls or Heston Blumenthal. So you have this basic activity that we and all other animals do, which is called eating, but then unlike all other animals, we do a lot of embroidery and embellishment on top of it. We make eating into a complicated, stylised activity of some kind. You have to wear clothes. But you don't have to come up with Dior dresses or Doc Marten boots or Chanel little black

frocks… So, once again we have an essential need – clothing ourselves – which we then do with intense sort of interest. We stylise
and embellish and ornament and decorate.[19]

Does this mean art is that which comes after the satisfaction
of basic needs? Bread first, art (and croissants) second? Rather,
Eno argues, art "is central to everything we do". Art is not a
material necessity; rather, it is something we do in response to a
need that is fundamentally human.

We can contrast this with Abraham Maslow's famous "hierarchy of needs", outlined in 1943 and adopted by marketing
agencies in the 1960s. It is only after the basic needs of food,
water, shelter, security, belonging, and esteem have been met
that we engage in various forms of "self-actualisation", including art.[20]

Basic material provision is crucial to any flourishing life;
without it, nobody is free. Lives of crippling poverty are not
conducive to participation in the creative arts. As "Doc" Tydon
says to Jock in the 1971 film *Wake in Fright*: "It's death to farm out
here. It's worse than death in the mines. You want them to sing
opera as well?"[21] But Maslow's "hierarchy" is saying something
else. Not just that a range of basic needs and social arrangements are needed for full human flourishing, but that it is *only
after* these needs are met that people can begin to think about
"self-actualisation", and art and culture.

This claim – food and shelter first, art later – involves an
index of progress familiar to Matthew Arnold and Edwin
Taylor. Only as history progresses and material civilisation
improves can (no longer "primitive") societies enjoy the arts.[22]
But locating art and creative expression only after basic material needs are met is anthropologically wrong. Throughout

history, as in this present age, lives are crippled by poverty and grinding labour, but it is not the case that these lives do not seek meaning, or latch onto symbols, words, rhythms, and melodies which articulate this meaning.

The world's oldest continuing living culture, Australia's First Nations people, shows a depth and complexity of artistic expression in the earliest recorded finds. Aboriginal rock paintings, as with those in pre-historic European caves, show a basic impulse to make symbolic or mimetic marks, movements, and sounds, coterminous with the extreme challenge of a dry continent or one creaking under the icesheet. Peasant icons, songs of work and grief, oral narratives passed on between generations of enslaved groups, collective markers or sacred spaces, liturgies and rituals – these have been present in the very earliest records of human existence. These suggest an ontological, evolutionary propensity to makes symbols, signs, and metaphors fundamental, and unique, to humans-in-nature.

Maslow's "hierarchy of needs" related more to neoclassical economics than any anthropological reality. As an argument for an ascending hierarchy of values beyond basic utility, it came into its own in the 1980s when it was linked to an argument about epochal change. We were now in a "post-scarcity" economy where the material means for the reproduction of life were assured. In this "post-materialist" society, we sought self-actualisation, meaningful experiences, and aesthetic choice through which we could shape our identities.[23]

The arrival of post-scarcity, post-materialist societies seemed to announce the "cultural economy". After the era of Fordist mass consumption, which for large parts of the population had made the material deprivations of the past a distant memory, we were now in the post-Fordist era of individualised, niche consumption. We were able to spend money on goods expressive of our identity while our everyday lives could be "aesthetisised".[24]

On the contrary, rather than being a universal truth, it is a way of thinking particular to our own modern civilisation that culture can only happen after the "essentials" have been taken care of. When Indigenous peoples talk about culture, it is of something foundational to their lives, inseparable from them. This has been the case historically for most societies and civilisations. Only in the eighteenth century does a space called the "economy" or the "sphere of needs" get separated out into an autonomous system unrelated to ethics and meaning, driven by "scientific" laws. It is this idea of the amoral, mechanistic "modern economy", imposed by colonial gunboats, that non-Western societies found so existentially shocking.[25]

In Europe, the idea of art and culture was one important source of opposition (there were others) to the economic and instrumental logic that came to define our lives in society. That, in the 1980s and 1990s, this very "anti-materialist" objection becomes a way to position culture as a foundation for a post-industrial economy, is as much part of the neoliberal revolution as New Public Management or reducing the welfare budget.

Art, as Eno describes it, is "central to everything we do", and, as anthropological studies show, it is coterminous with recognisable human existence. While we need a whole range of material and social arrangements to flourish as full human beings, this is not the same as saying we can only engage in art *after* these basic needs are met. An Australia Council survey in 2020 found that 98 per cent of the population engaged in some form of art and culture.[26] Art and culture are woven into the lives of the most deprived individuals and communities, and we would consider someone with no concern for even the smallest element of these as somehow dehumanised.

I have found Martin Hägglund's account of material and spiritual freedom very useful here.[27] All animals have to sustain their material life and to reproduce themselves. Life depends on fragile bodies, and sustaining them gives life purpose. All animals have the agency to satisfy the needs of their bodies, and all animals acquire a surplus of time, a certain material freedom, and time of play and relaxation beyond the immediate acquisition of these material needs (or avoidance of existential threat). Humans are subject to these material needs, but their purpose and agency are not set by the imperatives of material survival. The purposes of human lives are set by normative not natural imperatives. By "ought" not "instinct". These normative purposes, in turn, can be changed in the light of self-reflection. "As distinct from natural freedom, spiritual freedom requires the ability to ask which imperatives to follow in the light of our ends, as well as the ability to call into question, challenge and transform our ends themselves".[28]

Humans also generate surplus time, after material necessities have been met, but nothing tells them how they ought to use this time. They themselves must decide this. Material and spiritual freedom are inseparable – there is no spiritual realm apart from the material – but they are not the same. Spiritual freedom is a higher order of freedom; it is dependent on nature but transcends it. The way we lead our lives is not set by material necessity but set by us. To which I would add that culture, at its broadest, is the name we give to the collective patterning of our material and spiritual freedoms, patterns based not just on communication – all plants and animals communicate – but on symbolisation, forms of speaking about what we *ought* to do.

Necessity or luxury?

That's why the absence of art and culture from any transformative agenda has the potential to be so damaging. A narrow focus on basic material needs – material freedom – ignores the dimension of spiritual freedom, a radical existential freedom whose omission leaves a vacuum at the heart of the radical agenda. Ignoring culture does not make it go away, as the current right-wing monopoly of the "culture wars" shows only too clearly. Ernst Bloch, writing in 1930s Germany where the communists and social democrats were focused purely on the material economic struggle, observed that: "Man does not live by bread alone, especially when he does not have any".[29] In this way, Bloch was very clear about what happens when people feel their sense of meaning has been eroded, and the kinds of powerfully affective, atavistic symbols that can easily step into the ontological vacuum.

Individual consumption or communal luxury

Brian Eno's definition of "creative arts" is provocatively wide: "Symphonies, perfume, sports cars, graffiti, needlepoint, monuments, tattoos, slang, Ming vases, doodles, poodles, apple strudels, still life, second life, bed knobs and boob jobs".[30] This lets us into culture as a way of life, an entertaining formulation driven by alliteration and internal rhyming perhaps. Cultural critic Stefano Harney gives us a more precise evocation of art and culture as intimately interwoven with everyday life:

> Art is closer to people than at any other time in history. People make and compile music. They design interiors and make-over their bodies. They watch more television and more movies. They think deeply about food and clothes. They write software and surf the net of music videos and play on-line games together.

They encounter, study, learn and evaluate languages, diasporas and heritages. There is also a massive daily practice in the arts, from underground music, to making gardens, to creative writing camps. And with this there is production of subjectivities which are literally fashioned, which are aesthetic, which are created ... There is a massive daily register of judgment, critique, attention, and taste.[31]

This is an image of human flourishing that would be widely accepted in any account of social wellbeing, where provision for basic need has freed up time from the drudgery of labour and allowed for the possibility of self-realisation, or the full exercise of spiritual freedom. I want to interrogate this image a little.

The most immediate objection is that access to many of these services or spaces requires financial resources which are unequally distributed. But let's assume some kind of universal basic income scheme, or that a significant investment in universal basic services has freed up income for discretionary spending. Even in this case, coming out of four decades of neoliberalism, Harney's portrait can also be seen as an idealised image of a post-materialist consumer culture.[32] After forty years of individualised consumption economies, how far would a UBI- or UBS-fuelled creative flourishing exacerbate this social fragmentation? How far would this individualised creative self-realisation further undermine a sense of social solidarity?

Assigning culture and leisure to market-based discretionary spending glides over how their privatisation has been part of the "unpicking" of the welfare state. The shift from "mass consumption" to "personalised choice", while providing some gains in terms of individual autonomy, was also a deliberate and demonstrative shift away from public to private goods. It was a source of profit through the privatisation of much of collective cultural consumption, with a consequent erosion of public life. This, I argue, was part of its wider ideological project.

In response we need to look at where collective consumption can help rebuild social connectivity, civil society, local community, and a wider sense of public solidarity. We need to ask which of these services, spaces, or products should be collectively provided and enjoyed, and which are a matter of individual discretionary spending?

Collective provision means publicly financed or subsidised, but also to be enjoyed collectively rather than individually. In Chapter 5, we discuss the "cultural infrastructure", something that is collectively provided or guaranteed, for example communication systems, parks, libraries, and community centres (these are part of what the FEC call the "social infrastructure"). The question is not just one of efficiency or necessity. A common public communications infrastructure is more efficient, and parks and libraries are collectively provided (almost) by definition. But there are other social and political reasons why both collective provision and collective consumption should be encouraged.

The collective provision of cultural and leisure services, along with ensuring a certain quality of public realm, was long seen as an essential part of the welfare state and democratic citizenship. It was important for many of the "social liberal" and social democratic municipalities who first provided these spaces and facilities in the nineteenth and twentieth centuries, often at the same time as the infrastructure for water, gas, electricity, and public transport.[33] So, too, this democratic and collective access to aesthetic forms of self-realisation was what the Communards called "communal luxury".[34]

The personalisation of cultural consumption is not an inevitable technological outcome; rather, the technologies were deliberately framed around individual choice and convenience. Where collective consumption remains necessary, such as football and other sports events, cinemas, and festivals, the logic of commerciality constantly works against any sense of an empowered collective. I shall argue in the next chapters that it is the deliberate facilitation of collective consumption, rather than a narrow focus on "access and participation", that marks a transformative cultural policy.

The second question concerns the economy underpinning the complex array of products, services, and spaces evoked by Harney. Even if we provide some of these collectively, many will be supplied by the marketplace. And what kind of market? Are these to be small-scale, everyday, locally embedded markets, or massive franchises run out of a global headquarters somewhere?

The protection and promotion of locally embedded cultural and leisure economies, of the sort often evoked in the creative industries literature, requires political will. They no longer happen "organically". The hollowing out of the "creative city" by internationally mobile development capital, or the reorganisation of the most localised, mundane services by global platform companies, is well known. No evocation of cultural flourishing is realistic unless it comes with a clear sense of the political economy of culture. Just as artist spaces provided the gateway for gentrification, small-scale creative service providers can be quickly folded into large-scale franchise companies.

The flip side of markets is labour. Who is leading Harney's creative workshops or making the video games and movies? We have seen how conditions for cultural workers have been eroded, with declining incomes, less autonomy, and more precarity. Fixing this will require more than just enhancing employment rights and minimum wages, welcome as these might be. It means addressing ownership of intellectual property rights and how these are deployed throughout the production chain. It means confronting the multiple chokeholds the large cultural corporations now exert. I discuss this in Chapter 6.

Crucially, however, neither systemic regulatory changes nor these practical points of intervention can work if not undertaken as part of a collective endeavour. This means not just collective action by cultural sector workers, but also building connections to wider struggles against precarity and exploitation in the labour force, and in turn a recognition that culture is not an industry but a collective human need. If this is so, then it has radical implications for the political economy of culture, as we will discuss in the next two chapters.

Capabilities and citizenship

The third question for Harney's portrait concerns the unequal ability to participate in this creative flourishing. Do apple strudels and Ming vases, symphonies and tattoos, require the same cultural competence to enjoy them? Or "evaluating diasporas" the same as "surfing music videos"? This is not a question about which is "better", but rather an acknowledgement that different elements of this list require different amounts of time or prior "cultural capital", neither of which are equally distributed. This would not be changed by a UBI. In isolation from the democratic development of individual capacity, a UBI would exacerbate the inequality and fragmentation of creative consumption.

Brian Eno, the rock star from an art college, can move between symphonies and sports cars, but there are many for whom a Ming vase, a symphony, or a creative writing camp are closed books. This has long been a criticism of the "cultural omnivore" thesis, which argues that we all now see a rap song and a piano sonata, clubbing and going to the theatre, as equally valid. But some people are more omnivorous than others. They can move freely across the cultural register because they not only have the income and time, but also the requisite education and disposition to partake in creative flourishing.[35] We might see here the habitus of the "professional-managerial class", whose sense of "self-worth" often builds on a commitment to a (highly individualised) cultural self-development.[36] Again, there is no reason to restrict such potential for flourishing to the habitus of a particular class fraction, even if such restriction may often be the case in the current circumstances. The task, surely, is to make the potential for creative expression a democratic right and an essential part of social solidarity.

That is, access to culture needs to be ensured not via enhanced discretionary spending or a UBI, but by its promotion as a fundamental part of citizenship. Basic social needs are not to be understood just as the reproduction of material life, physiological urgency, or categorically opposed to wants, but rather as those things we cannot do without if we are to fully participate in society and realise our potential. We need material and spiritual freedoms.

In rejecting GDP as a measure of our welfare, both Raworth and the FEC – along with many others – refer to Amartya Sen and Martha Nussbaum's "capabilities" approach.[37] They look to human wellbeing and flourishing as the primary ethical objective of any society (Aristotle's *eudaimonia*). They emphasise substantive or positive freedom – not just the formal freedom to do something, but the means and resources that make that choice real. This requires an identification of what capacities are essential to empower humans. As Sen has it, "to choose a life they have reason to value".[38] These capabilities directly inform the idea of human rights, which should be accorded to everyone if they are to be able to live their lives in ways that fulfil their potential.

In contrast to the 2015 SDGs, the United Nations 1948 Universal Declaration of Human Rights, article 27.1 states: "Everyone has the right freely to participate in the cultural life of the community, to enjoy the arts and to share in scientific advancement and its benefits". This was reaffirmed in the 1966 United Nations International Covenant on Economic, Social and Cultural Rights, article 15.a, which notes the right to fully participate in culture and science. Human rights formulated in this way clearly overlap with T. H. Marshall's famous 1949 definition of social citizenship, where he describes the substantive welfare rights which were won after the civic and political freedoms acquired between the eighteenth and twentieth centuries. Social citizenship ranged from "[granting] the right to a modicum of economic welfare and security to the right to share to the full in the social heritage and to live the life of a civilised being according to the standards prevailing in the society".[39]

Participation in culture ("social heritage" and the "life of a civilised being") was envisaged as a universal human right, an essential part of citizenship. Martha Nussbaum's list of ten essential capabilities includes being able to use the senses, imagine, think, and reason, and to have the educational opportunities necessary to realise these capacities. Culture is used in the sense of "cultivation" and human growth, and includes artistic, musical, literary, religious, and scientific works.[40] Both the 1948 Universal Declaration and Nussbaum's formulations could have provided the basis for a 2015 SDG focusing on culture. Its absence speaks both to the strategic failure of UNESCO and to the neoliberal character of the SDG framing itself.

If we have a fundamental right to those capabilities we cannot do without if we are to fully participate in society and realise our potential, then our approach to cultural policy requires more than a display of available cultural goods and services before the choosing individual. To make real, informed choices involves more than disposable income. It requires, as the FEC argue, "reliance systems delivering essential services and social infrastructure which sustain all the various forms of individual expression and sociability".[41] It requires education in the broadest sense. This entails a systematic accordance of respect and recognition, a sense of self-worth, and a confidence in making choices. Currently, these are as unequally distributed as wealth and time.

Social philosopher Russell Keat talks about "cultural meta-goods", the acquired cultural capacities that allow one to make free, informed choices about other cultural goods.[42] This refers to education in its broadest sense, not just arts and cultural education, though the precipitous disappearance of these at a time of the privatisation of cultural consumption is no coincidence. Cultural goods themselves are part of that process of education, of self-development, part of the infrastructure, if you like, through which spiritual freedom is enhanced and expanded. They are:

> the more concrete and engaging representations of the various ways in which human life may be conducted, the nuanced depictions of social relationships and individual characters, which are to be found in novels, films, plays, TV drama, soap operas and many other cultural "products". What is crucial about these

cultural goods is that they enable us vicariously to extend our own range of experience, freeing us from the limitations imposed by the contingencies of our own existence, and thereby provide us with some understanding of the possibilities, dangers and attractions of lives we have not (yet) led, and some means of reflection on those which we already have. A certain critical "distance" is thereby made available, but in a way that relies mainly on things being "shown" rather than "said".[43]

The access to cultural meta-goods includes an environment where one is exposed to different cultural ideas and images – libraries, galleries, events, festivals, indie cinemas, free public online content, and so on, as well as a thriving local "independent" sector. It means an environment where citizens are held in respect, and institutions open themselves up to you. This is the "communal luxury" of the great state art galleries and museums, the grand libraries, theatres, and concert halls. It is the social and cultural infrastructure of community centres and local libraries, cinemas, and music venues. But it also means the railway and bus stations, shopping precincts, and public offices. Imagine, even the employment and social security services might be conceived of as citizen services rather than punitive regimes! It is the free wi-fi and information services, the open citizen platforms, and public media services made possible by communications technologies but long hived off from the commons. It means all those things evoking what Dan Hill calls "the quietly radical importance of everyday infrastructures".[44] It is "luxury" – "reimagined not as material abundance ... but as 'light', lux, the possibility for different expressions of human creative potentials".[45]

John K. Galbraith's "private affluence, public squalor", to which the FEC refer when talking of the decay of social foundations, equally describes the degradation of cultural citizenship. The privatisation of culture has gone hand in glove with the reduction in public investment in the individual and collective capabilities required to fully participate in that culture. Culture conceived both as collectively provided goods – events, activities, exhibitions, performances, environment – and as the daily exercise of "judgment, critique, attention, and taste" relies on the shared capabilities, the "cultural meta-goods", which allow individuals to make informed choices about "a life worth living".

As I will argue in the next chapters, culture needs to be conceived in direct relation to the social infrastructure – that essential pillar of liveability – which has been severely eroded in the last decades. But culture also has its own systemic functions, which require specific attention.

Dancing together

Culture is not just about the provision of goods and services to the sovereign consumer but a crucial aspect of citizenship and the empowerment required for the flourishing of human capabilities, of spiritual freedom. Culture is a part of the social foundations, an essential attribute of liveability, and a source of individual and community connectivity. It thus has systemic functions, of a similar order to those described by Nancy Fraser, as essential, even though disavowed, to the functioning of contemporary capitalist society.

Amongst some critics there has been a reworking of an older Marxist distinction between "material production" and the social superstructure, such that the latter is dependent on, and to some extent a function of, the former. With echoes of an old "base–superstructure" distinction, this model has taken off from the growing tensions between the working class (those in receipt of wages) and the professional-managerial class, which, though waged, has autonomous working conditions and is driven by educational credentialism. From this perspective, the institutions and professional labour of culture is paid for out of the social surplus. It is non-productive labour made possible by the productive labour which generates that surplus. Matt Huber, for example, suggests that culture is a "living space in the economy" for particular kinds of professionals "not wrapped up in necessary material production or surplus value production".[46] Quoting Hal Draper, he suggests:

> Contributions to the symphony orchestra, university, church, or opera association come out of the same fund as expenditures for butlers, yachts, private chefs, or fashionable paintings and also … prison wardens, generals, politicians, lawyers, judges, Boy Scout leaders, or asylum-keepers.[47]

This is not the place to get into the arcana of the Marxist theory of value, but this kind of objection raises some crucial questions on culture as necessity or luxury.

In its evocation of "material" production as uniquely generative of the social surplus – and the characterisation of this non-material realm as a merely functional outcrop of material production – it is a repetition of an old base–superstructure model which is highly problematic, and, I would suggest, damaging.

It is of course the case that without the production of the vital, material basics of life there can be no separate professional realm of intellectual labour. In this light, it serves to recall intellectuals to the physical drudgery of production on which their own autonomy rests. Annie Ernaux, in *A Woman's Life*, calls it a "blatant injustice" that her mother "spent all day selling milk and potatoes so that I could sit in a lecture hall and learn about Plato". As with Didier Eribon and, in a different register, Thomas Piketty, these are *mea culpas* regarding the failure of solidarity between a declining working class and an expanding intellectual ex-working class bent on escape into the cultural professions.[48]

This puncturing of the creative professional's sense of autonomous self-direction is accompanied by the revelation of their social role – part of the regime of social discipline and obfuscation, alongside priests and prison wardens. All well and good, but this can easily shade into an archaic, and I might say masculine, denigration of culture as secondary, mere decoration, to the world of work and material production.

The acknowledgement of the existence of a distinct intellectual caste or class is not the same as saying that culture is merely secondary to material needs. It is not true that the need for meaning, symbolic and aesthetic pleasure, comes only after some prior material satisfaction. The history of working-class popular culture suggests otherwise.

Rebecca May Johnson recounts the story of how Audre Lorde's mother, bringing her up in the Harlem of the 1930s and 1940s, was always in search of the butter (rather than margarine) that was never sold in the local shops. And how, knowing they would be excluded from Washington's segregated dining spaces, her mother would make an "exquisite picnic", full of "yellow iced cakes with scalloped edges called 'marigolds', that came from Cushman's Bakery", spiced buns, and "iced tea in wrapped mayonnaise jars". There were "piles of napkins and a little tin box with a washcloth dampened with rosewater and glycerine for wiping sticky mouths".[49] For Lorde, "our children cannot dream unless they live, they cannot live unless they are nourished, and who else will feed them the real food without which their dreams will be no different from ours".[50] As May Johnson comments: "Oppression takes place at every scale – in the spreading of butter on bread – and the kitchen is a site from which liberation can be imagined and practised and tasted in fragments".[51] This is a very different configuration of nourishment and dreaming to that of a steam-powered schema of material and non-material, base and superstructure.

There is also, in this revived base–superstructure, a conflation of a generic social surplus – which we as humans need to sustain our fragile bodies – with the technical distinction of "productive" and "non-productive" labour. It's a conflation that is very debilitating for a progressive cultural policy.

As we saw above, for Marx, the pianist is non-productive labour, the piano maker productive, because only the latter is valorising capital via a commodity. But this is no longer the case. The explosion of commodified cultural production does indeed involve productive labour, in that it brings returns to capital. The ethical-political contrast of a productive working class and an unproductive, surplus-consuming cultural-intellectual class no longer works. Disney is one of the largest corporations on the planet. The cultural industries are, on this account, productive of the surplus that pays unemployment benefit and housing benefit.

The bigger point is that, in Nancy Fraser's terms, capitalism is not simply an "economy", but a social system. Care and nurture, performed unpaid in the domestic setting, is, technically, non-productive labour. Yet it is essential if productive labour is to return to work each day and replenish itself. As Fraser

133

suggests, there are multiple resources required by capitalism – expropriated, extracted, or unpaid – without which it could not continue to operate. They are as constitutive of capitalism and its crises as are its economic contradictions, and form part of the grounds of any systemic opposition. While the focus on "point of production" is of great importance, the base–superstructure, material–immaterial distinctions of nineteenth-century Marxism are simply counterproductive.

The particular configuration of culture in industrial capitalism needs to be acknowledged. But the fact that a realm of culture has been separated out and given over to a particular professional class fraction cannot blind us to the systemic importance of culture to the meaningfulness of our individual and collective lives, and to the functioning and future evolution of our society. Historically, art and culture have been seized upon, often desperately, by some of the most deprived and oppressed members of capitalist society, and to dismiss it as "social surplus" is a fatal mistake.

The reduction of culture to industry that we have charted in this book is part of the systemic contradictions which mark our current conjuncture. It may not be the primary or the most important contradiction, as suggested by thinkers such as Herbert Marcuse and other "new left" thinkers, but it is systemic nonetheless.

What is the wider social function of art and culture? Eno again:

> You know, we live in a culture that is changing so incredibly quickly ... probably in a month of our lifetimes we have about the amount of change that there was in the whole of the 14th century. So we have to somehow come to terms with all of that. None of us have the same experiences: you know you might

134

know a lot about what's happening in cars and you might know a lot of what's happening in medicine and you might know something about mathematics and you might know something about fashion. None of us are at all expert on everything that's happening. So we need ways of keeping in synch, of remaining coherent. And I think that this is what culture is doing for us ... So, I'm starting now to propose the idea of culture as a sort of collective ritual, or a set of collective rituals that we're all engaged with.[52]

Eno is talking about more than human flourishing and self-actualisation; he is pointing to the *collective* importance of art and culture.

The most important thing is that we have been all together – that doesn't mean just "the artists", so called, it means everyone, it means all the people actually in the community, everybody – has been generating this huge, fantastic conversation which we call culture. And which somehow keeps us coherent, keeps us together.[53]

Culture as a "fantastic conversation" among ourselves keeps us coherent, together, and is crucial to our collective futures. It is part of how we adapt ourselves to change, individually and collectively. "What we tend to do", Eno says, "is we get a sense of what everybody else is thinking about things and we sort of work out our attitudes in relation to everybody else, as we generally think quite collectively".[54]

Culture, then, is a complex, multifaceted, ongoing public conversation about the future, and the past. One of the most fundamental and universal definitions of culture is that it is an enduring bond between past and future generations. Anglo-Irish conservative philosopher Edmund Burke famously described society as "a contract ... between those who are dead, those who are living, and those who are to be born". I would also see this as part of our "fantastic conversation". Importantly, it is one conducted as much through the senses, through the movement of bodies separately and together, through the emotions, desires, and imagination, through metaphor and sign, as it is through formal, "rational" speech. It is a conversation that mixes nourishment and dreaming, necessity and freedom, material and spirit.

The German Romantics thought the task of art was to "digest", to make sense of the dislocations of the present in order to orientate ourselves to a future.[55] Raymond Williams, in *Culture and Society* and *The Long Revolution*, envisaged this as an expanding democratic project, involving more and more people in Eno's "fantastic conversation". This democratic project is far more than "access and participation", the great shibboleths of recent cultural policy thinking.

When Eno talks of a "collective ritual" as keeping us "in synch" and "remaining coherent", he's referring to forms of patterning, of individual and group interactions, practices, and shared meanings which have always been central to the idea of culture. This is what is meant when people speak of culture and "social cohesion", ways of collectively organising and regulating social practices. It's what Confucius called "rites and music" (禮; Lǐ), the rituals through which a social order is formed and sustained.

This takes us back to the Latin roots of culture, *colere*, "to till, cultivate, or inhabit", later expanded to become the "nurturing of one's interests, spirit, and intellect". Or, as Wang Hui wrote of China: "[t]he Chinese concept of "culture" came together from the words *wen* and *hua*. *Wen* refers to natural patterns as well as the order of rites and music. *Hua* connotes the developmental stages of *wen* (birth, transformation, change)".[56]

Michel Foucault's later work spoke of cultivation as an ethical injunction to care for the self, a care which included the form-giving of aesthetics. In this he looks to the Stoics, who form the self as able to withstand any and all misfortunes. But his is a highly individualised cultivation, as were the Stoics themselves, separated from any concrete political project.[57] Cultivation – culture – refers to whole social formations, to a political-civilisational project beyond the self, and so care for self is a collective project.

Williams talks about this more general process, not of human perfection, which implies a known ideal, but of human evolution, of general human growth.

> For it seems to me to be true that meanings and values, discovered in particular societies and by particular individuals, and kept alive by social inheritance and by embodiment in particular kinds of work, have proved to be universal in the sense that when they are learned, in any particular situation, they can contribute radically to the growth of man's powers, to enrich his life, to regulate his society and to control his environment.[58]

He calls this a "general tradition which seems to represent, through many variations and conflicts, a line of common growth".[59] These are difficult words to read after a half century in which the concept of the "universal", and its implications in colonialism, patriarchy, class domination, and so on have been thoroughly aired. Indeed, Tony Bennet suggests he has caught Williams out in an inadmissible romanticism, and a Euro-centric one at that, simply by using these words.[60] But such postmodern relativism has led us to the alternatives, of the patterning of our lives performed by markets and contract law, the nudges of behavioural economics, or the algorithms of the contemporary click-on-demand economy and its cultural industry platforms.

We have given over these forms of patterning, these rituals and conversations, this dialogue between past and future, the care of self and others, the nourishment of dreams, to the small group of private owners of capital exclusively responsible for deciding capital investment in culture as an industry.

It is the consequent collapse of anything like Williams' tradition, especially in the last forty years, that is the source of so much contemporary anxiety, which adds alienation and anomie to the distributional inequalities of capitalism.[61] Williams, by his own admission, saw his early works as lacking a political analysis, which is why he turned more to the idea of a "cultural formation", in which the "many variations and conflicts" over our "line of common growth" could be more adequately addressed. Nevertheless, he remained committed to the idea.[62]

The conflicts over our common growth are currently running at fever pitch, with deep, destabilising divides running through many Western societies – as we can see in the theatrics of the culture wars, or the proliferation of media bubbles promoted by the privatisation of social media. There is no longer an uncontested canon or set of cultural hierarchies, as these, quite rightly, have been challenged on multiple fronts. It is the threat to these established hierarchies, of class, gender, race and nation, that lies behind much of the current culture wars. The far right sees the defence of a canon as a defence of a singular tradition against the eradication of all shared values, an objective it imputes to the post-sixties elites – or worse.[63] The answer is not some postmodern flattening, however liberating that might sound. The high stakes involved in our fantastic conversations and collective rituals, stakes around processes of individual cultivation and common growth, have not gone away just because voices have democratically multiplied. As Gillian Rose wrote in relation to challenges to the authority of enlightenment "reason":

> The only way forward [is] to make a virtue out of the limitation: the boundaries of legitimate knowledge are endlessly challengeable, corrigible, moveable, by God, by man, by woman. There is no rationality without *uncertain* grounds, without the *relativism* of authority. Relativism of authority does not establish the authority of relativism: it opens reason to new claimants.[64]

Art and culture are part of a common social life, and whether we acknowledge that and address it in policy and politics, or we devolve decisions to the "market" – if that's how we want to describe the kind of politically connected platform capitalism at work here – will make a huge difference to the way this interregnum evolves. We have no answers here, other than to state that art and culture, whatever their myriad manifestations, are somehow "in common", and that the forms of that art and culture are intertwined with the present and future prospects for human flourishing. The "rites and music", the patterned rituals of the social order, are endlessly contestable, just as our spiritual freedom sets us ends which can never be finally fixed. This is the democratic conversation of which culture is a central part. As Raymond Williams wrote in his essay on Welsh culture, "people have to, in the end, direct their own lives, control their own places, live by their own feelings. When this is denied them in any degree, distortions, compensations, myths, fancy dress can spread and become epidemic".[65] Culture has to be part of that democratic conversation. An interregnum, as we know from Gramsci, is ripe for myths and fancy dress. And worse.

Culture and the social foundations

Neoliberalism may be dead as a coherent political project, but many of its policy settings and cultural shibboleths remain. Similarly, it is not clear what shore we are sailing to, or what political forces will take us there. Neither the old post-war state nor free markets "commands the support or authority they once possessed. Political disorder and dysfunction reign".[1] Culture must find its role in this conjuncture.

Broadly aligning culture with public services – health, education, social welfare, basic infrastructure – rather than some knowledge economy growth sector moves us away from a "market citizenship" agenda of GDP and productivity-driven wage growth, educational meritocracy, and privatised consumption. But this needs to involve more than a vague invocation of culture's contribution to "wellbeing". Without a clear acknowledgement of the deeper causes of the crisis of liveability and generalised precarity, such wellbeing agendas remain purely ameliorative.

To help us think through this, I draw on the work of the Foundation Economy Collective (FEC), a loose grouping of scholars and activists in a conversation that has evolved since its early iteration.[2] The FEC break with the jobs and GDP-growth model of economic and social policy, disaggregate the economy into distinct zones in which only one is fully commercial-transactional, and put liveability at the centre of a long-term transformative vision. In adding social infrastructure to disposal household income and public services as a key pillar of liveability, the FEC provide a crucial foothold for a radical rethinking of cultural policy in the interregnum.

Yet culture must align itself with the social foundations at a moment when these foundations themselves are in crisis. Healthcare, education, public services, and infrastructures of all kinds have been severely damaged by neoliberalism. This, amid a generalised precarity described by economist James K. Galbraith as "a minority ensconced in a diminishing set of safe career paths or sufficient wealth not to bother worrying about [economic insecurity], and a majority living in persistent anxiety over the costs of health, housing, education, the quality of public services and other formerly ordinary attributes of middle-class life".[3]

The task, then, is not just to rethink culture's place in the social foundation schematically; we also need to identify its transformative role in the current conjuncture. That is, a new approach to cultural policy which contributes to our collective capacity to act. It means creating what Albena Azmanova called a more secure ontological "breathing space" in which, precarity at bay momentarily, to think and to imagine in common.[4] It would pivot culture from being a symptom of our systemic crisis to being a crucial part of our collective attempt to overcome it.

Culture is not an industry

Culture as public policy

This is a tall order. Cultural policy is caught between an expansive, idealistic view of its fundamental social role and the impoverished reality of its own intellectual, institutional, and political resources.

In 1982, coming off the back of the decade-long challenge to the "first world" by the newly independent countries, UNESCO attempted a comprehensive redefinition of culture. Moving away from a Euro-centric view of culture as "arts and letters", it embraced the anthropological:

> In its widest sense, culture may now be said to be the whole complex of distinctive spiritual, material, intellectual and emotional features that characterise a society or social group. It includes not only the arts and letters, but also modes of life, the fundamental rights of the human being, value systems, traditions and beliefs.[5]

UNESCO reaffirmed this definition in a commemorative conference in the same Mexico City location in 2022. However, such definitions of culture have proved far too expansive to provide an effective handle on actual policy. Cultural policy no longer "owns" culture at this broad anthropological scale. It barely owns culture as specific products and services, the commanding heights of which, as we saw, have become the fiefdom of large global corporations. Though flying the banner of culture as "everything that makes us human" or the "glue that holds society together", the actual cultural sector – should it be invited at all – turns up to the negotiating table confused, under-resourced, and marginal.

In the diplomatic manoeuvring around the SDGs in 2015, culture was left out. There were many reasons, but a recurrent argument was that culture was a "cross-cutting theme" rather than a distinct goal. A cultural diplomat involved in the 2015 negotiations recently told me during a conversation that culture was in everything: "how can we understand gender without culture, or food?" To which I replied, perhaps unhelpfully, "when was the last time you were invited to an agribusiness conference?" Culture is everywhere and nowhere.

The other foundational public service sectors have their expansive definitions. "Wellbeing" takes health out of the hi-tech hospital and into everyday lives. Precarity is bad for public health. Education takes us out of the schoolrooms and lecture theatres into lifelong learning, learning-in-common, and the knowledge society. Creativity itself was to permeate all our lives. What, viewed in this light, is not a social welfare issue?

Nonetheless, these public services agendas are pursued by a coherently identifiable set of government departments and international agencies, NGOs, philanthropic foundations, intermediary organisations, and the like. Culture-as-industry might have given some entry into the world of economic development, but meanwhile it has been systemically removed from the forums in which these wider global challenges are discussed. Health, education, and gender rights are there, but very rarely culture. As one ex-head of the Netherlands' environmental protection agency told me, culture lacked its own specific claims on public policy, its institutional presence barely visible:

> In the midst of the various problem agendas ... there is no clear place or storyline any longer for the role of culture – in the sense of creating and celebrating collective forms of imagination, communication, perspectives ... We must have a rich cultural sphere in itself ... for culture to be instrumental to these other agendas ... So why not start with redeveloping the storyline that in the

midst of the crises we find ourselves in, we urgently need a revival of a cultural sphere and that the current lack of this has been a big mistake … because it is producing a distrust in the future and a lack of collective imagination.

Culture will require a strong sense of its own specific contribution, and some robust institutional resources, if it is to enhance the "breathing spaces" of the commons from which the collective imagination of a possible shared future might take flight.

How, then, do we reassert culture's role in public policy?

Many who seek to give culture a distinct function have been tempted to add it as a measure or priority alongside the "economic". Advocacy such as the "fourth pillar" adds culture to the "triple bottom line" of economic, social, and environmental impact. But simply adding "culture" leaves "economy" unexamined, a "black box".[6] Like many such attempts, it is constantly surprised when the real bottom line turns out to be "economy" after all.[7] In this sense, we need to challenge what "economy" actually entails. It is not some ontological reality, a force of gravity to which all social reality must bend. Accepting "the economy" as a fixed category in this way is already to be trapped by it. There is now a growing reservoir of heterodox economics – heterodox to "neoclassical Econ 101"[8] – but, as I have tried to argue here, political reality itself is leaving that economic model behind.

We have already discussed Kate Raworth's "doughnut", with its social foundations based on the SDGs. In 2020, deep into the world's longest lockdown, a local Melbourne group created the "Melbourne Doughnut", which now included "arts and culture". The icon was a paintbrush, palette, and canvas.[9] This addition only illustrates the problem. We might add an art and culture icon, just like we might add a distinct culture SDG, but do we have a coherent idea of what "culture" is as an object of public policy?

At the 2022 Mondiacult conference, UNESCO called for a distinct culture goal to be added to the new set of SDGs due in 2030. It also declared culture a "global public good". After enumerating the "multiple, protracted, and multidimensional crises" facing the planet, it called for "a systemic anchoring of culture in public policies". But this grand declaration rapidly descended into a list of social and economic impacts, with culture

> an enabler and driver of resilience, social inclusion and economic growth from education, employment – especially for women and youth – health and emotional wellbeing to poverty reduction, gender equality, environmental sustainability, tourism, trade and transport, while also sustaining context-relevant models of economic and social development. [10]

This provides no grounds for cultural policy other than as an adjunct to these other social and economic policies, their priorities and rationale flowing directly from them. In what follows, I try to provide an analytical schema to frame culture's public policy role, and sketch how this might work in the current conjuncture.

The foundational approach

In order to make a start on this, I have found it useful to look to the work of the FEC. Their approach provides, for me, a balance between an analytical critique of the current conjuncture and a set of practical orientations to move us forward. As specified in their more recent book, building on a decade of collective investigation and debate, they set out to radically change the lens through which we view economic and social policy.[11] This does not entail a fully designed programme, but a project of incremental change that will require the work of a generation. Neoliberalism did not emerge overnight, fully formed, in the heads of Reagan and Thatcher. Neither did the thinking behind the New Deal and post-war social democracy.

Remaking the lens of existing economic and social policy thinking is a long-term prospect that will require high-level political agency – the central state will be crucial in any transformation – often in the policy "back room" rather than the ideological grandstanding of the "front office". But it also requires "a gradualist practice of adaptive reuse whereby the central state works round constraints and draws on distributed social innovation and initiative from the lower levels".[12] This local experimental practice needs to begin immediately.

This is not about carving out some post-capitalist enclave but applying a different economic lens in full recognition of the structural constraints on local spending, central government support, and the wider dynamics of a dysfunctional economic and social system.[13] We might see some prefigurative experiments, what Ernst Bloch called "concrete utopias", but we must also effect real, long-term changes in people's lives.[14]

The starting point is the pressing crisis of liveability: stagnant wages, declining public services, rising prices, increasing insecurity, and social disconnectedness. This is set against the model of "market citizenship", which holds that increasing GDP means creating more "good jobs" with better wages, providing higher incomes which can then be spent on privately supplied services, getting on the "housing ladder", and other discretionary wants.

The FEC critique the "supply-side" approach to growth, both as ineffective in providing these elusive "good jobs" and in assuming aggregate GDP will "will lift all boats". The FEC's goal is to reorient social and economic policy away from a GDP-centred, individualised jobs-and-wages growth to a focus on guaranteed collective liveability.

It is disposable household income, rather than wages per se, that should provide a key metric. Wages may be higher in London than, say, Wales, but then a great percentage of that income is, in London, spent on necessities (housing, commuting, childcare, and so on). Equally, public services – health, education, transport, welfare, infrastructure – are a crucial addition to household income. Better and cheaper public services mean more disposable income. They also provide the collective resources – education, social services, social infrastructure – which allow personal and community development, and in far more equitable terms than the injunction to "get a better job".

However, there has been a privatisation of basic services, now absorbed by a financialised regime of high return on investment, asset stripping, weak regulation, underinvestment, and a business model of cultivating political connections that Dylan Riley calls "political capitalism".[15] This has resulted in a massive transfer of wealth from the public to the private sector and has contributed to the impoverishment and insecurity of large sections of the population. GDP is indifferent to these developments. Indeed, as we know from the last decade, there is no necessary connection between GDP growth, profitability and general prosperity. The sluggish growth of the last decade has seen enormous profits accrue to a small percentage of the population.

A recent crucial addition to household disposable income and foundational services is social infrastructure. Experiences of social isolation during the pandemic, alongside local community surveys, have underscored the importance of "hard social infrastructure" which sustains all the many forms of sociability which have proven benefits for the psychological and physical health of individuals. We return to this below.

Disaggregating GDP

The FEC disaggregate the singular model of the economy as envisaged by GDP modelling. There is not one economy but multiple economic zones, which operate on different principles, have different structures and dynamics, and which should be valued in different ways. They outline a core household community economy (mostly untraded); a foundational ("material and providential") economy; an "overlooked" economy (sometimes combined with the former as "foundational economy plus"); and the "tradable competitive" economy (see Figure 4.1). The foundational economy has two components. There is the "material infrastructure" of energy, water, housing, public and private transport, cables and pipes, supermarkets and food, and retail banking and ATMs. That is, the "social-technical" networks connecting households to "reliance systems" which make everyday life possible and safe. Then, there are "providential services" such as education, health, social and community services, prisons and police, public administration, funerals, and public and social housing. FEC empirical studies have shown that the foundational economy makes up nearly a half of national economies on standard measures (employment, GVA), often more in particular places.[16]

Alongside the foundational economy is the "overlooked" economy of basic goods and services. Though not provided by

Culture and the social foundations

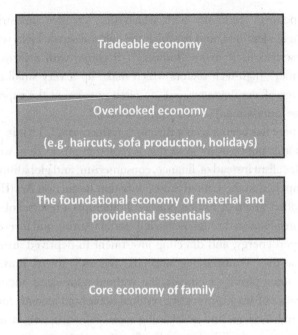

Figure 4.1 The FEC's zonal schema of the economy

the state, we now take these for granted as essential parts of any decent life. These include firms providing basic furniture, clothing, home maintenance, hairdressers, vets, hospitality, and recreation. These make up around a fifth of the economy, and, when added to the foundational economy (as FE+), account for between 60 and 70 per cent of national and local economies.[17]

Then there is the "tradable competitive" economy, purely commercial goods and services, which makes up between 30 and 40 percent of national economies. In the last forty years, this "tradable" zone became the paradigm for all the others, and the primary focus of government policy. It is this "tradable competitive" economy with which the "creative industries" strongly identified, and to which the cultural sector looks when it describes itself as an "industry". It comes with a focus on "frontier" high-tech sectors which make up a very small percentage of employment and are often pursued at the expense of the foundational or everyday economy.[18]

There has been a recent turn to "productivism". That is, "an economic policy framework that is rooted in production, work, and localism instead of finance, consumerism, and globalism",[19] exemplified in the United States' Inflation Reduction Act (IRA) and other green transition policies. It attempts a reversal of de-industrialisation through reshoring manufacturing and investing in green energy, and directing investment to deprived areas – such as the "Trump states" and UK "red wall" towns. It might have some positive elements, but without addressing underlying issues of wages, precarity, residual household income, foundational services, and a declining social infrastructure, it may involve more "political capitalism" and supercharge monopoly and concentration.[20] Inevitably perhaps, the IRA has already moved away from public infrastructure and services towards individualised consumption.[21]

FEC empirical studies have shown how the foundational economy is centred on supplying local economies, tending to employ locally.[22] Compared to the tradable economy, it is more employment-rich, and a larger proportion of its value-add goes to employees rather than companies or shareholders.[23] The foundational economy should not be seen as a low-wage, low-productivity economy – though parts of it are that – but includes highly capitalised and commercially successful businesses (large and small), as well as skilled workers and professionals.[24]

In addition, wages earned through the foundational economy are important, their value also in the services that they provide, which are key to wellbeing.[25] This is important, as it is often countered that foundational services are paid for out of the surplus generated by the transactional economy. This ignores the large-scale commercial nature of much of the foundational economy, as well as the extractive "rentier" nature of much of the transactional economy. More generally, it equates profit and productivity with the social surplus per se, and ignores (as Nancy Fraser argued) the extent to which this profitability relies on the (disavowed) inputs of the foundational economy for its sustainability. This includes the social infrastructure which the FEC now adds to the foundations of liveability. The hard infrastructure in which sociability, physical recreation, and creative expression take place is clearly part of Fraser's system of social reproduction, the failures of which are as much a part of the systemic crisis as those located in the "economy" so designated.

This disaggregation allows the FEC to break with models of economic development derived from the "commercial-transactional" zone – focused on efficiency, productivity, and maximisation of profit. The foundational economy, it suggests, ought not to be subjected to these rationales. High productivity – the ratio of capital investment over labour costs – is not always desirable, as reducing labour can be counterproductive, as we have seen recently in many sectors from aged care to the railways.[26] So, too, "efficiency", the maximisation of profitability, which cuts against the core purpose of these services.[27] More generally, "efficiency" has proved brittle in the pandemic, as "just-in-time" systems with little "slack" shut down rapidly. Resilience and adaptability derive from different principles, which, the FEC argue, need better recognition within the foundational economy.[28]

The importance of the foundational economy to a decent life in common means that principles of economic efficiency and growth, derived from the market-first, commercial-transactional model imposed by neoliberalism across all sectors of the economy and the public services, need to be reversed. The purpose of the economy should not be growth per se, but collective wellbeing, and should be judged accordingly.[29] Above all, the foundational economy needs to be assertively framed in this way, and the creeping financialisaton and commodification resisted or regulated.

The FEC are also aware of how the foundational economy has become increasingly dominated in its more profitable areas by the tradable and competitive economy – privatisation and outsourcing of basic services, linked to global finance seeking high returns. Promoting the foundational economy cannot mean generating "extractive" profits.

> When the pandemic is over, we need to rebalance away from the tradeable and competitive economy towards the mainly sheltered foundational economy producing daily essential goods and services which underpin liveability and sustainability. And, equally, accept that the financialised business models of public companies and private equity funds are an extractive intrusion on foundational activities which offer modest, steady returns on long term investment.[30]

The FEC note the move of finance into basic services, part of the process of privatisation and outsourcing noted above, which has done much damage to the provision of essential services. This is marked by the lowering of wages, squeezing of suppliers, rising debt, erosion of working conditions, and the reduction of service quality. Demands for efficiency and productivity are made at the expense of the actual value they are meant to deliver.[31] In the name of efficiency, government responsibilities are turned into contractable services, with deleterious consequences. The transformation of citizens into "consumers" has also changed our relation to these services, and undermined the very idea of citizenship.[32]

Implications for culture?

There are three clear and immediate implications for cultural policy.

First, the foundational approach provides a radically different lens for cultural policy, away from jobs and GDP growth towards a social and economic policy focused on enhanced liveability. Second, the disaggregation of the economy allows us to schematically understand culture as a complex, distributed system, only part of which is subject to the imperatives of profit and productivity. Third, the notion of the "social infrastructure" helps us to think of culture as essential to liveability while possessing its own distinct systemic contribution at a whole of society level.

Since the 1980s, art and culture have been pushed into, and gradually accepted, the position of a private consumption economy, an "industry" whose core default settings are those of the transactional-commercial economy. Culture-as-industry aligned itself uniquely with the transactional economy, a high-value but minority employment economic zone, in which fewer and fewer workers attain any degree of security. As a result, culture's high-touch, high-care, jobs-rich character has been squeezed into an efficiency-maximising, profit-driven, winner-takes-all competitive pyramid model. Small wonder, then, the panel of flashing red lights suddenly revealed in the pandemic – of precarity, low pay, debt, negligible entitlements, collapse of career structures, de-professionalisation, and so on.

Taking culture out of the transactional-industrial realm is not to assign culture uniquely to the publicly provided "providential" sector, nor to ignore the small-scale independent and larger commercial sector. Rather, it no longer takes the latter as exemplary for all culture, as if the ideal goal of public policy for culture was to move as much as possible from the subsidised to the fully commercial. In this model, those elements which clearly could not survive entirely on the market – arts and heritage mostly – were "market failures" which, on strict conditions, could be supported by taxpayer subsidy. Where culture was deemed to have a "social impact", it could also be supported, depending on how it met targets set by various social services, community, health, crime, and other policy agendas.

We need to position culture as a distinct part of the social system, as crucial and as complex as health and education. Culture, broadly understood as an object of public policy, is distributed across all of the FEC's economic zones – foundational, overlooked, transactional. This is similar to other foundational sectors. Energy, food, and water are highly complex systems, so too education and health. Education includes local childcare, primary and secondary schools, further and higher education, teacher training programmes, research institutes and councils, private schools and personal tuition, professional accreditation, publishing and media, "edu-tech", and related public administrative bodies. The health sector, too, has "Big Pharma", private hospitals, medical technologies, and big data (think Palantir), as well as a range of small-scale, "everyday" medical and wellbeing practices at local levels.

The specific challenge for culture is that, while these other sectors may be in dire straits, they are still accepted, just about, as public services. This allows political purchase through the demand to restore these sectors to the public and make them work for us. Currently, this kind of political demand is only minimally available to culture.

The task of taking culture out of industry and returning it to public policy needs to consist of more than assigning culture to "communities", or the fulfilment of social policy tasks such as mental wellbeing programmes, crime reduction, or getting kids back into school. Defining culture as an essential need and a fundamental right is a systemic proposition and will require new institutional, intellectual, and financial resources.

The social foundations include urgent, "vital" goods and services – water, utilities, shelter, food, and so on. Other foundational services are more enabling, providing for the substantive capabilities and positive freedom to make real choices – education, health, social services, and public administration. The "hard social infrastructure" (as discussed in the next chapter) provides spaces for social interaction, physical recreation, and creative expression. But if culture as a basic need involves capabilities we cannot do without if we are to fully participate in society and realise our potential, then we require a systemic approach to the provision of these basic services.

In Figure 4.2, I have used a broad, standard definition of the cultural sector to distribute it across the different economic zones.[33] The zonal distribution is not historically or anthropologically fixed, but is a result of specific historical evolution and deliberate government policy (such as the privatisation of public

Material	Providential	Everyday	Transactional
Communications	Public realm/built environment	Music/performance venues	Cinema chains
Fibre-optics	Parks	Dance clubs	Big concert venues
Telephony	Libraries	Small cultural retail	Commercial theatres
Built environment	Museums and galleries	Book shops	Commercial galleries
	Community centres	Small galleries and creative spaces	Big music festivals
	Performing arts	Independent cinema	Commercial radio
	Theatres (and screens)	Local radio	Screen (film and television)
	Festivals and events	Crafts	Games
	Public broadcasting	Cultural manufacture	Music industry
	Literature	Poetry clubs	Streaming services (music, television)
	Art education	Art supplies	Publishing
	Arts for health	Private music and art tuition	Large retail (bookshops, art, music, games)
	Community arts	Urban gardens and markets	Online retail (e.g. Amazon)
	Public art	Pubs and cafes	
	Community radio		
	Experimental cinema		
	Crafts		

Figure 4.2 Art and culture in the zonal economy

media or reduction in arts funding). Indeed, we might want, as a matter of policy, to deliberately move certain activities from one sector to another. Further, while culture may be a zonal mix – providential, overlooked, transactional – it is still subject to a holistic policy vision, based on its systemic social functions. There is a direct provision of basic services and infrastructures, but nurturing capabilities involves a complex set of institutions, as does culture's contributions to social connectedness and the spaces required to collectively reimagine a future.

This systemic approach applies not just to the publicly provided or guaranteed elements but also the "overlooked" and "transactional" zones too. One of the shortcomings of so many "community art" approaches is their tendency to write off the commercial sector and large cultural industries as beyond the local, and so beyond the pale. Reframing culture as foundational means taking care of the everyday and commercial sectors as much as community-based services. It is contradictory to work for community cultural infrastructures and programmes while having nothing to say about who produces the sounds, images, and stories which pour through our EarPods and screens into the deepest recesses or our individual, household, and community lives.

So, too, an arts policy conceived of as separate to a "creative industries" policy makes little sense. I once met a very erudite and radical Swedish arts minister, who was very clear about the transformative role of the arts. I asked her about the creative industries, to which she replied this was not her role, introducing me to the person responsible – a man in a suit with an MBA. As I argued in the Introduction, the whole thrust of post-war cultural politics has been concerned with the whole question of how they interact, and we need to put this back onto the table.

The FEC's economic zones are not geographically or onto-logically distinct. Local and community economies sit cheek by jowl with other forms of market-based (small-scale or global corporate) economic activity. "Home and community" might be mostly about gift and free exchange, but the communica-tion and entertainment devices which permeate these social spaces – often at the expense of civic networks – are manu-factured, programmed, and loaded with content by some of the most highly capitalised and globalised companies on the planet. These zones are articulated in complex ways, as with the solitary mushroom pickers in the forests of the American Northeast "doing it for the love of it", yet linked to a global value chain supplying high-end Japanese restaurants.[34] So, too, local cultural ecosystems are an essential part of the operations of global platform culture industries.

None of these different elements are "naturally" part of the state, or market, independent or not for profit. They are so as the result of a complex set of political struggles and choices about how we want to organise these systems, and for what defining purpose. Choosing to align culture with the founda-tional economy is not only about outlining a different kind of economic rationale or rationales. It is also about redefining cul-ture's wider social purpose and what it would take to achieve that purpose.

The discursive struggle

These are the stakes in what Tony Judt calls a "discursive strug-gle", a transformation in the imaginary of culture away from being a growth industry towards being foundational for our social system.[35] This is not just a question of policy; it requires a new "creative imaginary". It is to change the lens through which our creative selves are viewed, away from being "entrepreneurs of the self" in a networked capitalism to providing care or an essential social service. It might require a new sense of vocation, a "calling" that once underpinned a professional self that also has been thoroughly gutted by neoliberalism. It would require an epochal break from the individualised, competitive new spirit of "creative capitalism" installed in the 1970s and 1980s.

The creative industries agenda aimed to shift as much of the foundational and everyday economy to the transactional. The refusal, lodged at the heart of the economic and financial command centre of the neoliberal state, to countenance culture as anything other than an individual consumer economy provided the context for an accelerating defunding and privatisation of culture (and much else besides). This underpinned the cultural logic of creative entrepreneurship, creative hubs, creative cities, scaling up, and moving to export; seeing the world like a business opportunity. As Gary Gerstle notes, the neoliberal system might have gone but many of its cultural elements persist, such as self-entrepreneurship and the obsession with metrics so ingrained within the cultural sector.[36]

The gradual intellectual and political disinvestment from the neoliberal agenda should prompt the cultural sector to actively assert its importance to a new kind of socioeconomic imaginary. If we wanted to move the vast bulk of cultural activity away from the transactional to the everyday and foundational sectors, what kind of new imaginary would that require and stimulate?

The project of investing in culture as an expansion of individual citizen capabilities, as a basic right and as a thickening of the social infrastructure, would be undertaken at a time when the social fabric is in a highly distressed state. Michael Denning portrays the alliances of artists and working-class organisations in the New Deal era, and the post-war patterning of new left and old left, through the cultural infrastructure of the 1960s and 1970s. All fell victim to Reagan's neoliberal revolution.[37] Similar stories could be told in the UK or Australia, as a parallel contraction of working-class social and political organisation and cuts to culture budgets combined – as was intended – to make culture an individual consumer good.[38] As I tried to show in the Introduction, this underpinned the de-politicisation of culture and its reduction to creative economy.

Reimagining culture as part of the social foundations in a situation of social fragmentation and generalised precarity is a challenge.

This is not about some artistic intervention, after the fashion of "relational aesthetics", in which artists create situations which reconstruct or evoke a social connectedness lost in the wider society.[39] Nor can it be about the extension of the existing subsidised art system to "communities", driven by metricised KPIs of inclusion and participation, or hitting social agendas determined by health or social services. It requires a robust articulation of culture's own distinct worth. That is, understanding what it could bring to individuals and communities faced with the pressing exigencies of precarious living, while taking care of culture's institutional and systemic robustness after three decades of funding cuts.

This will involve working with communities, building up local economies and social infrastructure, stepping away from the "creativity bundle" towards forms of communitarianism, community wealth building, *restanza*, local job creation, co-ops and mutualism, new forms of municipalism, and so on.[40] These will require a lot of new capacity. But, as we shall argue, these initiatives cannot be done in isolation from strategic initiatives to rein in the power of the cultural industries and the platform companies. The quip "Goldman-Sachs doesn't care if you raise chickens" is a useful reminder here.[41] But building community capacity and tackling global corporations is not zero-sum.

Culture can be conceived of as providing a "breathing space", where creative capacity, artistic expression, aesthetic knowledge and sensibility might come into their own, making their particular claims on social meaning, on what it is to live in the world together. It is also the space, to quote the much-maligned Matthew Arnold, in his 1969 *Culture and Anarchy*, in which we might turn "through this knowledge ... a stream of fresh and free thought upon our stock notions and habits". This is not something that ChatGPT will do for us.

In this radical reworking of the "creative imaginary", we might hope to retrieve the promise of cultural work that was rerouted into the agenda of the creative industries. The promise of a democratisation of creativity, its availability to all and its permeation into everyday life, drew on older traditions of working-class struggle, dating back well before the new left and the 1960s. It was a tradition which hoped that all work might one day be invested with an aesthetic richness, a sense of meaning and purpose, in the spirit of John Ruskin's "art is an expression of man's pleasure in labour".[42] The restriction of such possibilities to the educated, professional creative class was a core failing of New Labour's vision for a "Creative Britain". So, too, the annexation of aesthetic pleasure to a rampantly individualised "post-material" consumer economy.

William Morris wrote of the separation between the "higher" and "lesser" arts, in which the first were associated with "useless luxury" and the latter with that "mass of shoddy, cheap goods" for the rest of us. The utopian promise that might animate a new cultural imaginary would have to involve a sense of shared social labour and pleasure in everyday production that makes society possible, and to which art and culture might contribute.

As Kristin Ross had it, "senseless luxury, which Morris knew cannot exist without slavery of some kind, would be replaced by communal luxury, or equality in abundance". If de-growth often comes in hair shirts and puritan austerity, "communal luxury" evokes a world "where everyone, instead, would have his or her share of the best".[43]

5

Cultural infrastructures

How then to take these first steps to a new kind creative imaginary, a new sense of purpose for culture outside the stifling confines of culture-as-industry? How do we outline culture's role in helping us cross the uncertain landscape in which we find ourselves, and to reaffirm its centrality to our lives together? In what follows I present a sketch for how we might do this. It's not a detailed policy prescription, nor is it anything like complete. Rather, it tries to suggest a basic orienting framework within which we can begin to reimagine culture and its policies as an essential part of our collective future.

In the last chapter I suggested culture was a complex, distributed system, and in this it is similar to other public service sectors, such as education and health, which also have complex mixed economies. But culture is both more distributed and more mixed, involving an extensive publicly funded cultural infrastructure, a complex ecosystem of freelancers and micro-businesses, and, dominating this motley flotilla, some huge global entities (five of the ten largest global companies are digital communications platforms dealing extensively in cultural commerce) which themselves now reach down into the minutiae of our everyday living and working.

In this chapter I will build on the disaggregated, zonal schema of the economy – household, social foundations, overlooked, transactional – while engaging with the recent FEC work on the social infrastructure as a crucial element of liveability. In addition to disposable household income and foundational services, the FEC see the social infrastructure – sociability, exercise, creative expression – as one of the three pillars of liveability. In a similar vein I will argue for a cultural infrastructure approach, one which is both part of that social infrastructure, and which contributes its own crucial and conceptually distinct elements.

As with the social infrastructure and foundational services, the cultural infrastructure has an immediate presence in the lives of households and local communities, sustained by complex systems of delivery, finance, skills, training, and research. Similar to education and communications, health, and social welfare, the cultural infrastructure provides society-wide functions without which our society could not function. And, as with these other social systems, cultural infrastructures now face serious erosion, as inequalities, budget austerity, deregulated planning, and the distortions of global platform monopolies have combined to undermine them.

In this chapter I will outline a rationale for cultural policy as a crucial dimension of individual autonomy and democratic citizenship. I first look at the household as a centre of cultural consumption and how the cultural infrastructure is crucial to sustaining their participation in culture as collective consumption. Then I examine the "hard" cultural infrastructure of the built environment and its utility "pipes", followed by the "soft" cultural infrastructure. I suggest that these infrastructures sustain the capacity for individual autonomy and freedom essential for any democracy, as well as connecting us to our pasts and opening up spaces for reimagining the future.

In the next chapter I will look at the system of production: at cultural work, sustaining the small-scale "overlooked" economy and confronting the commercial-transactional world of global corporations.

Fixing the cultural infrastructure

In *When Nothing Works*, the FEC introduce the social infrastructure as a crucial third pillar of household liveability, after disposable household income and foundational services:

> The first two pillars of liveability are about provision and systems which are manifestly necessary for human survival in a modicum of comfort and dignity, the third pillar of social infrastructure is about systems which are relevant for human flourishing through thriving social relations and positive emotional states.[1]

The social infrastructure provides for socialisation ("being together"), physical exercise, and creative expression. It is a combination of hard (for example, libraries, swimming pools, parks) and soft (for example, toddler groups and community choirs) infrastructure. For the FEC, "the role of social infrastructure is to sustain high functioning individuals who strengthen the resilience and capability of households". [2] That is, the emotional, physical, and interpersonal wellbeing provided by the social infrastructure is crucial to the ability of individuals to fully realise their capabilities. This is in the Senian sense, so that "a person has the ability to do or be certain things that she has reason to value".[3] In foundational thinking, however, this "freedom depends on reliance systems delivering essential services and social infrastructure which sustains all the various forms of individual expression and sociability".[4]

This account involves that combination of material and spiritual freedoms I discussed in Chapter 3. We must act, as with all animals, to reproduce our material lives, freeing ourselves from the most immediate necessity. But as humans we are also faced with the open question of how we should conduct our lives, seeking to pursue the ethical path which we have chosen to value. A flourishing culture is inseparable from the material freedom without which our lives are used up by the demands of necessity. Culture, at its broadest, describes the patterned collective space within which these ethical paths are framed, chosen, and sought, as well as the means used by individuals and communities to reflect on and modify these life choices. Cultural policy is thus concerned with nurturing the foundations on which humans can flourish, providing the symbolic means enabling the full exercise of their freedom to pursue their chosen ends.

Therefore, art and culture involve more than the mental health benefits of creative expression. They contribute to the individual's ability to reflect on her own ongoing process of self-realisation. Art and culture are tied up with our spiritual freedom and sense of autonomy. They also contribute to our shared social meaning, our multifaceted collective identities. It is impossible to think of the cultural infrastructure without an idea of social relationality of individual creative expression, and the society-wide function of culture as a "fantastic conversation ... keeping us coherent".

It is on these grounds that we should think about the relation between culture and democracy. There is a growing mass of data on inequalities and exclusions around class, gender

and ethnicity, in both cultural work and arts audiences.[5] This
has led to demands for what Mark Banks has called "distributive justice", calls for increased representation of these groups
through affirmative programmes of various sorts.[6] Much of
this is welcome, and I discuss it more in the next chapter. What
I will argue here is that such data sets on representation only
make sense within a clear framework for culture as part of the
social foundations. Rather than focus on distribution, Mark
Banks talks of "contributive justice", where everyone is given
the opportunity to contribute to society, performing paid or vol-
untary work that is meaningful in itself or (in the case of more
demanding or routine jobs) in what it contributes to society. In
cultural terms, everyone should have the right, should they so
wish, to be involved in some way in the production of culture.
This, for Banks, is key to building self-esteem and skills, in fulfilling the basic right to cultural expression and enjoyment, and as
part of democratic citizenship.

That is, the right to produce culture, should they so wish,
even if it is not paid work, should be extended to everyone. This
is a radical, cultural democratic approach to "participation" in
which the public cultural infrastructure is repurposed to allow
people to be more actively involved within it. It is this positive
approach, rather than getting caught up in the data of equitable social representation, that I propose here. Rather than argue
over the distributive justice of the existing system, we ought to
assert the right to culture, of positive freedoms, of contributive justice, and the need for the cultural system to reorganise
so as to accommodate these demands. Democracy here refers
not just to some equitable representation but to the more radical sense of active participation and the requisite capacity, as
autonomous citizens, to exercise this participation to the fullest.

Culture is not an industry

Fixing the cultural infrastructure does demand resources of time and money, but it also demands that we radically reconstitute it as part of the social foundations. This certainly involves the locally accessible cultural infrastructure of physical space and (relatively) organised social activity, and it also points to the system of cultural production which we will tackle in the next chapter. But we start at the level of the household, where much of the cultural formation of individuals takes place, and where the general process of the privatisation of culture has its primary target.

Household consumption and liveability

The household has itself become a centre of cultural (and other) consumption in ways that often actually undermine the social infrastructure. That is, the privatisation of material infra-structures – "the pipes" which carry energy, gas, water, communications, and so on – along with a range of providential services have implications not only for disposable income (services provided for profit, thus costing more) but also the very social infrastructure on which liveability also depends.

Households are key units of social reproduction, a complex mix of free, subsidised and highly commodified services, alongside "gift" economies (of money, time, care) and coerced or onerous unpaid labour. As such the household is always a site of struggle around free, subsidised and collectively provided services, a living wage, debt, care, gender rights, disability rights, and so on.

Households are also enmeshed in the consumer economy, from renovation, decoration, furnishing, food, "consumer durables", private tuition, cars, and so on. They are "asset units", where mortgages, rental income, pension schemes, wealth funds, and so on are managed.[7] From our perspective, they are also key sites of cultural consumption, with family media subscription and streaming packages (sports channels, Netflix, Spotify), books delivered via Amazon Prime, online ticket purchase, multiple internet-integrated screens, VR headsets, game consoles, smart speakers, and so on, along with the all-pervasive advertising and data extraction that keeps the whole thing ticking over.

Increasing income (higher wages, more equitable tax system) and reducing the cost of foundational services would increase disposable income. But in a system where global finance is heavily invested in the provision of these services on a commercial basis, on its own this would only serve to reinforce the household viewed primarily as a node in a system of commodity consumption. The same might be said of schemes for universal basic income.[8] In Nancy Fraser's account of the nineteenth-century household, the fight for a decent wage to provide for basic domestic reproduction was an essential one. But, as the domestic sphere was locked into a gendered division of paid and unpaid labour, the struggle was ultimately not emancipatory. So too, providing services in a manner that further privatises household consumption at the expense of any wider sense of social connection or solidarity is not an unalloyed advance.

That is why the social infrastructure is so important. In acknowledging that household liveability is embedded in a wider community, it opens up that liveability to a collective context rather than tie it to privatised household consumption. This privatisation goes back beyond neoliberalism and was often part of the post-war welfare state, predicated on the family as the primary unit of consumption.[9] As we know from the

169

model of the suburb developed in the post-war US, or the shopping mall, and on to the recent expansion of on-demand, "click and collect" services, material and providential infrastructures are regularly organised around profit-generating household consumption.

The impacts of increased levels of home consumption of culture on socialisation, physical exercise, and individual creative expression are complex and multiple. Certainly, home cultural consumption can enhance socialisation (think of the many online communities, communal gaming, and the enhanced connection to distant family and friends), just as it can enhance individual creative expression (think of music, film, publishing, and other creative making facilitated by digital equipment). But these practices are perhaps better understood not as individual acts of isolated cultural consumption and creative expression, but ones facilitated and made more meaningful in terms of a wider sociocultural context. The teenager's bedroom, full of devices for consuming, making, and sharing cultural practices and products, is a meniscus containing a whole world in miniature. Hers are not solitary acts but depend for their full flourishing on the wider sociocultural infrastructure.

Again, with Nancy Fraser, the crucial importance of this sociocultural infrastructure, without which cultural engagement and innovation would barely take place, is disavowed by a commercial sector that has no interest in providing for its upkeep and often seeks to further strip out its profitable elements – not least by the exploitation of the very traces left by that teenager in her bedroom.

The privatisation of household consumption often comes at the expense of communal forms of consumption and participation, which undermine the social infrastructure. We can see this in the rise of streaming and the decline of local cinemas, or home delivery and local restaurants. A recent survey of census data in Australia confirmed a loss of around 10,000 jobs from video stores. Though the civic contribution of these places varied, they often provided a first contact with a "curated" film experience, as well as a crucial social connection and animating otherwise deserted streets. Whatever financial value they brought to local communities has now been siphoned off to Netflix or Apple TV or Disney.[10] As we shall see in the next chapter, this applies to the cultural system writ large, which has strong tendencies towards monopoly and concentration.

One of the consequences of the pandemic was that some basic level of access to cultural consumption (internet, communication devices, screens) was acknowledged as an essential need. As a key item of household expenditure, making this more affordable and available is important. Broadband, mobile phones, computing devices, and various broadcast and streaming services are expensive. But simply making cultural consumption more affordable raises questions as to how that culture is to be provided or organised. Is this "essential need" to be met entirely by a for-profit commercial sector? If at least some forms of culture – such as a public streaming platform – were being provided as part of the social foundations, what kinds of culture would be provided and how would it be made? Would it be a subsidised private sector contract, or would there be more public involvement in culture's production as well as distribution? What kind of regulatory guidelines would there be? What kind of democratic accountability? (I discuss this in the next chapter).

Culture viewed entirely as a private consumption good thus undermines culture as part of a wider sociocultural infrastructure. To put it another way, the cultural infrastructure is not just "out there" in a local community but "right here" at the heart of the household. If the social infrastructure is, as the FEC argue, about sustaining "high functioning individuals who strengthen the resilience and capability of households",[11] that is, citizens equipped with Senian freedom and the capacities to flourish and realise themselves, then we must see cultural capacity as a crucial part of this citizenship. Household cultural consumption acquires its fuller meaning in a social context, in those sites and occasions for discussion, argument, learning, and exchange. As well as for collective celebration, or sub-cultural bonding. Harney's utopian vision in Chapter 3, if it is not to describe an individualised consumer paradise, builds on this cumulative process of self-reflection and exploration made possible by culture. These capacities are built not just on disposable income but also on the education, access, recognition, and respect that would allow the full exercise of these cultural faculties. This is why social isolation is not compensated for by individual cultural consumption but rather exacerbated by it.[12]

In Chapter 3 I spoke of cultural "meta-goods", those educational (in the broadest sense) goods which allow people to make their own judgements of value (cultural or otherwise) and of the broader vision of the "good life" they seek to pursue. For Russell Keat the value of culture as a meta-good is its contribution to our ongoing judgement of the value of other goods and of the coherence and meaningfulness of our lives. These meta-goods include formal education (schools and universities) as well as the informal cultural infrastructures (local galleries, dance schools, film events) I discuss below. But cultural goods are themselves part of our ongoing education, an individual and collective conversation about human flourishing and meaning. Which is why the cultural system is an essential part of any democratic public sphere.

At the same time, we need also to emphasise the role of the social and cultural infrastructure in the strengthening not just of the household but the community itself, its capacity as a site of citizenship, to act as a commons, to provide a breathing space in which to imagine our individual and collective futures. This is the public sphere in its most palpable sense, rather than some abstract invocation of a "fourth estate" or parliamentary deliberations. From this perspective we might see that the privatisation of cultural consumption is not just an effect of profit-seeking but is part of a wider political project.

Thatcher's aim to change the nation's "heart and soul" was famously founded on the privatisation of public services and the promotion of the family over "society". We can recall Will Davies' the "economy is cultural ... markets, property rights, work and consumption produce distinctive identities and affects, not as side-effects ... but as integral components of how they operate".[13] The privatised household is a political project, one in which cultural consumption has been fully complicit.

Since the 1980s, the privatisation of the material infrastructure of communications, followed by a convergence of telecoms with "content" companies, has underlain much of the shift of culture from public to private consumer goods.[14] There has been a wholesale privatisation of the public sphere since the 1980s. It was continued by the take-off of commercial Web 2.0 after the dot-com crash, and the subsequent rise of "platform capitalism".[15] The gains in social connectivity, collective creativity, and access to knowledge opened up by these new technologies have to be set against the profound contribution their privatisation has made to social fragmentation and isolation.[16] We have become far more aware of the results of that privatised public sphere over the last decade, its fragmentation and individualising effects, the mobilisation of anger and reaction, and its regime of data extraction and surveillance.[17]

The political and ideological consequences of the privatisation of the public sphere are equally clear, with the creation of a group of billionaires of unprecedented power and wealth. Platform capitalism has sparked talk of "techno-feudalism" – the platform bosses the new lords of the manor, with us their serfs.[18] Whether neo-feudalism or not, the giving over of the internet public sphere to a small group of Silicon Valley entrepreneurs has revealed the "double truth" of neoliberal freedom. As William Davies outlines, this is not the "freedom to choose on the market" but the "higher order" freedom of the "founders", that is, "the freedom to construct whole social worlds".

> This was a freedom that was especially valued by Austrian conservatives, such as von Mises and Joseph Schumpeter. But in the form taken by [Peter] Thiel and others, it is far closer to a political capacity than an ordinary economic one; far closer to "positive liberty" than "negative liberty". It is the freedom to create the very conditions of ordinary people's freedom.[19]

The parallel erosion of journalism and independent media, the ongoing transformation of universities to corporate entities, and the marginalisation of arts and humanities within these are of a part with this erosion of the public sphere. In these circumstances, looking to the social and cultural infrastructure at a local level is a practical first steppingstone in a wider revival of a democratic culture.

Hard infrastructure: buildings and pipes

Recent work on the social infrastructure has emphasised the hard, physical requirements necessary for the generation of Putnam's social capital.[20] Even bowling alone requires a bowling alley. This includes Ray Oldenburg's "third spaces" – "Cafés, Coffee Shops, Bookstores, Bars, Hair Salons and Other Hangouts at the Heart of a Community" – and public spaces too.[21] Kelsey and Kenny define social infrastructure as:

> those physical spaces in which regular interactions are facilitated between and within the diverse sections of a community, and where meaningful relationships, new forms of trust and feelings of reciprocity are inculcated among local people. These physical spaces may be public and free to use, such as libraries, parks and youth centres, or they may be provided in commercial spaces, for instance pubs, cafés and restaurants.[22]

This recent work is symptomatic of the long-term erosion of the physical social infrastructure, exacerbating Putnam's portrait of the decline in "social capital".[23] However, the FEC rightly criticise these approaches for failing to factor in the other pillars of liveability – disposable income and services – which have a direct impact on the viability of local social infrastructures. Wealthier areas can sustain these better through private spending; poorer areas require public investment. The erosion of social connections has been far more marked in working-class rather than middle-class areas. These approaches also fail to explain just how this situation came about, Klinenberg especially not having much to say about policy solutions. So too, Kelsey and Kenny are concerned with the Conservative government's "levelling up" agenda, but barely discuss the impact of the post-GRC austerity measures launched by then chancellor George Osborne in 2011.

However, the issue is not simply one of public disinvestment but also private extraction. Since the 1980s there has been a transformation in urban planning regimes in favour of real estate companies. The proliferation of out-of-town shopping centres in the 1980s, the swamping of local areas with chain micro-supermarkets in the 1990s, the massive acceleration of "up-market" city centre apartments, or the unregulated escalation of online shopping and delivery services, amongst others, have all undermined the social infrastructure. The "crap towns" books speak to this.[24]

The privatisation of culture and leisure services, either through austerity (sports and community centres, swimming pools, libraries) or expanded home consumption (cinemas, bookshops, music streaming), are of a part with this erosion of the social infrastructure. But so too is the valorisation of selected cultural elements of the urban infrastructure by development capital for cultural consumption and "creative industries", under the sign of "urban regeneration". The agenda broadly dubbed the "creative city" has resulted in a highly distorted form of urban development.

There's now a political and socio-geographical divide between shiny metropolis and peripheral "crap towns", in which the social mobility promised by the creative economy required that you physically relocate. Preferably with a university degree. The popular cultural "coming-of-age" narrative is about those who "got out" to go to university, and those "left behind". The Conservative promotion of boot-strap entrepreneurship and New Labour's educational meritocracy urged that the best way of improving your chances was to leave these decaying communities behind.[25] "Get on your bike" and "swop your toolbox for a laptop" had its creative equivalent in Billy Elliot's leap from doomed mining village to the Royal Ballet. The story of the last decade is the growing desperation of both the aspiring creatives who did get out (debt, precarity) and those who stayed put in "dead-end" jobs. It is also one of the fracturing of political solidarity between these two forms of desperation. For the Conservatives, the working-class resentments of the "red wall" towns were wedged against the educated cosmopolitans of the metropolitan centres (as with the Trumpian "rustbelt states") in a clear "divide and rule" strategy.

This divide is replicated in the urban space itself, where highly capitalised urban centres like Manchester's are surrounded by areas of deep deprivation.[26] Owen Hatherley's tours through the ruins of the urban renaissance so loudly proclaimed by Richard Rogers in the early 1990s, and by Charles Landry's creative city manifesto, are salutary. Gleaming lottery-funded cultural icons stand out like islands in a degraded cityscape, where most of the collective aspirations of post-war planning have been destroyed or privatised. The glass and steel cathedrals of postmodern culture are surrounded by "non-place" brick boxes and the abandoned, cast-off urban developments of what architect Rem Koolhaus called "junkspace".[27]

The creative city valorised certain symbolic and cultural aspects of the city, while abandoning others, especially the mundane social.[28] It prioritised the marketing benefits of "iconic" buildings, an "edifice complex" which focused on buildings rather than the people and programmes required to animate them.[29] Governments rarely build hospitals without thinking of the doctors, nurses, technicians, and other workers required to make them function. This happens regularly in culture, where an endless supply of artists is assumed. Money for hard infrastructure is often listed under "arts funding" but most of it goes to construction and consultants.[30] It sucks money out of everyday cultural infrastructures. The apotheosis of Manchester's music scene, according to Andy Spinoza, the city's official hagiographer, is the

> £600 million worth of new arts and entertainment facilities being opened this year. A £385 million arena, Co-op Live, next to Manchester City's football ground. Then there's Factory International ... venue for cutting-edge culture is costing £211 million — £100 million pounds of which has been given by the Conservative government.[31]

Though cultural projects are routinely required to show direct economic impact (jobs created, local spend), this is only occasionally applied to the edifice, whose aspirational visitor spending figures supplied by the consulting accountancy firms are rarely held to account post-opening.[32] On the other hand, the benefits to the private sector in the form of linked commercial development (hotels, leisure, retail, apartments) is not recouped by the cultural sector and is rarely even attributed to them on their "impact assessment".

The cultural sector is crucial to the various indexes of "liveability" and "vibrancy" for those cities seeking to attract global "footloose" personnel. Yet, as with public transport, public investment in culture is seen as an expense, a taxpayer subsidy, whereas the businesses which depend on this "vibrant city", in hospitality, retail, leisure, and real estate, are seen as somehow wealth creating.

The one-sided focus on "iconic" buildings and "starchitects" is a distorted, disavowed tribute to the intimate connection between the built environment and civic space. The laying out of buildings associated with art and culture, or with learning and public administration, is itself a civic gesture, a statement about the importance of the public realm. From the grandiose schemes of Baron Haussmann's Paris, Vienna's *Ringstrasse*, Victorian London, Chicago's "City Beautiful", or the colonial piles of Calcutta or Shanghai, to the smaller towns and cities which followed them, the physical–aesthetic form of the material infrastructure attempted to shape a new public realm.

The built environment is not just functional infrastructure but can make manifest the public services it helps deliver – hence the great nineteenth- and twentieth-century hospitals, schools, universities, train stations, post offices, and "people's palaces". The expressive form of the built environment is an intrinsic part of that service, at its best emphasising transparency, access, and citizenship. The degradation of the public realm – private affluence and public squalor – is not just a result of the diversion of funds from public services but also expresses quite clearly that these services are residual, given on sufferance to the losers in the great race, and a drain on resources not to be exacerbated by comfy seats or artists' murals.

As Kieran Long, Director of ArkDes, the Swedish National Centre for Architecture and Design, has it:

> It is architecture and design's task to give form to a societal idea (like justice) through the creation of a setting for people to encounter that idea (like a courthouse). We see in our public buildings and spaces (our park benches and metro trains; a hot dog kiosk and a monument to the dead) what we are made of. Design cannot avoid this assignment – it either embraces the task, or it unwittingly displays, or even conceals, society's prejudices and weaknesses.[33]

The built form is part of the necessarily collective provision of services we associate with networks or "reliance systems" (trains, telephony, water, electricity). You can't build your own city! But to this functional necessity we can add the delivery of beauty, pleasure, delight, prestige, and respect via a shared public realm that no individual could afford to buy. The great social housing complexes of modernism, the stations and parks, the boulevards and shopping complexes also provide a collective service through their design aesthetic. This concern with collective aesthetics is what the Communards, as Kristin Ross tells us, called "communal luxury".[34]

This is not to argue for a return to the beaux-arts tradition, or even the grand designs of heroic modernism. Long-term social and cultural changes point us in new directions. Designing communal luxury for the twenty-first century is an exciting challenge and would follow less Le Corbusier and more the architect collective *Assemble* or the French duo of Anne Lacaton and Jean-Philippe Vassal, whose "adaptive reuse" is central to the pragmatics of the foundational approach.[35]

This inevitably points beyond the built environment to the "pipes". As Timothy Mitchell and others have shown, physical infrastructures and markets are both highly constructed.[36] The decisions made about the reliance systems of water, housing, electricity, and food supplies are shaped by political economy as much as any technical necessity. The modern city, from the mid-nineteenth century on, aimed to give shape to these services technically and financially, politically, and (as in modernism) aesthetically. These issues now apply to the communication systems which now permeate the physical infrastructure of the city in complex ways. How these "pipes" (and the protocols which structure them) have been formed as natural monopolies (or monopsonies), leading to a privatisation of the public sphere, will be discussed more in Chapter 6.[37]

Cultural infrastructures

This is not just about the privatisation of consumption, as discussed above, but also the shaping of the democratic space of the city. The rise of vendor-led "smart city" agendas as well as the now normalised saturation of the urban realm by surveillance, smart systems, embedded platforms, and so on has presented dauntingly technical and commercial challenges to traditional urbanism. As Adam Greenfield has pointed out, such technologies are often directly antithetical to democratic public space.[38] What Dan Hill calls "street as platform" and Sarah Barnes "platform urbanism" both set out the challenges for a democratic enhancement of public space rather than a profit-driven enclosure.[39] I cannot discuss this in detail here, but a cultural policy concerned with the social and cultural infrastructure must engage with this dimension.

More generally, as design theorist Dan Hill has argued, we need to radically flip the idea of infrastructure away from a purely technical issue towards a socially grounded, adaptive approach. Technics cannot be thought of apart from everyday social infrastructures. And here culture too will be required to play a greater role. Quoting Raymond Williams, Hill suggests this moves us closer to art: "Everything we see and do, the whole structure of our relationships and institutions, depends, finally, on an effort of learning, description and communication. We create our human world as we have thought of art being created".[40]

But before leaving hard infrastructure, we should point to the most foundational element of all, land. The fair distribution of land has been central to emancipatory struggles the world over.[41] Structures of ownership are crucial to social and cultural infrastructures. In this context, the massive process of land privatisation that Brett Christophers has recently charted speaks to the enormous task confronting any real transformative agenda.[42] While we can't discuss this here, seeking out new forms of ownership, reasserting public ownership, and redistributive land taxation might also need to be added to the language of cultural policy.

Cultural infrastructure

The concept of cultural infrastructure has been around for some time in cultural policy. In formal terms, it is a combination of buildings and facilities with the institutional capacity required to make them operational.[43] This lends itself to an "asset inventory" approach, which is useful but limited. This can be broadened to include the "soft infrastructures" which include organisations and institutions, training and education, festivals and events, and so on. It includes libraries, galleries, and museums; community arts and craft centres; dance, theatre, and music schools; radio stations; arts and craft classes; independent cinemas; music, theatre, and other performance venues; festivals and events; online publishing; recording studios, film production facilities, and creative workspaces.[44]

There are also various art and cultural programmes repurposed from elsewhere, such as arts for health, or arts education and training, university research, cultural heritage, CCI economic development, and so on. These are set within the funding programmes of local, regional, and national government, which sustain this highly complex ecosystem, often built up over centuries. Many of these are difficult to disentangle from the social infrastructure. Parks and libraries, for example, were long associated with a popular cultural mission.[45] Sport too is about culture as much as it is about physical exercise, though mostly governed via a different set of institutions. I don't want to get into this here, but somebody needs to write a parallel book, *Sport is Not an Industry*.[46]

The funded cultural infrastructure intersects in complex ways with the "overlooked" zone of small independent not-for-profit projects and spaces, volunteers and unpaid artists, and those small businesses behind the record shops, bookshops, music pubs, nightclubs, indie cinemas, small private museums and galleries, cafes, and restaurants. These are highly dependent on planning, urban development regimes, zoning regulations, and other "technical" issues.

Deeper still, culture's soft infrastructure refers to the shared knowledge, traditions, patterns of sociability, and genres of business practices which bare the weight of history and have effects on a city's adaptability and mutability. The creative city agenda, though often reduced to real estate-led gentrification, also attempted to reorient these deeper "structures of feeling" towards a more open, innovative, future-oriented culture. In this it joined with the creative industries in seeing local cultures as primarily valuable as sources of economic development. I will discuss this more in the next chapter.

I prefer infrastructure to "ecosystem", mainly because the former concept emphasises construction and maintenance, rather than the latter's sense of organic evolution and self-regulation. Introduced during a period of deregulation in favour of the real estate market and the privatisation of public assets, "ecosystem", though useful in certain circumstances, is somewhat ideologically tainted.

A functioning cultural infrastructure requires money, skills, time, and effort. It involves a mix of salaried workers, contract workers, and volunteers, plus cross-over workers from health, social services, education, and training. This latter might be an "arts for health" project, or youth inclusion, or an economic development-led "creative hub". It might include public, philanthropic, and sponsorship funding, perhaps with a university or another institutional involvement.[47]

This is a very fragile ecosystem and has suffered austerity cuts along with the rest of the public service sector. While some "reliance systems" quickly show stress when they are underfunded – food, water, electricity, transport – others, such as education and culture, take a long time for their emergency lights to blink red. It is very easy for governments to cut such esoteric, specialist services as archives, or art storage, or those extra hands in the outreach department. Cutting "luxuries" in hard times usually means culture budgets, or leaving cultural workers out of consideration, as often happened in the pandemic.

I've outlined some of the reasons for this in previous chapters – economic rationalism, market citizenship, individualised cultural consumption, as well as culture's own failures of legitimation and sense of purpose. Turning this around requires a robust assertion of the public value of culture. The cultural infrastructure requires investment in facilities, people to run and deliver programmes, and interlocking networks of education and training, research and documentation, communication, evaluation and debate, and the administrative and political capacity to take care of these infrastructures and ecosystems.

Funding for the cultural infrastructure, for the last few decades, has been based on various iterations of economic benefit. Jobs and growth; tourism spend; inward investment; attraction of skilled workers; innovation spillovers; catalytic creative inspiration; R&D for cultural commercialisation; bringing the socially excluded into the workforce. And so on. As we saw in the last chapter, in the zonal schema of culture, the creative industries agenda has sought to drive as much as possible from the social foundations into the transactional-commercial. The burden of investment in the cultural foundations is, we are told, borne by the private sector and made possible by the wealth they generate.

As I argued in the last chapter, the social foundations and small-scale local economies employ around 70 per cent of the working population in most cities and regions. Yet culture-as-industry looks to the highly extractive, and mostly non-locally owned, minority commercial sector for its exemplar and sign of success. We have yet to do a full mapping of the zonal cultural economy, but we already know its transactional sectors are extremely geographically concentrated, in the metropolitan centres, and in specific zones of these centres. The publicly funded social and cultural infrastructures and the small-scale overlooked "third spaces" which grow around them are what most people encounter in their everyday lives. Yet this is routinely marginalised, or rendered economically instrumental, in our public discourse.

It is this discursive capture, by an economic development language antithetical not only to cultural value but social value too, that we have to flip if we are going to have a chance at rebuilding the cultural infrastructure on which a flourishing democracy depends.

Asserting the public

The cultural infrastructure is crucial to individual and communal wellbeing, a dimension of the social infrastructure without which the rights and capabilities needed to fully choose one's life cannot be guaranteed. A resuscitated cultural policy needs to actively engage in the discursive struggle to reassert public value over private profit, and to return culture to the public realm rather than leave it to market citizenship. The UN's recent invocation of "public goods" and "common goods" should be seen as part of this discursive struggle to end the default model elaborated in the 1980s – culture as a combination of private consumption economy with pockets of "market failure", hemmed in on all sides by onerous and disciplinary metrics.[48]

The market cannot guarantee the sustainable continuation and flourishing of such cultural infrastructures. Indeed, given free reign, as it has been, it is actively detrimental to them. The combination of a withdrawal of local and national state funding, alongside the depredations of development capital, large-scale cultural industries, and platform capitalism has pushed them to the brink. This crisis concerns not just the immediate hard and soft infrastructures but the systemic services which underpin these – arts and cultural education at schools through to professional creative training of all kinds; large and small institutions which sustain the circulation of creation, critique, and experiment; a cultural public sphere of criticism, evaluation, and debate; a public media with a commitment to democratic values and the participation of the commons, and so on.

The discursive struggle should insist on the positive value of collective provision. There is a public good involved in communally shared events and activities, as there is in the enhanced quality of the environments in which social life takes place. It is not just that some cultural and leisure goods need to be delivered collectively (libraries, parks, swimming pools) but that the collective nature of the (free or partially subsidised) provision is itself part of the value of these public goods. Not only is collective provision a public good in itself, enhancing citizenship, but public subsidy, as Mariana Mazzucato suggests, can often "crowd in" private provision – which is why urban regeneration schemes most often have some kind of publicly subsidised culture at their heart.[49] The challenge is to retain this "value-added" for the public realm rather than it being seen as a "loss leader" to stimulate the for-profit sector.[50]

Crucial to this assertion of public goods and public value is a reclaiming of democracy. For two decades arts and cultural institutions and organisations have adopted, willingly or not, goals of participation, engagement, and access as part of their "social licence". Yet despite all the metrics demanded of cultural organisations, "policy-based evidence" is the norm, these metrics rarely influencing strategic decisions.[51] Rather, politicians, driven by the failure of culture's social licence to which they themselves have so often contributed, see increased ticketing numbers as a primary vindication. "Cultural democracy" is frequently reduced to "bums-on-seats", the public sector version of neoliberalism's "every penny a vote".[52] In this context the kinds of invisible work required to sustain cultural infrastructures so easily get sidelined.

Three points of intervention might help turn this around.

First, I propose that rather than an endless process of "mapping" or social impact metrics, multiple dashboards and indicators substituting for thought and evaluation, we can start with a simple audit of cultural infrastructure. This is not an itinerary of cultural facilities and organisations, though these would be included. Rather, it is an attempt to map the extent to which each citizen has access to the foundational services (especially education) and cultural infrastructures necessary for the effective exercise of the right to full participation in art and culture.

Such a right is enshrined in the 1948 UN Declaration of Human Rights and the 1966 International Covenant on Economic, Social and Cultural Rights. It is part of that expanded "social citizenship" we spoke of in the Introduction. What resources and what capabilities would be required if households and individuals are to participate fully in art and culture, and to realise their potential within it? Do they have access to any form of arts (music, drama, visual art, design) education in local public schools? What kind of local arts and cultural facilities are available? Are there music venues, libraries, indie cinemas, bookstores, record shops, performance spaces, rehearsal spaces, and meeting spaces within reasonable distance? Which areas fare worse/better than others.

Such an audit would have to be linked to benchmarks of minimum national and local government provision, as a right to culture and mark of democratic citizenship. This has long been claimed by cultural rights groups, such as the United Cities and Local Government and interventions such as the Charter of Rome.[53] It used to be pursued by UNESCO before they took their own detour into the creative economy.

Such an audit would identify funding requirements for those areas lacking the basic minimum social and cultural infrastructures, to "level up" perhaps. This would have to be more than just redistributing an existing art and cultural budget, getting rid of a metropolitan opera house to fund something "up North". Such a comprehensive audit, based on access to cultural resources and the acquisition of capabilities rather than access to cultural goods, could form the basis of a real process of radical cultural policy making, driven by citizen assemblies and a (local and national) government commitment to reimagine art and culture as foundational for democratic citizenship.

The results of such an audit might show up a set of social and geographical divisions that are somewhat more complex than "red wall" versus "metro" areas. For while these divisions are real, the causes are by no means simply the outcome of the college-educated "precariat" or even the "professional-managerial class" (the "Brahmins") hogging all the funding. It can also be laid at the feet of the more hard-headed "merchants" who insist on tax cuts, the privatisation of services, and punitive welfare regimes while remaining able to – voluntarily obviously – finance a rich social and cultural infrastructure for their own areas.

The pillars of cultural equity and access, with clear democratic lines of responsibility – taking back control – could form a site of solidarity around which "red wallers" and precarious "metros" might stand together. For the spiritual freedom promised by culture is meaningless outside of the material freedoms guaranteed by foundational solidarity and liveability. The degradation of the local social and cultural infrastructure – crap towns – is as deeply felt as other forms of cost-of-living challenges. The promise of economic regeneration via culture is now a busted flush, and we need – urgently – to move on.

Second, though participation and engagement are increasingly demanded, the ability of citizens to affect the decisions taken by governments over priority cultural investments, levels of funding, and programming has been limited. This lack of democracy is reflected in the boards that oversee many of the key institutions and agencies of the cultural infrastructure. Such boards often become sites for the accumulation of cultural capital for the wealthy, with the stipulation for "skills-based" appointments acting as cyphers for the business, legal, and financial expertise with which these elites are associated.[54] The growing reach of philanthropy within the public sector already begins to distort the public space in which "arts" governance is supposed to operate.

Finding new forms of citizen consultation and involvement would be crucial to the implementation of a radical reform agenda for arts and culture. It would involve actively promoting a wider social catchment for boards and broadening the "skillset" away from business and finance to those reflecting the people who work in and use these institutions. Participatory budgeting has been building up a large body of knowledge but is barely applied to arts and culture budgets.[55] So too citizen assemblies, charged with addressing strategic planning, should be on the agenda. Many of these ideas come out of social movements in the Global South, concerned about reasserting social rather than economic development value. The growing voices of indigenous peoples have also been crucial here. But this is also occurring in movements around community wealth building and the "new municipalism", which we discuss in the next chapter.[56]

Again, the goal here is not to achieve some numerically representative sample but to provide a space in which participation can be active, rather than the tokenistic levels of Sherry Arnstein's "ladder of citizen participation". But this will be impossible unless culture aligns itself with the reform of the social foundations. Art and culture cannot, by themselves, solve a democratic deficit in which social inequality and the collapse of household liveability prevents the majority from having any sort of time for these things. "In the final analysis", the Uruguayan writer Eduardo Galeano once said, "it doesn't bother anyone very much that politics be democratic as long as the economy is not".[57]

Third, we might embark on a project of inflecting the existing cultural infrastructure towards the social, but in a way that does not reduce the specific value of culture to health and wellbeing, or an arm of social services. Thinking of the FEC commitment to "adaptive reuse", and to the power of *restanza*, or "staying in place", this project to radically rethink the cultural infrastructure would run in tandem with the necessary work on cultural democracy and national audited standards of effective cultural rights.[58]

The growing acknowledgement of the importance (and erosion) of the social infrastructure is mirrored in the opening up of local cultural infrastructures to communities in a way that can often prefigure a real democratisation of culture. While the mechanistic-bureaucratic end of "access and participation" can be onerous and irrelevant, the parallel emphasis on community outreach and engagement – local schools and communities, disabled and older people, anti-racist and women's groups, refugees and homeless, queer and trans rights, and so on – has been transformative for many organisations. These are incredibly under-resourced but have helped us radically rethink not just what cultural organisations do but how we might understand arts and culture's relation with everyday life.[59]

Indeed, many creative hubs and spaces, whose funding model is predicated on creative industries and entrepreneurship, are in practice key parts of the local social and cultural infrastructure. Rather than "start-up" spaces landing like UFOs from another brighter, more successful galaxy, they often attempt to embed themselves in a community. Multifunctional, social, educational, and celebratory, they can be central to the small ecosystems of not-for-profits and micro-businesses we will discuss in the next chapter. But they are also an essential part of the wider sociocultural infrastructure. Though the "creative city" discourse presented these regenerative effects as a harbinger of a new creative economy, we might flip this and see them as a disavowed contribution to the social and cultural infrastructure.[60]

The same might be said of "creative improvement districts", and related concepts, where investment and care for local infrastructures are set within a framework dominated by metricised economic outcomes – much like the Kelsey and Kenny report.[61] Using the concepts of social and cultural infrastructure as essential to active, engaged, empowered, autonomous citizens, such creative hubs and creative improvement districts might be reoriented to what, effectively, has often been their real, sociocultural purpose.

The intersection of social and cultural infrastructures can be driven by need. As liveability declines, the social infrastructure often delivers foundational services, community centres providing respite from domestic violence and from sleeping rough. Equally, many local arts and cultural groups now run food-banks. Museums and libraries ask the government for help with their energy costs, as people seek the heating they can't afford at home. Indie cafes have phone-charging posts for delivery riders. As the climate crisis worsens, cultural centres rethink their role as places of refuge for communities.[62]

Recently, urban theorist and activist Adam Greenfield proposed the idea of the "lifehouse" as a distributed (social and material) infrastructural capacity,

> a place in every three-four city-block radius where you can charge your phone when the power's down everywhere else, draw drinking water when the supply from the mains is for whatever reason untrustworthy, gather with your neighbors to discuss and deliberate over matters of common concern, organize reliable childcare, borrow tools it doesn't make sense for any one household to own individually, and so on, and that these can and should be one and the same place.[63]

He was responding to *Guardian* columnist Simon Jenkins' proposal to use the 51,000 decommissioned and empty churches, each of them generally "the most prominent, not to mention magnificent, building in almost every English town and village". The churches could be used not merely to fill "the gaps in an increasingly dilapidated welfare state" but to "reconnect them to the surrounding communities from which the decline in worship has distanced them". Throughout history, "these buildings have offered their publics ceremony and memorial, peace and meditation, charity and friendship, quite apart from faith".[64] Greenfield says:

> communities need places to observe the rituals of lifestage and season that bind us together. Such observances are a considerable part of how we invest places with meaning, and there is no reason why church buildings, suitably desacralized, cannot serve that purpose into the indefinite future, as parish churches have done in this land since time immemorial.

Whatever the pragmatics surrounding English churches, here is a concrete evocation of the socially embedded function of a cultural infrastructure. They can – and should – intersect with social functions, but culture brings a specific space of meaning, celebration, communal identification, and collective ritual. These might be the breathing spaces, the moment set back from immediate exigencies of precarity, the endless "hustle", in which a different self and new world might be imagined.

Jenkin's distinction between "welfare state" function and wider cultural purpose is important. Much current socially embedded arts and cultural practice is hobbled by "social impact metrics" which are not only onerous in themselves but are set to agendas that are not those of culture. Their specific value so often disappears as cultural projects are shoe-horned into crime reduction, mental health, climate change communication, community health, and other (very worthy) agendas. This has roots in the cultural sector's need to demonstrate "social relevance" in lieu of other justifications for public funding, and it reflects a wider lack of confidence in its own purpose. So too, the impact of various forms of postmodernist, social justice, and post-humanist critique has also given an edge to the accusation of "elitism" thrown at the arts. While often guilty as charged, as publicly funded bodies they carry this weight while the private sector actors who ravage working-class communities, or the super-rich who extract wealth from owning the means of popular cultural production, go unmolested.

The specific value of culture to the social infrastructure, with which it intersects but also extends, needs to be positively embraced, not smuggled in as a social programme by default. This stripped back sense of culture's purpose, evoked by Jenkins (and Greenfield) points to the wider, systemic functions of culture as collective memory and connection to pasts, of its nurturing of diverse identities in a common space. Often labelled "heritage", culture in this sense can contribute to provide the institutional patterning within which individual autonomy can flourish. But this autonomy only makes sense in terms of a viable future, of the creation of the new in ways that are not the "eternal recurrence of the same" but which illuminate the territory of different, possible worlds. The systemic function of culture is to mark our changing connection to the past, to provide a space of respite from the present exigencies, to keep us together, coherent, and to imagine a future.

Economics, as Kim Stanley Robinson suggested in his 2020 book *Ministry of the Future*, simply cannot deal with the future.

But culture can. One of the most fundamental and universal definitions of culture is of an enduring bond between past and future generations.[65] The inability of neoclassical and neoliberal forms of economic reasoning to measure, and thus value, this intergenerational connection is one of the contributory reasons for the multiple world-wide systems stress that we now face. Culture-as-industry is the face of this collapse of the future.

Conclusion

When asked why Manchester had produced such a rich popular culture since the 1970s, DJ and author Dave Haslam answered: "Penguin Modern Classics".[66] I take this as a synecdoche of a cultural infrastructure in which access to cheap books – and records, gigs, magazines, and visual arts – was part of the "popular modernism" of which Mark Fisher spoke.[67] That is, the infusion into working-class lives of a kind of modernist sensibility, an ethos in which the future was there to be made, and that people previously excluded could now make a contribution. This grew from a combination of material and spiritual freedom. It involved a confluence of free education, cheap health, cheap (sometimes free) housing, and easy welfare, combined with the meta-goods of public culture, and spaces of rough and ready communal luxury. Limited as they were, these provided not just material and cultural resources but a space of recognition in which it was okay for working-class kids to pick these things up and run like hell with them.[68]

The creative industries were part of the way in which these aspirations were annexed into a programme of jobs, growth, and market citizenship, available not to the many but to the few. There is no necessary reason to counterpose this forward-looking popular modernism to an older working-class solidarity.[69] This popular modernism itself was predicated on forms of social and cultural citizenship without which it could not have existed. Andy Spinoza assigned Manchester's creative ascent to the moment the city turned against "welfarism" and adopted a "business friendly approach".[70] On the contrary, Manchester's "culture-led renaissance" was unthinkable without the social and cultural infrastructures of "welfarism" – which the private sector had little intention of renewing.

The kind of radical reinvention I evoke here would have to be local, adaptive, experimental. It would have to nurture locally based actors, providing education and support to allow access and participation. It would require programmes of "contributive justice", providing multiple opportunities to actually produce culture rather than consuming it, even if these may not lead to full-time jobs. It would need to focus on that local ecosystem not as an economic engine but to encourage what the FEC call *restanza*, a staying in place. The answer may no longer be to either "go to uni" or get stuck in life, but to stay, or return, and build solidarity alongside a creative future.

6

Culture and economy

The argument I have been making in this book is that culture-as-industry has run its course, failing to deliver the political influence and resources it promised. The economic Trojan Horse devoured its cunning occupants. Culture-as-industry does still remain in play, however. In the UK, NESTA, an endowment trust founded in the same year as the creative industries rebrand, has weathered austerity and cuts to culture budgets, a relatively wealthy patron while other cultural research entities tightened their belts. NESTA have been powerful proselytisers for the creative industries. So too have the academic research funding agencies, where programmes for "creative industries" give far greater credibility with a sceptical government and allow individual academics to demonstrate "industry engagement" in ways other parts of the arts and humanities find difficult. But it is clear the creative industries moment is an ebbing tide.

While the funded CCI agencies proclaim "building back better" and the "pivot to digital", many in the subsidised sector have drawn a line between themselves and the more commercial CCI.[1] Claims for the social and community benefits of art and culture gained prominence in the pandemic, stressing their

197

alignment with the ethos of "care" and "wellbeing". Politicians are now prepared to state more boldly these social and community benefits, over and above the economic. It's a paradigm shift marked by UNESCO's recent adoption of the idea of culture as a "global public good" and pushing for culture to become a stand-alone sustainable development goal.

But this reckoning with culture-as-industry has only just begun. The shock impact of the pandemic on cultural workers, the hit to their livelihoods and to their self-esteem as governments often ignored or trivialised their plight ("why not just retrain"?), disabused many of their confident creative industries persona. There has been a new concern with the plight of "cultural labour", and a resurgence of the sense that art and culture are largely unviable outside government subsidy. But the more confident reassertion of the role of art and culture is still absent, with often bitter debates over whether the arts council should even exist.[2]

In this chapter I will argue that we need a real alternative to culture-as-industry, for the decline of the creative industries agenda will leave art and culture exposed unless it develops a new purpose and rationale. Though many reaffirm the social benefits and the need for government subsidy, this remains a weak "market failure" argument for culture. We must be far more robust and make claims for public investment in culture as a crucial contribution to our collective prosperity. Equally, that culture as public service needs a radical overhaul if it is to deliver on this promise.

There is the danger that carving out subsidised art and culture from the wider "commercial sector" will also be a limiting strategy. One the one hand, it puts the local bookshop or indie cinema on the same level as Ticketmaster, Amazon, or Netflix, ignoring the very real conflicts and differences at play here. The local cultural infrastructure necessarily involves the small-scale "everyday" economy of culture, alongside the social infrastructure of public parks and local cafes, libraries, and pub venues. It is as much under threat as the subsidised arts sector, needing urgent care and attention. Part of the response is to find ways of addressing the precarity that is now rife in the freelance and casual sector. While independence and autonomy are crucial in art and culture, this is barely possible in a state of ontological insecurity. The publicly funded cultural sector has a role to play here, as has the provision of foundational services and new forms of labour regulation. I also suggest that universal basic services and job guarantee schemes might be better than universal basic income.

At the same time, we have to address the issue of small-scale local cultural economies. This can no longer be imagined though standard CCI models of "SME clusters" and I suggest that we look more to ideas of the commons and embedded economies as a more sustainable approach. While the CCI cluster model maintained elements of the utopian promise of creative work in the creative city, this is no longer a viable option and needs radical reframing. Debates around community wealth building, community economies, citizen platforms, and cultural co-operatives are becoming far more attractive alternatives.

Part of this unsustainability relates to the more predatory nature of the commercial-transactional sector which now penetrates far below the commanding heights, reaching down into the heart of local, community, and household cultural economies. We need new ways of framing this sector, which retains part of the older "business model" identified by cultural political economy scholars in the 1980s and 1990s, but with some disturbing new additions. New forms of monopoly and concentration, rentierism, intellectual property regulation, and the mass extraction of user data, much of it linked to the rise of the new "platform capitalism", have transformed global cultural industries. I suggest how we might approach what some have called a "new feudalism", and how we might understand the current crisis of culture as part of a wider systemic crisis.

Social investment in culture

Many working in arts and culture have long been sceptical about "cultural and creative industries", certainly after the global financial crisis and the austerity that followed. Those working in subsidised arts and culture mostly ignore it or use it as and when needed. Anyone familiar with the arts and cultural sector will know its hand-to-mouth, cunning pragmatism, where one renders unto Caesar whatever Caesar wants if it means getting that grant. The grant you need to survive. Given the general antipathy to cultural funding by many governments – the UK out front – many are content to huddle under the protective umbrella of the creative economy, with all those jobs and wealth and innovation metrics, simply in order to keep their heads above water.

Even under the direct banner of "CCI" lots of good work gets done. Those creative hubs or innovation spaces, skills development and networking events, technology access and grants for micro-businesses – they do have some real social, cultural, and economic impact, generating small ecosystems of activity and inspiration through the resources they bring. But their direct economic benefit, which used to be the stuff of headline metrics and elaborate impact charts, has been tempered by these social and educational "spillovers", and their language is increasingly uncomfortable with the gung-ho industry language of a pre-austerity, pre-pandemic, pre-cost of living crisis world.

The move to a more open acknowledgement of the social benefits of culture, and that these require government subsidy is gathering pace, but mostly it is done by (re)installing the separation between subsidised and commercial. The growing interest in a "UBI for artists" has been justified in terms of the arts being commercially unsustainable and requiring public support. The arts deal in one-off artefacts or in live performances, involving high costs that cannot easily be recovered. The cultural industries, on the other hand, recoup their high costs of production by mass reproduction, each additional digital copy tending to near zero. The arts find it hard to increase productivity – bigger audiences, more performances, reproductions of scale – and are stuck in the old 1960s "cost disease" trap – costs going up, but income remaining static.[3] But such a separation, based on a subsidy/industry distinction, is problematic.

While separating publicly funded art and culture from the creative industries might be a welcome reaffirmation of the role of public subsidy, its claim on funding remains justified as "market failure". It is art and culture's *non-industrial* nature that is given as the main reason for subsidy, rather than positively embracing them as key areas of public service. It leaves commercial viability as culture's ideal default position. But we do not provide public health simply on the grounds that not everyone can pay for private cover. Or public education while assuming that ideally everyone should go to a private school. There are positive, egalitarian, collective, and social justice principles underpinning such public provision that art and culture should embrace, rather than talk about "market failure". Indeed, we need to acknowledge more forthrightly that contemporary capitalism has proved itself systemically incapable of providing for a wide variety of basic social and environmental needs. Why then should we assume "the market" as the default for cultural provision?

Neither does the idea of "market failure" challenge the basic framing of public provision as "unproductive spending". Cultural funding, in this view, like much other foundational spending, is made possible by the wealth generated by the "productive" part of the economy, that is, the commercial-transactional. In this way it is easy for the cultural sector to return to the mendicant mentality dependent on "the real economy" for its money. This chimes with the rise – and active courting – of philanthropic funding in culture over the last decade. We need a more robust and positive assertion of culture's public role.

As I suggested in Chapter 4, the combined employment in the foundational economy – material and social infrastructure and the "everyday" economy – is around 60 per cent of the total nationally. Outside of the metropolitan centres it is more like 70 per cent. Yet culture-as-industry looks to emulate the high-growth, high-returns commercial-transactional sector even though the combined state spending and employment figures for health, education, and social services dwarfs the levels seen in the arts. The Arts Council of England accounts for 0.05 per cent of the UK government budget.[4] The UK government spent GBP4.6 billion on culture in 2020/21. On education it spent almost twenty-five times as much (GBP116 billion), on health GBP220 billion, and social benefits GBP231 billion.[5] On the most pragmatic level, perhaps art and culture should try and align themselves with a public services sector that receives

123 times the funding of culture? But the argument must go beyond such pragmatics.

In neoclassical and neoliberal economics, state spending on services is framed as being paid for by the "productive" – i.e. profitable – sector of the economy. But, as we learned in the pandemic, the most useful and essential parts of our society are often the least profitable and their workers the least remunerated. Many profitable sectors are not useful, and often quite damaging. Large parts of the hyper-profitable finance sector are parasitic on the public service sector. As I argued in Chapter 2, this "productive" economy relies on a whole set of disavowed systems – education, domestic labour, environment – without which its profits would be impossible. So too, "productivity", which is the ratio of capital to labour, was revealed as a poor indicator of actual real-world efficiency, as many residents of aged care were to find out to their cost. Indeed, even assuming the profit-driven sector pays the taxes it ought to, this does not mean that the money invested in services is somehow paid for out of such taxes. As Jason Hickel suggests:

> In reality, there is no reason that public production needs to rely on "funding" from prior private production (as if corporations somehow produce money, which of course they do not). Any government that has sufficient monetary sovereignty can mobilize public production directly, simply by issuing public finance to do it. As Keynes pointed out: anything we can actually do, in terms of productive capacity, we can pay for. And when it comes to productive capacity, high-income economies already have far more than they need. Deploying public finance simply shifts the use of this capacity from corporations to the public, where it can be used for democratically ratified social and ecological objectives, rather than for capital accumulation.[6]

Similar arguments characterise approaches to the "social invest-ment state", whose advocates

> emphasise future fiscal returns from the welfare state, arising from higher tax revenues and avoided costs. This enables the care economy to be reframed in hybrid terms as social infrastructure that can be invested in to build public wealth. Rather than the state as taxer-spender managing aggregate demand in the pre-sent, the state becomes a "social" investor managing social value (wellbeing) over the long-term.[7]

We can see this in the shift to place-based development, in which, as with foundational thinking, it is household consump-tion, social infrastructures, care, health, and education that are stressed not just export-oriented transactional economies.[8] This general approach can also be found in the current mix of green transition politics, in the new "productivism" which links the green transition to local economies and social welfare, and in the newer global development paradigms which emphasise education, health, social welfare, and essential infrastructure rather than industrial development.[9] In contrast to these, yet again culture-as-industry lies like a whale beached out of time.

Using this perspective, investment in the cultural infra-structure would not be some subsidised crutch for culture as market failure but rather a crucial social investment in public wealth, both now and over the longer term. As a form of social investment, we need to be arguing for more and better pub-lic funding for culture. The vision for growing a cultural infra-structure should be seen as social investment in public wealth building, one that requires a new set of principles, procedures, and policy tools. Culture as infrastructure, as with other foun-dational services, involves the provision of public goods, which are "non-rivalrous", in that just because "region 'A' has them does not mean that region 'B' has been denied them. Promoting the growth of the foundational economy breaks with the conventions of locational tournaments and zero-sum games and reduces the scope for territorial competition between cities, regions and countries".[10] This breaks with the entrepreneurial vision of the "creative city", in which towns and cities seek to become "winners" in a generalised competitive process.

Such an approach will require an expanded political and administrative capacity to deliver and evaluate this investment. It will require intensive knowledge of the relevant area, and close collaboration with other public service agencies. But rather than art and culture being brought on towards the end of any strategic vision, it will have to be involved, as an equal, in the planning stage. However, this cannot simply be a top-down professional-led process but requires new forms of citizen involvement and democratic participation, as I suggested in Chapter 4.

This implies a new capacity of the public sector to engage in strategic policy co-creation. Public sector innovation has now generated different "innovation labs".[11] As described by Geoff Mulgan, then head of NESTA, they involve "experimentation in a safe space at one remove from everyday reality, with the goal of generating useful ideas that address social needs and demonstrating their effectiveness".[12] Some version of these public sector innovation labs could be the kernel of cultural participatory planning. But they would require serious scaling up to a strategic public service delivery level. This in turn requires the building of public service capacity, such as that evoked by Mariana Mazzucato's "missions" or Brian Eno's figure of the bureaucrat, "stabilising knowledge, keeping things running, and sometimes innovating quite radically".[13] Such experimentation and co-creation will present real challenges for the ability of the public sector to listen, learn, fail, and adapt.[14] The cultural sector, devastated by cuts, will also need time to develop the capacity to learn how to listen and to experiment. So too the academic research sector that supports them.

It will need to develop innovative approaches to local development, such as that coming out of foundational thinking and "deep place" analysis. This can be found in the FEC's work in Wales, but also in many different experiments in community economics and related approaches.[15] This approach takes the specificity of place seriously, as well as acknowledging the real challenges to citizen involvement in co-design and implementation given differences in power and knowledge, as well as long-standing demoralisation and passivity. A recent summary of "deep place" suggested three critical social domains where change should be sought, in "atmosphere", "landscape", and "cultural horizon".[16] These evoke the close knowledge and commitment to place that were one of the original promises of the creative city agenda.[17] Such an engagement with the social and cultural infrastructure would require a new capacity of "situational leadership", "able to promote debate, diversity of responses and not be afraid of experimentation and failure".[18] There are long-standing practices of community arts, place-based cultural development, and participatory culture which would be a vital contribution, strongly aligned with other foundational agencies.

If culture is to be part of the social essentials, as well as a vital contribution to social innovation and experimentation, it will require new jobs in the sector. The jobs will be highly qualified and should be properly remunerated. The foundational economy generally is not just about low-paid, low-skilled work ("taxi drivers and hairdressers", as one "head of innovation" had it recently[19]), though it includes these, whose needs should be properly addressed. Health and education include many low-paid jobs but also a highly skilled workforce with credentialed professional expertise. Developing the cultural infrastructure under the aegis of participation and co-creation requires a wide range of skills and experience. Cultural infrastructures need technical and administrative workers, artists and cultural professionals, outreach workers, policy specialists, as well as education and training programmes to develop local employment pathways.

This means moving to properly structured employment in the publicly funded cultural infrastructure, rather than the "efficiency dividend" of staff reductions and outsourcing, each new set of casual jobs carrying a diminishing level of rights and security. It means reducing casual work and bringing jobs in-house where feasible and desirable. It means proper rates of pay and security, access to training and development, as well as the social rights of health and social insurance. This will increase costs but secure the better prosperity and (real) productivity of those professionals employed in art and culture. It means establishing the sector's educational needs and gaps in provision and being able to map out a professional career advancement structure. Careers in art and culture need not be as institutionally structured as in medicine or law or academia, but some viable career path needs to be mapped out and supported.

The revival of a flourishing professional cultural sector, within the new democratic dispensation I outlined in the last chapter would add to local prosperity and liveability on multiple social, cultural, and economic registers. The significant increase in public investment would go directly into the local economy, as does much else in the foundational sector, rather than the often extractive high-value (GDP or GVA) sectors local government so often seek to attract and whose increase they take as a (false) proxy for community prosperity. Culture is a social investment.

Living and working in the cultural infrastructure

This social investment would not be entirely focused on large formal cultural organisations. These work within a larger dispersed and "disorganised" ecosystem of small-scale cultural outfits, businesses, and independent artists and other workers. Though generically described as freelancers, the choice of such a career practice can be as much by necessity – the reality of casual work – as by choice. They operate within the penumbra of the larger funded organisations, for commissions and other temporary collaborations, as well as more commercial sector work. In addition, they seek employment in related sectors – such as education – or in those that provide the requisite flexibility, such as hospitality. The policy talk is of ecosystems, but, like insects or healthy soil bacteria, these freelance, indie cultural scenes are slowly disappearing.[20]

It is this that lies behind the growing concern with cultural labour. In Chapter 1 I argued that, for New Labour, it was participation in the new creative workforce that made up for the cultural democratic deficit in which social democratic citizenship was reframed as "market citizenship". The creative class were set to inherit the earth, now they are rubbing shoulders with its wretched.[21] The reduction of full-time cultural employment after a decade of cuts, alongside the growing precarity of both public and private sector jobs, has met stagnant wages, a rising cost of living, growing levels of debt, and reduction in welfare services that has had a devastating impact. The pandemic only highlighted this.[22]

This reflects wider shifts in which educational capital – arts and culture are amongst the highest-qualified sectors – has given way to the "asset economy".[23] That is, the returns to education in the form of (supposedly) higher wages is offset by debt, unaffordable housing, minimal pension and insurance, and stalled wages rises. There has been a widespread de-professionalisation of cultural workers, as the standard definitions of a profession – control over entry credentials, identifiable career path, social status, autonomy at work – cease to apply.[24] Cultural workers are in the process of exiting Thomas Piketty's public professional-managerial "brahmins". Given that the professional-managerial class are salaried, it is the high degree of autonomy over the work process that distinguishes them from the working class.[25] How far such autonomy can be said to exist in the cultural sector is moot. Certainly, it is hanging by a thread. Similar things might be said of other professions – education especially – but it is well advanced in the cultural sector. The emergence of new forms of generative AI might be the tipping point for many. There's no doubt however that large numbers of cultural workers make up that section of the "professional-managerial class" Matt Huber terms "proletarianising".[26]

Many pandemic responses were able to support publicly employed cultural workers (and administrators) but even in Germany, where they were explicitly valued from the beginning of the crisis, it was difficult for those not formally employed.[27] Since 2010 proposals have grown to regulate precarious "platform" employment, with new kinds of online "freelancer" co-ops emerging.[28] Calls for better regulation of the use of temporary and casual staff are growing, as are those asking for scrutiny of outsourced contracts which make responsibility for the conditions of work difficult to monitor.[29] Full-time employment in the sector has declined rapidly, the obverse of the rapid rise in freelancing.[30] After the great claims for the "creative economy" as the future of work, cultural workers are now looking to other regulatory benchmarks of "decent work" based on the SDGs or International Labour Organisation campaigns.[31] Certainly, unionisation and collective bargaining are now increasing in the cultural sector, breaking with the individualised ethos diagnosed by Angela McRobbie and others.[32] Some realignment with "blue collar" work, also radically precarious, might be the other side of culture's turn to the social infrastructure.

However, the shift to "culture is a job just like any other" needs caution. Of course, cultural labour involves routine, tiresome, dirty, repetitive tasks just like other jobs. And people need it to pay the bills. But the overemphasis on culture as labour can easily act as an alternative "economic justification", a focus on the needs of the workers rather than the value they actually create.[33] Nurses and doctors are also, in this sense, "jobs just like any other". But they are also jobs we value, unlike, say, arms traders or private equity dealers. Rather than position cultural workers as "vulnerable" and in need of protection, the argument might be to sustain a complex cultural sector as a crucial element of the social foundations.

A general sense of precarity and insecurity, driving us to accept bad jobs and long hours, has resulted in calls for universal basic income (UBI). Here some kind of unconditional payment is given to everyone to spend as they wish, relieving them from the necessity of bad jobs and freeing their time to do caring, volunteering, socialising, or passion-driven "labours of love". The attraction for artists is clear. It would provide a minimum to live on while doing their own creative work, without the pressure of grants, second jobs, or onerous demands to show that one is "seeking work". There is an experiment running in Ireland currently.[34] There are fierce debates on UBI. They concern its overall affordability as its payments are, by definition, not targeted, making universal basic services (UBS), from this perspective, a better option.[35] Others focus on its individualisation, and its characterisation of work as something we might wish to escape from. Some elements of these critiques are important for culture.

It might be that some targeted basic income for artists scheme would work. It is selective and so perhaps akin to a fellowship scheme. The Irish experiment will tell us a lot here. However, I would suggest that any such scheme must be accompanied by the provision of decent wages, pensions, and insurance for salaried and contract workers. But more fundamentally we would need to ensure the "universal basic services" of health, housing, education, welfare, and transport.[36] The FEC model of liveability – disposable income, foundational services, social infrastructure – is applicable to the cultural sector itself. Higher wages in the sector are of course important, as would be any basic income. But without free or affordable services these would be pretty much wiped out. The purpose of a basic income would be to allow people to choose a low-income career as an independent artist. But, as Alex Niven argues, we need to look at:

> the fundamental inability of our society to provide basic forms of
> security – in education, housing, welfare and employment – if we
> are to understand why it is now so difficult for young innovators

in all the arts to achieve breakthrough .... Far from being the enemy of creative freedom, social security in the widest, deepest sense is the practical means by which personally liberating – and, ultimately, socially useful – imaginative ideas are given the space to grow.[37]

The best cultural policy might be universal basic services.[38]

More fundamentally, proponents of UBI see it as a break from the work-consume-work treadmill. It would encourage us to consume less, to restrict our needs, but be rewarded by time now freed from wage-labour. It raises the possibility that everyone, should they so choose, can now participate in the emancipated cultural life of free self-realisation evoked by Stefano Harney. However, given the system of individualised consumption we have had for forty years (at least), and the erosion of social cohesion, how would such liberation work without promoting further fragmentation?[39] Outside a coherent social and cultural infrastructure, would a UBI approach not further encourage social atomisation?[40]

Work needs to be done, and it is not clear how a UBI will ensure that socially necessary labour happens. We need teachers and nurses and farmers and people to empty bins. We need people far away in the "planet of slums" and the sweat factories of the Global South to produce the cheap commodities on which we can spend our basic income. Can we really have "UBI in one country"? Perhaps a more socially equitable way of allocating and sharing the hard, difficult jobs can be devised. UBI will not do this. How are we to ensure adequate spending on the social and cultural infrastructure, within which this discretionary spending is to take place and without which its use would be much diminished? The cultural infrastructure needs cleaners and administrators and full-time programmers and curators and performers and educators, by which any monetary capacity conferred by basic income can be made real and meaningful.

While the "moral virtue of work" has been used to cram people into boring, demanding, and dangerous jobs, stealing our time for the purposes of profit, this is not to say that work in itself is an evil to be escaped. Hard and dirty jobs can come with a wider sense of being socially necessary, meaningful labour, and with respect and recognition (as nurses and care workers receive, even if only rhetorically) this work too can be fulfilling.[41] We will never escape from the need to provide for our material foundations, though we can allocate this work fairly. It is not clear how UBI schemes, where meaningful work is that done for free and the rest paid drudgery, will ensure the equitable allocation of work.

What I am concerned about here, aside from the financial-administrative technicalities, is that individuation of cultural self-realisation it seems to promote, and the opposition of work and freedom which is both inequitable and philosophically questionable. However, what it does point to, from a point of view of cultural policy, are issues around who gets to do cultural work, who gets to participate in art and culture, in a highly unequal and increasingly stressed society. Cultural work still does represent good work. Just about. But access to it is highly unequal. If we are to promote what we have called, following Mark Banks, "contributive justice", then any basic income scheme is inseparable from the provision of cheap basic services and the investment in the social and cultural infrastructure. Otherwise, in seeking only to distribute income, we are returning to the meritocracy of talent at the expense of the idea of the common good, which underlay the political programmes of Clinton and Blair.[42]

Culture is not an industry

Much more targeted and affordable is the idea of job guarantee (JG), which would be far more useful to the cultural sector. This recalls older histories associated with the US New Deal of the 1930s, but also other schemes in the US in the 1970s, and in the UK (Enterprise Allowance) that provided a basic level of income to artists.[43] In basing itself on the right to a job and the responsibility of governments to ensure full employment, the JG would provide a crucial platform for organising cultural infrastructure projects which would mobilise professionals and amateurs with a range of skills. This, to my mind, is far more useful for the common good, and more politically feasible, than a UBI.

The everyday ecosystem

If I argue for a counter movement from the transactional-commercial towards the foundational, this is not to suggest some "renationalisation" of culture. There is a place for public cultural provision, but the total absorption of culture into subsidy is neither feasible nor desirable. There are good reasons why most of health and education should be primarily delivered by the state. There are good reasons why much of culture should not be delivered by the state. What might this mean for culture?

As with social infrastructures, cultural infrastructures rely not just on formal, publicly funded spaces and programmes but also on small-scale private, independent, or not-for-profit actors. Record shops, bookshops, music pubs, nightclubs, cinemas, small private museums and galleries, indie project-based artists, as well as a host of small to micro cultural businesses. Just as these small-scale cultural activities sustain a large part of the more "formal" culture system, so too does the small-scale "everyday" economy supplement precarious cultural employment through all the small-scale "everyday" jobs in hospitality, retail, and other jobs that can mix flexibly with their main cultural work. Artists and cultural workers are sustained by the local everyday economy, which provides income while they "learn by doing", engage in projects and events, try things out, start businesses, open their own spaces, and run magazines and online platforms. In turn, these are vital elements for the sense of activity and environment, of atmosphere and open horizon so valuable to the sense of place.

Tony Judt quipped that the railways might need to be organised by the state, but not necessarily the sandwiches.[44] For urban design theorist Dan Hill, Judt's statement "suggests where the dynamics of the market are best deployed – *the sandwiches end of things* – and where the idea of public value, shared ownership and civic governance is just too important, valuable and, frankly, complex to be left to the simplified heuristics of the private sector".[45]

Is the non-publicly funded cultural infrastructure about the railway or the "sandwich end of things"? It's a fuzzy dualism, as these everyday economies are only partly about markets, producing not only commodities but public goods. The everyday cultural ecosystem combines the small-scale transactional with elements of a gift economy or unpaid "sacrificial labour".[46] It is not only essential to the wider economy of art and culture but produces "public goods" – education, exposure, creative expression, sociability, excitement, pride of place, and so on. Indeed, these public goods are often the basis for the profits taken by real estate, high-end hospitality, and retail, who have been the main beneficiaries of creative city strategies.

Public policy should concern itself with this everyday economy as part of its care for a civic culture. Instead, it is *overlooked,* routinely ignored by policy makers who look for bigger investors, large chains, or branches of corporations headquartered elsewhere. The benefit these latter bring in terms of employment is often doubtful, and the impact in terms of local rents and real estate ownership – either as gentrification or dereliction – is damaging to the everyday economy.[47] Urban planners, along with real estate, construction, and corporate retail/hospitality actors, take for granted the small-scale, local cultural economy that acts as a source of "vibrancy" even while their own operations contribute to its demise.

So while we might welcome a healthy independent, unpredictable, low-risk and rumbunctious local everyday cultural ecosystem at the "sandwich end of things", the space in which that ecosystem thrives requires public care and attention. These local urban systems are in fact "co-created" by public sector investment and small-scale cultural activity. A foundational approach to the cultural ecosystem would see these small-scale local activities not as residual, or "meanwhile" (waiting for some "real investment"), but as a zone to nurture and protect, to grow and make flourish. This involves planning and zoning regulations, rent protection, and the provision of good, localised material infrastructures – an attentive approach to the publicness of the built environment.

At the same time, these local small business economies present some distinct challenges to any foundational approach. In a paper on Morriston, a small town in Wales, the FEC authors pose the following question:

> The implication from Morriston is that social infrastructure should be prioritised in any plans for foundational renewal. Beyond that, we have complex issues about which foundational

goods and services are citizen rights, which services should be free, full cost priced or subsidised, what are the appropriate business models of for profit and not for profit providers and how should the central and local state tax and spend as we move towards a society where all have access to the foundational goods and services they need to flourish.[48]

These questions urgently need to be asked of the cultural infrastructure. This is not only about the limits of state spending – what can we pay for and what not – but about the nature of culture. No-one would want the cultural infrastructure to be pre-planned by local government officers. But if the cultural infrastructure is a "mixed economy", where does the network end and the sandwiches begin? There's the rub. To extend the metaphor a little, are the sandwiches provided by the local corner cafe or street van, or by a multinational food chain using Chilean avocado and Finnish smoked salmon, assembled by a Ghanaian migrant worker somewhere near Lille? Are they part of the local everyday economy or a global corporate supply chain? Local everyday economies have been increasingly integrated into global value chains. As an FEC collaborator suggests, a transformative programme for the overlooked sector would require us to "strengthen, convert, and pursue differentiated policies for different business models", to "strengthen small and medium-sized enterprises, while strictly regulating multinational companies, which extract rents from non-essential local provisioning".[49]

One answer is the strengthened publicly funded social and cultural infrastructure, whose own purchasing and commissioning power has a lot of impact on the clusters of independents and SMEs that work around them. As with community wealth building initiatives, there is a lot of scope for local governments to help sustain a local SME sector.[50] Working to connect the everyday economy with the social foundations means valuing these SMEs not just as "local jobs and businesses" but as contributing to the civic qualities of our towns and cities, the power of the commons, and the health of the arts and cultural system. Again, the capacity of the everyday cultural ecosystem depends on the "meta-goods" of education and training, formal and informal and on the three pillars of liveability.

Many projects are trying to do this, but they inevitably have to badge it as creative industries. A project such as Factory in Manchester or the Roundhouse in London have both secured large-scale funding for arts and cultural training programmes, often targeted at "disadvantaged groups". One obvious objection is why schools and further and higher education have had their funding cut in these areas, and how far these large-sounding grants are drops in the ocean of a properly funding creative education system. But even so, these programmes would be far better framed as social investment in the cultural infrastructure rather than a contribution to one of the UK's "economic success stories" despite all the evidence about the realities of work in the sector.[51]

SME economies

A closer connection with a publicly funded cultural infrastructure is only one side of the issue. A local SME economy will necessarily be trading outside the local area, and, especially in the cultural sector, with very dispersed partners and clients. The challenges faced by this more "distributed" cultural economy, and nurturing more robust businesses, are very complex.[52]

Culture and economy

The original impetus for the cultural industries agenda in the 1990s came from Labour-run municipal governments and was built on claims for the transformative role of SMEs and the networked milieux which supported them. The "creative city" agenda, when concerned with new forms of production rather than consumption, has focused on an urban infrastructure able to facilitate networking, serendipitous encounter and collaboration, and rapid access to diverse, niche skills via agglomeration economies and "creative clusters" (or "quarters", "hubs", "precincts", and so on).[53] It was a programme based on a belief that the SME sector could animate local economies and provide a third way between the (now defunct) Soviet-style state planning and free-wheeling US corporate capitalism. By the end of the 1990s it was clear that the "SME moment" was temporary, part of a wider process of reorganisation around new forms of global corporate supply chain integration. As we shall see, this applies to cultural industries too.

The creative industries agenda relied heavily on an account of SME clusters operating as a necessity for "cognitive-cultural capitalism". The very nature of "cognitive-cultural" production demanded technically and aesthetically skilled, autonomous individuals and small companies able to work flexibly in highly fluid projects and teams. As with the "good work" arguments of New Labour, the cultural economy was a benign economy. It provided good, economically sustainable jobs and beneficial "externalities". It increased the demand for well-paid skills, catalysed further innovation, worked symbiotically to enhance or "regenerate" the urban environment, and resulted in a rich cultural environment.[54] It was within these clusters that the "creativity dispositif" of highly motivated, self-managed entrepreneurial subjects was to flourish.[55] Creative cities became a "social factory" where everything from historical memories, urban environment, forms of play and socialisation were to be part of the innovative creative milieux. To effectively nurture a local cluster required sophisticated and well-informed policy makers delivering a high-level industrial policy, which by necessity included the management and provision of social and cultural "meta-goods".

This has failed. I've noted the ongoing separation of "talented individuals" from the ownership of the intellectual property they create. This is part of a long-term shift of income from labour to capital, and the diminution of autonomy at work. Whatever space of relative autonomy or bargaining power cultural workers managed to acquire from the 1990s has been severely curtailed. What David Hesmondhalgh calls the era of the "complex professional" – autonomous professionals working inside and between the large corporations – might be turning into something else.[56] The accelerating circulation of projects and project workers, abruptly halted by the pandemic, has turned large parts of the cultural sector into an exhausted "projectariat".[57]

Culture–economy win–win was impossible in the frame of neoliberal public management. The rejection of industrial policy and the dismantling of state capacity made the kinds of sophisticated policy making required for this agenda impossible. The vision required to deliver on such a policy became less and less available as industrial, social, urban, and indeed cultural planning was subjected to narrow econometric calculations, city administrations were cut and hamstrung, and the creative industries were reduced to the baldest "return on investment", "jobs and growth" requirements. As the urban realm became increasingly dominated by investment capital, the idea of protecting localised creative SME economies because of their sociocultural externalities quickly evaporated. Start-ups and global platforms, and their spatial manifestations exemplified by WeWork, became the dominant policy imaginary.[58]

More worryingly, the ways in which the digital economy reaches down into the local, the communal, the personal, the familial has meant that extraction now starts earlier than ever. This can be seen in the music industry, where what had previously been gift ecologies – bedrooms, sharing communities, small creative spaces – are far more easily integrated into the platform supply chains.[59]

It is precisely against the impact of the commercial-tradable economy on local "everyday" economies that much of the new thinking on community economies, the "commons", local doughnuts, wellbeing, circular and sustainable economies, and so on is aimed. The political agenda is one of equity, sustainability, and community-building, for both the promotion of local economies *and* for their de-commodification, or for the value generated to be better retained and shared locally.

The zonal schema itself has conceptual antecedents in Fernando Braudel's work, especially his distinction between localised markets, often governed by "moral economies" rooted in custom, and large-scale mercantile capital, increasingly backed by the state.[60] Others in the FEC tradition have used cluster theory to re-evaluate Marshallian "industrial districts". They evoke not an economy with "benign externalities" but a form of development,

> derived from virtuous interaction between "a community of people" and a "community of firms" in specific institutional settings. Accordingly, rather than mere productive environments,

industrial districts were distinctive milieux in which a community of people lives and establishes the greater part of daily social relationships. Hence, localities were understood as "complete" societies, with interdependence between economic structures, political institutions and civil society.[61]

How to govern such localised markets to ensure they deliver jobs and wealth, but also the texture of everyday life, and to find the correct articulation with the public provision of material and providential services is a crucial challenge and one to which cultural policy ought to be a key contributor. Rather than promote yet another version of the creative city, we need to start with an acknowledgement of the realities of place, to begin the long, hard slog of adaptive reuse towards new forms of shared prosperity. What I have called the cultural infrastructure works precisely at this juncture of economic structures, political institutions and civil society, for this is also where active citizens are formed, common identities negotiated, and imaginations applied to a collective future.

Aside from the provision of basic services and income, there are other policy tools. The promotion of co-operatives, asset sharing, and freelancer platforms. The creation of citizens media and locally based digital platforms. It means changing the imaginary. Why, for example, call the collection of hand-to-mouth live venues, animated by musicians barely making a living, and yet central to the social and cultural lives of so many, a "music industry"? This network of community-based arts and cultural venues could be organised on a far more equitable and sustainable basis through community co-ops,[62] backed by real local government investment and not voucher schemes or other forms of "stimulation". Why is Factory or the Roundhouse about jobs in the UK's creative "export industry" rather than a public intervention in developing local skills and jobs in our essential cultural infrastructure?

The everyday economy is about the continual making and remaking of places and our goal should be the retention of this public value for communities rather than real estate and corporate retail and hospitality. It is as much an essential a part of the right to the city as the collective consumption of foundational services. And ultimately, these calls for the reorientation of urban economies and urban planning towards sustainable and socially equitable development must be underpinned by the idea of "the commons" – that the wealth of the world is a commonwealth, and that policy should flow from this, rather than the absolute, exclusive rights of private property. Without such a challenge there is no such thing as "postcapitalism".

Cities are powerful economic engines, but ultimately their purpose is to allow us to live and flourish. Rather than a marginal, "overlooked" everyday economy in which our "vibrant" cultural infrastructure is dependent on a rickey set of failing local businesses, we ought to see everyday culture as the warp and weft of the city. Not only the warp and weft: conceived at its widest, from the material and social foundations, and the textures and meanings of everyday life, through science and art, to the city's complex collective and contested endeavours, culture is surely the ultimate goal of the city.

Taking on the heights

Leaving culture-as-industry means we can finally confront the industries of culture. To do this would be to pick up again the radical political trajectory of the post-war years, in which an expanding concept of cultural democracy met an accelerating privatisation and industrialisation of culture. The last confrontation was in the GLC years, 1979–86, in which economic development and cultural policy united to experiment with a local cultural economic strategy. They asked the question, if most culture is produced outside the subsidised sector, then what sense has a cultural policy that does not address this commercial production of culture? That experiment was quickly closed down. But in any event, it was a local (albeit Greater London) strategy. At the same moment, at the national and global scales, the convergence of computing and communications and the accelerated privatisation of public culture began an arc that, right now, is approaching its apex.

The process of concentration and monopoly, extraction and exploitation in the cultural industries has reached unprecedented levels. It has also come with a genetic splicing of the classic cultural industry model with the rentier model developed out of platform capitalism. The cultural industries had a distinct "business model". A dispersed workforce ("motley crew"), a volatile market ("nobody knows nothing") where nine out of ten products fail, an exponential return to scale ("winner takes all"), and a tendency for cultural goods to become public goods ("make financial hay whilst the sun shines").[63] Cultural political economy scholars have spent many years tracing the outline of this model across its various regulatory, technological, and sociocultural evolutions.

But since the late naughties the rise of the platforms to almost total dominance of distribution (and in some cases production) of online content and related logistics and delivery has been based on models of "get big fast" in order to create monopolies (or monopsonies), with exponential returns to scale. Huge markets, accompanied by various forms of consumer lock-in, are allied with the extraction of data from these consumers in ways with which we are now mostly familiar. The role of intellectual property rights has massively increased since the late 1990s. This is no longer just about copyright but huge numbers of patents and micro-patents that cover software, protocols, operating systems, algorithms, data feeds, and so on.[64] This allows the platforms to stay way ahead of smaller, later competitors who have little chance of reaching the scale of data collection and computing power available to the giants. It also allows them to effectively charge "rent" (economic actors receiving rewards "purely by virtue of controlling something valuable") on those systems, platforms, and infrastructures.[65]

One of the classic lines of tension in the cultural industries is that between the need of creatives for some kind of autonomy and that of financial management for control. In the 1990s, theorists of post-Fordism saw in the fluid networks of cultural SMEs the cutting edge of a new high-skill high-touch creative economy. Like the privileged artisans of a pre-industrial world, these postmodern artisans could name their price. Certainly, these agglomerated districts of highly paid skilled creative workers exist, but they are now integrated globally with those second and third tiers of the "franchise capitalism" we discussed in Chapter 1.[66] Through these means the traditional struggle of owners and managers to restrict the autonomy of skilled work, classically analysed by Harry Braverman, finds new expression.[67]

This system, though very new, also displays characteristics of an older "commercial capitalism". As in the eighteenth and nineteenth centuries, global capital is able to control the terms and flows of trade not through direct employment but via a complex system of intermediaries, agents, compradors, and (in the original sense) entrepreneurs.[68] It is maintained across a set of fragmented jurisdictions, creative hubs, production factories, mass render centres, and a slew of low-paid routine "creative" producers.

> In its quest for market expansion, the tech industry increasingly carves away at and lays claim to tasks that once were protected as the proper domain of professional judgement in every occupation from business management, medicine, and the criminal justice system to national defense, education, and social welfare. Deeply entrenched jurisdictions and human institutions are nothing but transient compromises awaiting the automation of their most routine tasks and sometimes their entire work domain.[69]

To which we might add the cultural sector, which is intermixing with the "cybertariat" whose production of digital goods (algorithms and AI) involves "a continuum of unpaid, micropaid and poorly paid human tasks".[70]

The consequences have been charted across different branches of the cultural industries, and we quoted Rebecca Giblin and Cory Doctorow, who outlined the massive levels of concentration now in operation.[71] In response they call for systemic answers, not just tweaking copyright, or digital locks, or even bringing back anti-trust laws. Other responses include transparency rights, so we know who gets paid what and on what grounds. Collective action, a crucial precondition to overcoming an atomised workforce and with growing momentum as the individualised glamour of the "creative entrepreneur", wears thin. Time limits on copyright, and other ways of turning around a system that once upon a time was there to protect creators and now enslaves them. Radical interoperability to end the lock-ins and lock-outs so central to the business models of devices and operating systems. A minimum wage. Taking back collective ownership, building citizen platforms, promoting shared tech and new forms of common production.

A systemic response is a long way off, as it would require building a political imaginary around culture which, as we know, has atrophied. And any such response would have to be global. This archipelago of creative districts, edge-of-town production, home-working freelancers, hot-desking digital nomads, denizens of creative hubs – all might once have been interpellated by the allure of their little corner of creative modernity.[72] But dreams are fading. The promise of a global creative economy by which the Global South would catch up to the Global North has receded. In 2022, 95 per cent of the global trade in cultural services (where money is) goes to the Global North.[73] But again, in industrial capitalism, the "proletariat was physically copresent, densely packed in factories. Digital warehouses and click farms sometimes have these qualities, but increasingly less so. As crowdsourcing platforms take over, members of this digital precariat are more and more individualized and isolated from one another".[74]

The arc I spoke of began with the definitive defeat of the New World Economic Order, and the New World Information and Communications Order.[75] A concerted attempt by newly independent nations to challenge the dominance of the old colonising countries over global flows and terms of trade was beaten back in the late 1990s by the Global North, led by the US. The defeat not only led to debt-stalled development but the installation of the legal-regulatory apparatus of enforceable intellectual property rights which organises the global economy of which culture is a part.[76] Taking these back and asserting economic sovereignty for the Global South is the work of a generation.[77]

Culture is not an industry

Since the 1990s, the global culture industry has become an integral part of global capitalism. Perhaps nowhere else in this system is the descriptor "neo-feudalism" more apt, as huge cultural conglomerates and their avatars now have almost unchallenged power over the collective imagination of humanity.[78] As culture industries they are currently at the end of a period of massive over-production in screen content, a windfall for writers and actors, producers and technicians. And platforms. The classic trajectory has now set in – glut, slump, lay-offs, elimination, more concentration.[79] The rapidly established dependence on the platforms across the global will mean the slump will hollow out local strategic capacity as well as make cultural workers redundant. The cultural industries have little interest in sustaining a creative ecosystem. A corporation is more like "an immortal colony organism… Its sole imperative is to do whatever it can get away with to extract maximum economic value from humans and the planet".[80]

We have heard much of "postcapitalisms" but at its core capitalism means that the owners of private property get to make the investment decisions on behalf of society. The anarchy and destruction which this is now producing across the globe is why states are stepping in to try and direct investment to the green transition and alternative energy. We desperately need a similar move in culture. Regulation. Breaking monopolies. Opening up proprietary algorithms and AI software. Socialising the databases. Re-affirming the various UN declarations and conventions on cultural rights and that culture is not a commodity like any other. It means affirming Culture is Not an Industry.

Culture is how we remember the past and imagine the future. It is part of how we become free individuals in a democratic society. We need it, at least the promise of it, if we are the take those stepping stones across the uncertain landscape of the present. Neoliberalism might be dead, but as Russian radical Alexander Herzen wrote after the 1848 revolution, "the departing world leaves behind it not an heir but a pregnant widow. Between the death of one and the birth of the other much water will flow by, a long night of chaos and desolation will pass". [81]

We would do well to avoid this.

Melbourne–Adelaide–Hanoi–Tours, June 2023

Acknowledgements

I would first like to acknowledge my partners in crime in the Reset Collective, especially Tully Barnett, Emma Webb, and Satu Teppo, along with Jessica Alice, Maggie Tonkin, Sam Whiting, Christie Anthoney, and many others who contributed to the thinking behind this book. And to Julian Meyrick, the book impossible without the many walks up and down the Melbourne rivers during the long pandemic lockdown(s). Huge thanks to Sebastian Olma, who had the faith throughout and helped publish my Reset book in Dutch with Starfish Books. Thanks to Susan Luckman at Creative People Products and Places for the extensive support given to me during this time, and also to the University of South Australia's Creative Unit, for providing me the space and time to think. Enormous thanks to unofficial editorial support from Kate Oakley, as well as to Mark Banks and Dave Hesmondhalgh for their long-suffering indulgence of my ranting and raving over the years. And the same thanks to Avril Joffe and Cornelia Dümcke, who gave me some global perspective. Not forgetting Al Rainnie for his constant supply of articles from far-flung disciplinary boundaries. Appreciation for early proofreader Ben Booker, and to Dalton Bruyns who designed all the Reset publications. The book was

Acknowledgements

finished while I was a Presidential Fellow at the Centre d'études supérieures de la Renaissance, University of Tours, helped over the line by delightful dinners in Philippe Vendrix's rose garden. Special appreciation for Karel Williams and Julie Froud, editors of MUP's *Manchester Capitalism* series, providing steady hands on the wheel as we approached deadlines at breakneck speed. And finally, to you, O long-suffering one. It's done now (until the next one).

Notes

Introduction: culture and democracy

1 UKRI (2023) "UK's creative industries benefit from significant funding boost". www.ukri.org/news/uks-creative-industries-benefit-from-significant-funding-boost.

2 Justin O'Connor and Xin Gu (2020) *Red Creative: Culture and Modernity in Modern China*. Bristol: Intellect.

3 Justin O'Connor (2023) "UNESCO's 2005 Convention: from creative economy to sustainable prosperity?" in Chris Bailey, Elena Theodoulou Charalambous, and Geert Drion (eds.), *Cultural Governance in the 21st Century*. London: Routledge.

4 J. Hartley (2005) "Creative industries", in J. Hartley (ed.), *Creative Industries*. Oxford: Blackwell, 1–41, p. 5.

5 John Harris (2004) *The Last Party: Britpop, Blair and the Demise of English Rock*. London: Harper Perennial.

6 Owen Hatherley (2011) *Uncommon*. London: Zero Books. pp. 7–8; Harris, *The Last Party*.

7 Robert Hewison (2010) "'Creative Britain': myth or monument?" *Cultural Trends International Conference: A "Golden Age"? Reflections on New Labour's Cultural Policy and its Post-Recession Legacy*. www.tandfonline.com/sda/1175/audioclip-transcript-ccut.pdf.

8 Andreas Reckwitz (2017) *The Invention of Creativity*. Cambridge: Polity; O'Connor and Gu, *Red Creative*, ch.1; Oli Mould (2018) *Against Creativity*. London: Verso; Rob Pope (2005) *Creativity: Theory, History, Practice*. London: Routledge; Philip Schlesinger (2017) "The creative economy: invention of a global orthodoxy", *Innovation: The European Journal of Social Science Research*, 30:1: 3–90.

Notes

9 Cf. Thomas Meaney (2023) "High-flown English", *Sidecar New Left Review*, 31 May. https://newleftreview.org/sidecar/posts/high-flown-english.

10 François Matarasso (2022) "Cultural policy in a post-political age", *Parliament of Dreams*, p. 1. https://parliamentofdreams.com/2022/08/05/old-words-6-cultural-policy-in-a-post-political-age-2021-22/.

11 Arran Gare (2007/8) "The arts and the radical enlightenment: gaining liberty to save the planet", *The Structurist*, no. 47/48.

12 For a heavy-duty philosophical account, cf. Andrew Bowie (2013) *Aesthetics and Subjectivity*, 2nd edition. Manchester: Manchester University Press. For an entertaining introduction, cf. Andrea Wulf (2022) *Magnificent Rebels: The First Romantics and the Invention of the Self*. New York: Knopf.

13 Raymond Williams (1981) *Culture*. London: Fontana, p. 126.

14 Edward Tylor's 1871 book *Primitive Culture* defines culture as: "that complex whole which includes knowledge, belief, art, law, morals, custom, and any other capabilities and habits acquired by man as a member of society" (1:1). It is often opposed to a book of two years earlier, Matthew Arnold's 1869 *Culture and Anarchy*, which defines culture as "a pursuit of our total perfection by means of getting to know, on all the matters which most concern us, the best which has been thought and said in the world". That is, arts and letters.

15 Cf Tony Bennett (1998) *Culture: A Reformer's Science*. London: Sage, pp. 92–101.

16 Raymond Williams (1989 [1958]) "Culture is ordinary" in his *Resources of Hope* (1989) London: Verso. pp. 91–100; on "a whole way of life", Raymond Williams (1983 [1976]) *Keywords: A Vocabulary of Culture and Society*, 2nd edition) London: Fontana, pp. 76–82.

17 Culture as an anthropological "whole way of life" is being used when we talk of "organisational culture", or the values of different national or ethnic "cultures", or the "culture of sexism" or "systemic racism".

18 Think of how the counter-reformation Church used "popular culture" to secure the legitimacy of the Catholic Church in the later sixteenth century while continuing to patronise the tradition of the fine arts developed in the Renaissance. Cf. Kenneth Clarke's TV series *Civilisation*, Part 6.

19 Raymond Williams (1961) *The Long Revolution*. London: Chatto and Windus; for a contemporary overview see: Jilly Boyce Kay (2021)

Notes

"A life lasts longer than the body through which it moves: an introduction to a special Cultural Commons section on Raymond Williams", *European Journal of Cultural Studies*, 24:4: 1009–1020.

20 The idea of a functional separation of different social sub-systems, explored extensively by Max Weber, is foundational to social science's account of modernity. See also Raymond Williams (1977) *Marxism and Literature*. Oxford: Oxford University Press, pp. 11–20.

21 Marshall Berman (1983) *All That Is Solid Melts into Air: The Experience of Modernity*. London: Verso.

22 Nicholas Garnham (2000) *Emancipation, the Media and Modernity*. Oxford: Oxford University Press. Which is not to say the public sphere is not problematic. Nancy Fraser (1990) "Rethinking the public sphere: a contribution to the critique of actually existing democracy", *Social Text*, 25/26: 56–80.

23 Cf. Justin Clemens (2020) "Après moi le déluge: artists after art", *Arena Quarterly*, 3 September.

24 Michael Denning (2004) *Culture in the Age of Three Worlds*. London: Verso, p. 80.

25 Stuart Hall and Paddy Whannel (2018 [1963]) *The Popular Arts*. Durham, NC: Duke University Press.

26 Mark Fisher (2014) *Ghosts of My Life: Writings on Depression, Hauntology and Lost Futures*. London: Zero Books.

27 Hartmut Rosa (2013) *Social Acceleration: A New Theory of Modernity*. New York: Columbia University Press.

28 Oscar Negt and Alexander Kluge (1993 [1972]) *Public Sphere and Experience: Towards an Analysis of the Bourgeois and Proletarian Public Sphere*. Minneapolis, MN: University of Minnesota Press; August Girard (1982) "Cultural industries: a handicap or a new opportunity for cultural development?" in UNESCO, *Cultural Industries: A Challenge for the Future of Culture*. Paris: UNESCO.

29 For a recent account see John Merrick (2021) "Good bourgeois subject: a post-mortem of the 20th century democratization of art". *Soft Punk*, 27 October. http://softpunkmag.com/criticism/good-bourgeois-subjects.

30 Owen Hatherley (2020) "The government of London", *New Left Review*, 122: 81–114, p. 94; Cf. Franco Bianchini (1987) "GLC R.I.P. 1981–1986", *New Formations*, 1: 103–117.

31 *Ibid.*, p. 95.

32 *Ibid.*, p. 97.

Notes

33 Stephanie Kelton (2020) *The Deficit Myth: How to Build a Better Economy*. London: John Murray; Kate Raworth (2018) *Doughnut Economics: Seven Ways to Think Like a 21st Century Economist*. London: Random House. It has its own "action lab" https://doughnuteconomics.org. *Time* magazine asks if the "Amsterdam Doughnut" could "replace capitalism". https://time.com/5930093/amsterdam-doughnut-economics/.

34 Luca Calafati, Julie Froud, Colin Haslam, Sukhdev Johal, and Karel Williams (2023) *When Nothing Works: From Cost of Living to Foundational Liveability*. Manchester: Manchester University Press.

35 *Ibid.*, p. 10.

36 FEC (2018) *Foundational Economy: The Infrastructure of Everyday Life*. Manchester: Manchester University Press.

37 *Ibid.*, p. 8.

38 Thomas Meaney (2022) "Fortunes of the Green New Deal", *New Left Review*, 138: 79–101. The article introduces an extensive thread on debating green strategy.

39 Wendy Brown (2017) *Undoing the Demos: Neoliberalism's Stealth Revolution*. Princeton, NJ: Princeton University Press; Colin Crouch (2004) *Post-Democracy*. Hoboken, NJ: John Wiley; Alex Hochuli, George Hoare and Philip Cunliffe (2021) *The End of the End of History*. London: Zero Books; Peter Mair (2013) *Ruling the Void: The Hollowing of Western Democracy*. London: Verso.

40 Luc Boltanski and Eve Chiapello (2005) *The New Spirit of Capitalism*. London: Verso.

41 Thomas Frank (1997) *The Conquest of Cool: Business Culture, Counterculture and the Rise of Hip Consumerism*. Chicago: University of Chicago Press.

42 See, for example, Bungacast (2022) *OK Bunger: The Problem of Generations*. https://bungacast.com/2022/11/15/ok-bunger-the-problem-of-generations-full/.

43 Helen Andrews (2021) *Boomers: The Men and Women Who Promised Freedom and Delivered Disaster*. New York: Sentinel.

44 Stuart Jeffries (2021) *Everything, All the Time, Everywhere: How We Became Postmodern*. London: Verso

45 Francis Fukuyama (1989) "The end of history?" *The National Interest*, 16 (Summer): 3–18, p. 18.

46 Simon Reynolds (2011) *Retromania: Pop Culture's Addiction to Its Own Past*. London: Farrar, Straus and Giroux

47 David Throsby (2017) "Culturally sustainable development: theoretical concept or practical policy instrument?" *International Journal*

of Cultural Policy, 23:2: 133–147; Kim Stanley Robinson (2020) *The Ministry of the Future*. London: Orbit Books .

48 Emily St John Mandel (2015) *Station Eleven*. New York: Vintage Books.

1 Creative industries

1   William Davies (2015) *The Limits of Neoliberalism: Authority, Sovereignty and the Logic of Competition*. London: Sage, p. 4.

2   David Parrish (2007) *T-Shirts and Suits: A Guide to the Business of Creativity*. Liverpool: ACME.

3   Department of Culture, Media and Sport (1998) "Creative Industries mapping document", p. 1. www.gov.uk/government/publications/creative-industries-mapping-documents-1998.

4   Richard Florida (2012) *The Rise of the Creative Class, Revisited*. New York: Basic Books, p. 25.

5   David Edgerton (2018) *The Rise and Fall of the British Nation: A Twentieth-Century History*. London: Penguin.

6   Julian Meyrick (2023) "Undoing Australian Cultural Policy: the 1976 IAC Inquiry into the Performing Arts". *Performance Paradigm*, 17.

7   John Meyercough (1988) *The Economic Importance of the Arts in Britain*. London: Policy Studies Institute.

8   Christopher Hood (1991) "A public management for all seasons?". *Public Administration*, 69: 3–19.

9   Eleonora Belfiore (2004) "Auditing culture: the subsidised cultural sector in the New Public Management", *International Journal of Cultural Policy*, 10:2: 183–202; Julian Meyrick, Tully Barnett, and Robert Phiddian (2018) *What Matters? Talking Value in Australian Culture*. Melbourne: Monash University Press.

10 David Graeber (2015) *Bullshit Jobs: A Theory*. New York: Simon & Schuster.

11 David Throsby (2012) *The Economic of Cultural Policy*. Cambridge: Cambridge University Press; John Holden (2004) *Capturing Cultural Value*. London: Demos; Françoise Matarasso (1997) *Use or Ornament: The Social Impact of Participation in the Arts*. Stroud: Comedia.

12 Steven Hadley (2021) *Audience Development and Cultural Policy*. London: Palgrave Macmillan.

13 *Culture Counts*. https://culturecounts.cc/company. Cf: Phiddian, Robert, Julian Meyrick, Tully Barnett, and Richard Maltby (2017)

Notes

"Counting culture to death: an Australian perspective on culture counts and quality metrics', *Cultural Trends*, 26:2: 174–180.

14 Luca Calafati, Julie Froud, Colin Haslam, Sukhdev Johal, and Karel Williams (2023) *When Nothing Works: From Cost of Living to Foundational Liveability*. Manchester: Manchester University Press.

15 Steve Redhead (2004) "Creative modernity: the new cultural state", *Media International Australia*, 112:1: 9–27; Robert Hewison (2014) *Cultural Capital: The Rise and Fall of Creative Britain*. London: Verso; David Hesmondhalgh, Kate Oakley, David Lee, and Melissa Nisbett (2015) *Culture, Economy and Politics: The Case of New Labour*. London: Palgrave.

16 Jo Caust (2003) "Putting the 'art' back into arts policy making: how arts policy has been 'captured' by the economists and the marketers", *International Journal of Cultural Policy*, 9:1: 51–63; Judith White (2017) *Culture Heist: Art versus Money*. Sydney: Brandl and Schlesinger.

17 Often credited with inventing the creative industries but it does not use that term, preferring cultural industries. This is mostly wishful thinking from the group of academics who promoted the term – post 1998 – in Australia.

18 Mark Leonard (1997) *Britain™: Renewing Our Identity*. London: Demos, p. 6.

19 Mic Moroney (1998) "Anyone for cultcha?" *Irish Times*, 27 October. www.irishtimes.com/culture/anyone-for-cultcha-1.207768.

20 Kate Oakley (2011) "In its own image: New Labour and the cultural workforce", *Cultural Trends*, 20: 3–4: 281–289. Abstract. Noel Thompson (2002) *Left in the Wilderness: The Political Economy of British Democratic Socialism since 1979*. Chesham: Acumen; see also his (1996) "Supply side socialism: the political economy of New Labour", *New Left Review*, 1:216: 37–54.

21 Richard Barbrook and Andy Cameron (1996) "The Californian ideology", *Science as Culture*, 6:1: 44–72.

22 Ridley Scott (1984) "Apple Macintosh commercial for Super Bowl". www.youtube.com/watch?v=2zfqw8nhUwA. See also Mark Fisher (2023) "Luxury communism", *Making and Breaking*, 2.

23 Cf. Daniel Stedman Jones (2018) "The neoliberal origins of the Third Way: how Chicago, Virginia and Bloomington shaped Clinton and Blair", in Damien Cahill, Melinda Cooper, Martijn Konings, and David Primrose (eds.), *The Sage Handbook of Neoliberalism*. London: Sage, 167–178. Cf. Daniel T. Rodgers, (2012) *Age of Fracture*. Cambridge, MA: Belknap Press; Nancy Fraser (2017) "From progressive

Notes

neoliberalism to Trump – and beyond", *American Affairs*, 1:4: 46–64; Oliver Nachtwey (2018) *Germany's Hidden Crisis: Social Decline in the Heart of Europe*. London: Verso; Michel Feher (2018) *Rated Agency: Investee Politics in a Speculative Age*. Boston, MA: MIT Press; Niklas Olsen and Daniel Zamora (2019) "How decades of neoliberalism led to the era of right-wing populism". www.jacobinmag.com/2019/09/in-the-ruins-of-neoliberalism-wendy-brown.

24 John Quiggin (2018) "Neoliberalism: rise, decline and future prospects", in Damien Cahill, Melinda Cooper, Martijn Konings, and David Primrose (eds.), *The Sage Handbook of Neoliberalism*. London: Sage, 143–153.

25 Sam Binkley (2018) "The emotional logic of neoliberalism: reflexivity and instrumentality in three theoretical traditions", in Damien Cahill, Melinda Cooper, Martijn Konings, and David Primrose (eds.), *The Sage Handbook of Neoliberalism*. London: Sage, 580–595, p. 581.

26 For a longer account see Kate Oakley and Justin O'Connor (2015) "Cultural industries: an introduction", in Kate Oakley and Justin O'Connor (eds.), *The Routledge Companion to the Cultural Industries*. London: Routledge, 1–32.

27 Kevin Kelly (1998) *New Rules for the New Economy*. London: Fourth Estate.

28 Perry Anderson (1984) "Modernity and revolution", *New Left Review*, 144: 96–113.

29 W. Terrence Gordon (2003). *Understanding Media: Critical Edition*. Corte Madera, CA: Gingko Press, p. 16.

30 Thompson, *Left in the Wilderness*.

31 Scott Lash and John Urry (1994) *Economies of Signs and Space*. London: Sage; Richard Florida (2002) *The Rise of the Creative Class*. New York: Basic Books.

32 Department of Culture, Media and Sport, "Creative Industries mapping document", p. 1.

33 NESTA (2013) *A Dynamic Mapping of the Creative Industries*, p. 24. https://media.nesta.org.uk/documents/a_dynamic_mapping_of_the_creative_industries.pdf.

34 A recent succinct definition by Will Davies: "that collective prosperity is only an effect of the efforts and ingenuity of businesses, investors and workers. If the economy stagnates, that must be because something is holding these institutions and individuals back – most likely government, but also trade unions and collectivist values. The job of

the state, from this perspective, is to ensure that entrepreneurs, investors and employees all have clear incentives to exert themselves as much as possible". Will Davies (2022) "Trussonomics will be a reckless exercise in slashing the state when there's nothing left to cut", *The Guardian*, 5 September. www.theguardian.com/commentisfree/2022/sep/05/trussonomics-reckless-exercise-slashing-state-thatcherism.

35 Land, in the form of public cultural infrastructure – galleries, museums, libraries, community spaces, venues, and so on – was provided by national or local states, sometimes by philanthropy. Creative spaces – incubators, hubs, shared workspaces, and so on – were provided by a mix of public investment and private developer capital. Of course, as we shall see, rather than developers adding an essential factor to creative production, it was more often that creatives were adding new value to development capital, a process mostly covered by the term "gentrification".

36 Florida, *The Rise of the Creative Class*, p. 25.

37 Cf. Thomas Frank (2022) "What the hell, America". www.youtube.com/watch?v=VWKsTzHwIsM.

38 C. Wright Mills (1959) "The Cultural Apparatus" in the BBC's weekly magazine *The Listener*, November 1959 and broadcast on the "Third Programme". Cf. Kim Sawchuck (2001) "The Cultural Apparatus: C. Wright Mills' unfinished work", *The American Sociologist*, 32:1, 27–49; Michael Denning (2010) *The Cultural Front: The Laboring of American Culture in the Twentieth Century*. London: Verso.

39 Cf. Barbara and John Ehrenreich (1979) "The Professional-Managerial Class", in Pat Walker (ed.), *Between Capital and Labor*. Boston, MA: South End Press. pp. 5–45; Eric Olin Wright (1978) "Intellectuals and the working class", *Critical Sociology*, 8:1: 5–18; Catherine Liu (2021) *Virtue Hoarders: The Case Against the Professional-Managerial Class*. Minneapolis, MN: University of Minnesota Press; Barbara Ehrenreich (2020) *Fear of Falling: The Inner Life of the Middle Class*. New York: Pantheon Books; Thomas Piketty (2020) *Capital and Ideology*. Cambridge, MA: Belknap Press.

40 Binkley, "The emotional logic of neoliberalism", p. 581.

41 Cf. Andreas Reckwitz (2017) *The Invention of Creativity*. Cambridge: Polity; Justin O'Connor and Xin Gu (2020) *Red Creative: Culture and Modernity in Modern China*. Bristol: Intellect. Ch.1; Oli Mould (2018) *Against Creativity*. London: Verso.

42 William Hutton (2007) *The Writing on the Wall: China and the West in the 21st Century*. London: Little, Brown, p. 311.

Notes

43 *Ibid.*, p. 171.

44 Hesmondhalgh, Oakley, Lee, and Nisbett, *Culture, Economy and Politics*.

45 O'Connor and Gu, *Red Creative*; Hye-Kyung Lee (2018) *Cultural Policy in South Korea: Making a New Patron State*. London: Routledge.

46 John Howkins (2001) *The Creative Economy: How People Make Money from Ideas*. London: Penguin.

47 Piketty, *Capital and Ideology*.

48 Gérard Duménil and Dominique Lévy (2011) *The Crisis of Neo-liberalism*. Cambridge, MA: Harvard University Press; Feher, *Rated Agency*.

49 Matthew Huber (2022) *Climate Change as Class War*. London: Verso, pp. 109–142.

50 Jenna Burrell and Marion Fourcade (2021). "The society of algorithms", *Annual Review of Sociology*, 47: 213–237.

51 Rebecca Giblin and Cory Doctorow (2022) *Chokepoint Capitalism: How Big Tech and Big Content Captured Creative Labor Markets and How We'll Win Them Back*. Boston, MA: Beacon Press, p.1.

52 *Ibid.*, p. 258.

53 Herman Schwartz (2022) "From Fordism to franchise: intellectual property and growth models in the knowledge economy", in Lucio Baccaro, Mark Blyth, and Jonas Pontusson (eds.), *Diminishing Returns: The New Politics of Growth and Stagnation*. Oxford: Oxford University Press. https://uva.theopenscholar.com/files/hermanschwartz/files/schwartz-ch2-bbp.pdf.

54 Jodi Dean (2020) "Neofeudalism: the end of capitalism?", *Los Angeles Review of Books*, 12 May. https://lareviewofbooks.org/article/neofeudalism-the-end-of-capitalism/.

55 Evgeny Morozov (2022) "Critique of techno-feudal reason", *New Left Review*, 133/134: 89–126. https://newleftreview.org/issues/ii133/articles/evgeny-morozov-critique-of-techno-feudal-reason (Jodi Dean's response: https://newleftreview.org/sidecar/posts/same-as-it-ever-was); Cédric Durand (2022) "Scouting capital's frontiers", *New Left Review*, 136.

56 Cecilia Rikap (2023) "Capitalism as usual? Implications of digital intellectual monopolies", *New Left Review*, 139: 145–160.

57 Justin O'Connor (2021) "Music as industry", *Loudmouth*. https://musictrust.com.au/loudmouth/music-as-industry/.

58 "Under political capitalism, raw political power, rather than productive investment, is the key determinant of the rate of return. This new

form of accumulation is associated with a series of novel mechanisms of 'politically constituted rip-off'. These include an escalating series of tax breaks, the privatization of public assets at bargain-basement prices, quantitative easing plus ultra-low interest rates, to promote stock-market speculation—and, crucially, massive state spending aimed directly at private industry, with trickledown effects for the broader population." Dylan Riley and Robert Brenner (2022) "Seven theses on American politics", *New Left Review*, 138: 5–27, p. 6.

59 For construction spend as the main component of "arts recovery" spending in Australia, see Jessica Pacella, Susan Luckman, and Justin O'Connor (2020) "Fire, pestilence and the extractive economy: cultural policy after cultural policy", *Cultural Trends*, 30:1: 40–51.

60 Isaac Rose (2022) "Against the Manchester model", *Tribune* magazine, November. https://tribunemag.co.uk/2022/11/against-the-manchester-model.

61 Bruce S. Tether (2022) "Creative clusters and sparse spaces: Manchester's creative industries and the geographies of deprivation and prosperity". Discussion Paper, Creative Industries Policy and Evidence Centre. https://pec.ac.uk/discussion-papers/creative-clusters-and-sparse-spaces.

62 *Ibid.*, p. 12.

63 Harry G. Frankfurt (2005) *On Bullshit*, Princeton, NJ/Oxford: Princeton University Press, p. 1; cf. Eleonora Belfiore (2009) "On bullshit in cultural policy practice and research: notes from the British case", *International Journal of Cultural Policy*, 15:3: 343–359.

64 Manchester City Council (2018) *Our Manchester Industrial Strategy*. www.manchester.gov.uk/downloads/download/7156/our_manchester_industrial_strategy, p. 36.

65 FIRE – Finance, Insurance, Real Estate. Hugh Morris (2023) "A new British arts venue tracks its city's changes". www.nytimes.com/2023/06/23/arts/design/factory-aviva-studios-manchester.html.

2 Culture goes missing

1 Mark Fisher (2009) *Capitalist Realism: Is There No Alternative?* London: Zero Books.

2 For example: Asia Development Bank Institute (2022) *Creative Economy 2030: Imagining and Delivering a Robust, Creative, Inclusive, and Sustainable*

Recovery. www.adb.org/publications/creative-economy-2030-imagining-and-delivering-a-robust-creative-inclusive-and-sustainable-recovery; OECD Local Economic and Employment Development (2022) *The Culture Fix: Creative People, Places and Industries*; UNCTAD (2022) *Creative Industry 4.0: Towards a New Globalized Creative Economy*; UNESCO/Abu Dhabi Department of Culture and Tourism (2022) *Culture in Times of COVID-19. Resilience, Recovery and Revival.* https://unesdoc.unesco.org/ark:/48223/pf0000381524.locale=en.

3 United Nations (2021) *Our Common Agenda.* www.un.org/en/un75/common-agenda.

4 Mark Banks and Justin O'Connor (2020) "'A plague on your howling': art and culture in the viral emergency", *Cultural Trends*, 30:1: 3–18; Cornelia Dümcke (2021) "Five months under COVID-19 in the cultural sector: a German perspective", *Cultural Trends*, 30:1: 19–27; Avril Joffe (2021) "Covid-19 and the African cultural economy: an opportunity to reimagine and reinvigorate?", *Cultural Trends*, 30:1: 28–39.

5 Thomas Meaney (2023) "Fortunes of the Green New Deal", *New Left Review*, 138: 79–102.

6 Justin O'Connor (2022) *Reset: Art, Culture and the Foundational Economy.* https://resetartsandculture.com/wp-content/uploads/2022/02/CP3-Working-Paper-Art-Culture-and-the-Foundational-Economy-2022.pdf.

7 Tim Jackson (2021) *Post Growth: Life After Capitalism.* Hoboken, NJ: John Wiley; Kate Soper (2021) *Post-Growth Living: For an Alternative Hedonism.* London: Verso.

8 Mark Banks (2023) "The unanticipated pleasures of the future: degrowth, post-growth and popular cultural economies", *New Formations* 107/108: 12–29.

9 FEC (2021) "Meeting social needs on a damaged planet: Foundational Economy 2.0 and the careful practice of radical policy", *FEC Working Paper* 8, p. 14. https://foundationaleconomycom.files.wordpress.com/2021/01/fe-wp8-meeting-social-needs-on-a-damaged-planet.pdf.

10 Raymond Williams (1975) *Keywords: A Vocabulary of Culture and Society.* London: Fontana, 76–82, p. 77.

11 Cf. Tony Bennett (1998) *Culture: A Reformer's Science.* London: Sage; Justin Lewis and Toby Miller (2003) *Critical Cultural Policy Studies: A Reader.* Oxford: Blackwell; Toby Miller and George Yudice (2002) *Cultural Policy.* London: Sage.

12 Cf. Barbara and John Ehrenreich (1977) "The New Left and the professional managerial class", *Radical America*, 11:3: 7–24; Barbara

Notes

Ehrenreich (1989) *Fear of Falling: The Inner Life of the Middle Class.* New York: Pantheon Books; Matthew T. Huber (2022) *Climate Change as Class War.* London: Verso; Catherine Liu (2021) *Virtue Hoarders: The Case Against the Professional-Managerial Class.* Minneapolis, MN: University of Minnesota Press.

13 Luc Boltanski and Eve Chiapello (2005) *The New Spirit of Capitalism.* London: Verso.

14 Thomas Piketty (2020) *Capital and Ideology.* Cambridge, MA: Belknap Press.

15 See the podcast by the Aufhebungabunga group (2022) *OK Bunger: The Problem of Generations.* https://bungacast.com/series/generations/.

16 Wolfgang Streeck (2021) "In the superstate", *London Review of Books,* 44:2, 27 January: "The public sphere of capitalist democracies today tends to be moralised in a way that obstructs the formation of collective interests, which are replaced by safe symbolic spaces for self-defined rights-bearing minorities. Radical politics becomes reduced to struggles, often adjudicated by the courts, by ever smaller groups for control over their symbolic representation. Instead of coalition-building and majority-formation, postmodern politics of this sort gives rise to social fragmentation."

17 Mark Fisher (2014) *Ghosts of My Life: Writings on Depression, Hauntology and Lost Futures.* London: Zero Books; Phoebe Braithwaite (2019) "Mark Fisher's popular modernism", *Tribune* magazine, 18 January. https://tribunemag.co.uk/2019/01/mark-fisher-kpunk-popular-modernism; Matt Coloquhoun (2020) *Egress: On Mourning, Melancholy and Mark Fisher.* London: Repeater Books.

18 Mark Fisher (2023) "Designer communism", in Seb Olma and Justin O'Connor (eds.), *Making & Breaking III: Communal Luxury.* https://makingandbreaking.org/article/designer-communism.

19 Branko Milanović (2023) "Robotics or fascination with anthropomorphism", Global inequality blog, 3 March. https://branko2f7.substack.com/p/robotics-or-fascination-with-anthropomorphism? See also his (2019) *Capitalism Alone.* Cambridge, MA: Harvard University Press. See also Danny Dorling (n.d.) "A review of Branco Milanović's Capitalism and Global Income Inequality", www.dannydorling.org/?p=8970. Milanović proposes a "paleo-leftism" i.e. "reduce the political and economic power of the top 1 percent, fund public goods, increase taxes for the rich and large companies, and improve the national political climate". "Can globalization be improved" 14 September 2021. http://glineq.blogspot.com/2021/09/can-globalization-be-improved.html.

Notes

20   For a detailed discussion see Jackson, *Post Growth*. For the full extract: https://en.wikipedia.org/wiki/Robert_F._Kennedy%27s_remarks_ at_the_University_of_Kansas.

21   The Geneva Charter for Well-being (2021). Geneva: World Health Organization.   www.naspa.org/files/dmfile/Geneva-Charter-for-Wellbeing_2022.pdf.

22   Kate Raworth (2018) *Doughnut Economics: Seven Ways to Think Like a 21st Century Economist*. London: Random House. There's a Doughnut Economics "action lab", https://doughnuteconomics.org. *Time* magazine asks if the "Amsterdam Doughnut" could "replace capitalism". Ciara Nugent (2021) "Amsterdam is embracing a radical new economic theory to help save the environment. Could it also replace capitalism?" https://time.com/5930093/amsterdam-doughnut-economics/.

23   United Nations Sustainable Development Goals. https://sdgs. un.org/goals.

24   David Oks and Henry Williams (2022) "The long slow death of global development", *America Affairs*, 20 November. https://americanaffairs journal.org/2022/11/the-long-slow-death-of-global-development.

25   Daniela Gabor (2021) "The Wall Street consensus", *Development and Change*, 52:3: 429–459.

26   Gaya Herrington (2021) "Update to limits to growth: comparing the World3 Model with empirical data". https://advisory.kpmg.us/articles/ 2021/limits-to-growth.html. For the original: www.clubofrome.org/ publication/the-limits-to-growth.

27   Ann Pettifor (2020) *The Case for the Green New Deal*. London: Verso; Kate Aronoff, Alyssa Battistoni, Daniel A. Cohen and Thea Riofrancos (2019) *A Planet to Win: Why We Need a Green New Deal*. London: Verso. On the EU, https://ec.europa.eu/info/strategy/priorities-2019- 2024/european-green-deal_en. On China, cf. Pierre Charbonnier (2020) "For an ecological realpolitik", *e-flux journal* 114. www.e-flux. com/journal/114/365035/for-an-ecological-realpolitik.

28   Mariana Mazzucato (2013) *The Entrepreneurial State*. New York: Anthem Press; Mazzucato (2018) *The Value of Everything: Making and Taking in the Global Economy*. London: Random House.

29   Mariana Mazzucato (2021) "A new global economic consensus", *Project Syndicate*, 13 October.

30   Adam Tooze (2018) *Crashed: How a Decade of Financial Crises Changed the World*. London: Penguin Random House; Geoff Mann (2017) *In the Long Run: Keynesianism, Political Economy and Revolution*. London: Verso;

Notes

Stephanie Kelton (2020) *The Deficit Myth: How to Build a Better Economy*. London: John Murray; Robert Skidelsky (2018) *Money and Government: A Challenge to Mainstream Economics*. London: Random House.

31   Ilias Alami, Adam Dixon, and Emma Mawdsley (2021) "State capitalism and the new global D/development regime" *Antipode*, 53:5: 1294–1318. https://doi.org/10.1111/anti.12725.

32   Laurie Macfarlane (2020) "A spectre is haunting the West – the spectre of authoritarian capitalism", *Open Democracy*, 16 April; Paolo Gerbaudo (2021) *The Great Recoil: Politics after Populism and the Pandemic*. London: Verso; Toby Green and Thomas Fazi (2023) *The Covid Consensus: The Global Assault on Democracy and the Poor – a Critique from the Left*. London: Hurst.

33   UNESCO (2023) "Modiacult: Final Declaration. Article 2". www.unesco.org/sites/default/files/medias/fichiers/2022/10/6. MONDIACULT_EN_DRAFT%20FINAL%20DECLARATION_FINAL_1.pdf.

34   Adam Tooze (2022) "Welcome to the world of the polycrisis", *Financial Times*, 29 October. www.ft.com/content/498398e7-11b1-494b-9cd3-6d669dc3de33.

35   Cf. the argument in J. K. Gibson-Graham (2006) *Postcapitalist Politics*. Minneapolis, MN: University of Minnesota Press.

36   Wolfgang Streeck (2014) *Buying Time: The Delayed Crisis of Democratic Capitalism*. London: Verso.

37   Wolfgang Streeck (2016) *How Will Capitalism End?* London: Verso, p. 41.

38   Quinn Slobodian (2018) *Globalists: The End of Empire and the Birth of Neoliberalism*. Cambridge, MA: Harvard University Press.

39   Robert Putnam (2000) *Bowling Alone: The Collapse and Revival of American Community*. New York: Simon & Schuster Ltd. It was based on a 1995 essay. For an update, post internet, see Anton Jäger (2022) "From bowling alone to posting alone", *Jacobin*, 12 May. https://jacobin.com/2022/12/from-bowling-alone-to-posting-alone.

40   Anthony Giddens (1991) *Modernity and Self-Identity* Cambridge: Polity, pp. 75–79.

41   Keir Milburn (2019) *Generation Left*. Cambridge: Polity Press; Alison Pennington (2023) *Generation F'd*. Melbourne: Hardie Grant Books.

42   Jo Littler (2017) *Against Meritocracy: Culture, Power and Myths of Mobility*. London: Routledge; Michael Sandel (2020) *The Tyranny of Merit: What's Become of the Common Good?* London: Allen Lane.

43   Martin Wolf (2023) *The Crisis of Democratic Capitalism*. London: Penguin Press, p. 111.

Notes

44 Alex Hochuli (2021) "The Brazilianization of the world", *American Affairs*, 5:2: 93–115, p. 114.

45 Streeck, *How Will Capitalism End?* p. 41.

46 Fisher, *Ghosts of My Life*, p. 1.

47 Alex Hochuli, George Hoare, and Philip Cunliffe (2021) *The End of the End of History*. London: Zero Books.

48 Slavoj Zizek (2002) *Welcome to the Desert of the Real*. London: Verso.

49 Göran Therborn (2022) "The world and the left", *New Left Review*, 137: 23–73.

50 Cf. Amitav Ghosh (2021) *The Nutmeg's Curse: Parable for a Planet in Crisis*. Chicago: University of Chicago Press.

51 Nancy Fraser (2022) *Cannibal Capitalism*. London: Verso.

52 Karl Polanyi (1944) *The Great Transformation*. New York: Farrar and Rinehart.

53 Michael Denning (2004) *Culture in the Age of Three Worlds*. London: Verso, p. 80.

54 Cf. famously Richard Hoggart (1957) *The Uses of Literacy*. London: Penguin.

55 William Davies (2017) "Populism and the limits of neoliberalism", *LSE Blog*, 30 April. https://blogs.lse.ac.uk/europpblog/2017/04/30/essay-populism-and-the-limits-of-neoliberalism-by-william-davies.

56 Ronald Butt (1981) Interview with Margaret Thatcher in the *Sunday Times*, 3 May. www.margaretthatcher.org/document/104475.

57 Cf. John Hartley (1999) *Uses of Television*. London: Routledge.

58 Dominic Sandbrook (2016) *The Great British Dream Factory: The Strange History of Our National Imagination*. London: Allen Lane.

59 *Inter alia* Andrew Ross (2004) *No-collar: The Humane Workplace and Its Hidden Cost*. Philadelphia, PA: Temple University Press; Mark Banks (2007) *The Politics of Cultural Work*. London: Palgrave Macmillan and (2017) *Creative Justice: Cultural Industries, Work and Inequality*. Lanham, MD: Rowman and Littlefield; David Hesmondhalgh (2018) *The Cultural Industries*, 4th edition. London: Sage; John T. Caldwell (2023) *Specworld: Folds, Faults, and Fractures in Embedded Creator Industries*. Oakland, CA: University of California Press.

60 Antonio Negri (2018) *From the Factory to the Metropolis*. Cambridge: Polity; Maurizio Lazzarato (2014) *Signs and Machines: Capitalism and the Production of Subjectivity*. Los Angeles, CA: Semiotext; Maurizio Lazzarato (2017)

Notes

Experimental Politics. Work, Welfare and Creativity in the Neoliberal Age. Cambridge, MA: MIT Press.

61　Kristin Ross (2015) *Communal Luxury: The Political Imaginary of the Paris Commune.* London: Verso. On digital platforms and surveillance, Sharon Zuboff (2019) *Surveillance Capitalism: The Fight for a Human Future at the New Frontier of Power.* London: Profile Books.

62　In the US 1950s, the highest rating shows reached two-thirds of households; in the 1980s, still about a third. Now the most popular shows reach fewer than one in ten. Benedict Evans (2023) *The New Gatekeepers.* www.ben-evans.com/presentations.

63　Stuart Jeffries (2021) *Everything, All the Time, Everywhere: How We All Became Postmodern.* London: Verso.

64　Jurgen Habermas (1989) *The Structural Transformation of the Public Sphere.* Cambridge, MA: MIT Press. Cf. *Theory Culture and Society* (2023) Special Issue: A New Structural Transformation of the Public Sphere? 39:4.

65　Hesmondhalgh, *The Cultural Industries*; for a recent overview see Michael Chanan (2022) *From Printing to Streaming: Cultural Production under Capitalism.* London: Pluto Press. Still relevant is Raymond William's (1980) *Culture.* London: Fontana.

66　Cf. Jeremy Gilbert and Alex Williams (2022) *Hegemony Now: How Big Tech and Wall Street Won the World (and How We Win It Back).* London: Verso.

67　Howard Caygill (1990) *The Art of Judgement.* Oxford: Blackwell.

68　Terry Eagleton (2023) "What's your story?" *London Review of Books,* 45:4: 16 February. See also his (1991) *Ideology of the Aesthetic.* Oxford: Blackwell.

69　See, for example, Seb Olma (2016) *Autonomy and Weltbezug: Towards an Aesthetic of Performative Defiance.* Breda: Avans Hogeschool; Arran Gare (2007/8), "The arts and radical enlightenment: gaining liberty to save the planet", *The Structuralist,* 47/48: 20–27; Andrew Bowie (2003) *Aesthetics and Subjectivity: From Kant to Nietzsche.* Manchester: Manchester University Press.

70　Pierre Bourdieu (1993) *The Field of Cultural Production: Essays on Art and Literature,* edited and introduced by Randal Johnson. New York: Columbia University Press, 1993.

71　Cf. Emma Webb (2023) "Crying through our singing", in Seb Olma and Justin O'Connor (eds.), *Making & Breaking III.* https://makingandbreaking.org/article/crying-through-our-singing/.

3 Necessity or luxury?

1 A list compiled recently by Jason Hickel (2023) "Universal public services: the power of de-commodifying survival". www.jasonhickel.org/blog/2023/3/18/universal-public-services.

2 Anna Coote and Andrew Percy (2020) *The Case for Universal Basic Services*. Cambridge: Polity, p. 12. They draw on Len Doyal and Ian Gough (1991) *A Theory of Human Need*, 1st edition. London: Red Globe Press.

3 *King Lear*, Act 2, scene 4.

4 Karl Marx and Friedrich Engels (2022 [1846]) *The German Ideology*. London: Penguin.

5 Cf. Anna Coote (2020) "Universal basic services and the foundational economy", *FEC Working Paper* 7. https://foundationaleconomycom.files.wordpress.com/2020/10/ubs-and-fe-working-paper-wp7.pdf.

6 FEC (2020) *What Comes after the Pandemic? A Ten-Point Platform for Foundational Renewal*. www.researchgate.net/publication/343110880_What_Comes_after_the_Pandemic_A_Ten-Point_Platform_for_Foundational_Renewal.

7 Göran Therborn (2009) "The killing fields of inequality", *Soundings*, 42:4: 579–589. www.researchgate.net/publication/235388737_The_Killing_Fields_of_Inequality.

8 Which is not to deny the exigencies of the immediate vital threat.

9 Luca Calafati, Julie Froud, Colin Haslam, Sukhdev Johal, and Karel Williams (2023) *When Nothing Works: From Cost of Living to Foundational Liveability*. Manchester: Manchester University Press, p. 112.

10 Theodore Adorno, Friedrich Pollock, and Greta Adorno (2021 [1942]) "Theory of Needs", *New Left Review*, 128.

11 Hannah Arendt (1998 [1958]) *The Human Condition*. Chicago: University of Chicago Press. Chapter on labour.

12 Tim Jackson (2021) *Post Growth: Life After Capitalism*. Hoboken, NJ: John Wiley, p. 14.

13 As Anna Coote and Andrew Percy acknowledge in their invocation of Durkheim, cf. *The Case for Universal Basic Services*, p. 12.

14 Matthew T. Huber (2022) *Climate Change as Class War*. London: Verso.

15 Nancy Fraser and Axel Honneth (2003) *Redistribution or Recognition: A Political-Philosophical Exchange*. London: Verso.

16 Luc Boltanski and Eve Chiapello (2005) *The New Spirit of Capitalism*. London: Verso; Eve Chiapello (2004) "Evolution and

co-optation: the artistic critique of management and capitalism", *Third Text*, 18:6: 585–594.

17 For an explicit rejection of this see Erik Baker (2022) "New Left review: who did neoliberalism?" *N+1 Magazine*, 42: Spring. www.nplusonemag.com/issue-42/reviews/new-left-review.

18 See also Michael Denning (2004) *Culture in the Age of Three Worlds*. London: Verso.

19 "Brian Eno's BBC Music John Peel Lecture 2015". www.bbc.co.uk/programmes/p033smwp.

20 Abraham H. Maslow (1943) "A theory of human motivation", *Psychological Review*, 50: 370–396. For an attempt to retrieve Maslow's hierarchy of needs from marketing, see Mike Ratokovic and Gina Sosteric (2020) *Eupsychian Theory: Reclaiming Maslow and Rejecting the Pyramid – The Seven Essential Needs*. https://doi.org/10.31234/osf.io/fswk9.

21 *Wake in Fright* film (1971) Dir. Ted Kotcheff.

22 Edward Tylor's 1871 book *Primitive Culture* and Matthew Arnold's 1869 *Culture and Anarchy*. See the Introduction, note 14.

23 Ronald Inglehart (1977) *The Silent Revolution: Changing Values and Political Styles among Western Publics*. Princeton, NJ: Princeton University Press.

24 Mike Featherstone (1991) *Consumer Culture and Postmodernism*. London: Sage. Perhaps the more persistent damage done by simplistic use of Pierre Bourdieu's work is how the experience of art has been reduced to sociology, an expression of distinction and class habitus only. Against Bourdieu's critical intention, this quickly become a sociology of taste, the radical class analysis sloughed off to leave an analytics of market segmentation.

25 Justin O'Connor and Xin Gu (2020) *Red Creative: Culture and Modernity in Modern China*. Bristol: Intellect. Ch. 2; Amitav Ghosh (2021) *The Nutmeg's Curse: Parable for a Planet in Crisis*. Chicago: University of Chicago Press; Arran Gare (2007/8) "The arts and the radical enlightenment: gaining liberty to save the planet", *The Structurist*, no. 47/48.

26 Australia Council (2020) *Creating Our Future*. https://australiacouncil.gov.au/advocacy-and-research/creating-our-future.

27 Martin Hägglund (2019) *This Life: Why Mortality Makes Us Free*. London: Profile Books.

28 *Ibid.*, p. 175.

29 Ernst Bloch (1991 [1935]) *Heritage of Our Times*. Cambridge: Polity Press.

30 "Brian Eno's BBC Music John Peel Lecture 2015".

Notes

31 Stefano Harney (2012) "Creative industries debate: unfinished business: labour, management, and the creative industries", in Mark Hayward(ed.), *Cultural Studies and Finance Capitalism*, London: Routledge, 100–120, p. 433.

32 This is not a critique of Harney's paper. This quote was part of a wider argument with which I am very sympathetic. I have merely torn it out of context to illustrate a point.

33 On social liberals, see Tristram Hunt (2005) *Building Jerusalem: The Rise and Fall of the Victorian City*. London: Metropolitan Books.

34 Kristin Ross (2015) *Communal Luxury: The Political Imaginary of the Paris Commune*. London: Verso.

35 Richard A. Peterson (1992) "Understanding audience segmentation: from elite and mass to omnivore and univore", *Poetics*, 21:4: 243–258; Alan Warde, David Wright, and Modesto Gavo-Cal (2007) "Understanding cultural omnivorousness: or, the myth of the cultural omnivore", *Cultural Sociology*, 1:2: 143–164.

36 Anthony Giddens (1991) *Modernity and Self-Identity*. Cambridge: Polity. pp. 75–79; on working-class "worth" cf. Beverley Skeggs (2011) "Imagining personhood differently: person value and autonomist working-class value practices", *Sociological Review*, 59:3: 496–513.

37 Amartya Sen (1999) *Development as Freedom*. New York: Knopf; Martha Nussbaum (2011) *Creative Capabilities: The Human Development Approach*. Cambridge, MA: Harvard University Press.

38 Sen, *Development as Freedom*, p. 3.

39 T. H. Marshall (1963) "Citizenship and social class", in *Citizenship and Social Class and Other Essays*. Cambridge: Cambridge University Press, p. 23.

40 Martha Nussbaum (2007) "Human rights and human capabilities", in *Harvard Human Rights Journal*, 20: 21–24. https://wtf.tw/ref/nussbaum.pdf.

41 Calafati *et al.*, *When Nothing Works*, p. 113.

42 Russell Keat (2000) *Cultural Goods and the Limits of the Market*. Basingstoke: Macmillan. Also Mark Banks (2007) *The Politics of Cultural Work*. London: Palgrave Macmillan; David Hesmondhalgh (2010) "Russell Keat, cultural goods and the limits of the market", *International Journal of Cultural Policy*, 16:1: 37–38.

43 Keat, *Cultural Goods*, 10.

44 Dan Hill (2020) 'The quietly radical importance of everyday infrastructures". https://medium.com/slowdown-papers/30-the-quietly-radical-importance-of-everyday-infrastructures-f6e588d88d24. See also

Notes

talk given to the Reset Collective, https://resetartsandculture.com/2021/08/05/reset5-dan-hill-slowdown-reimagining-the-infrastructures-of-everyday-life.

45 Alberto Toscano (2023) "'Everything can be made better, except man': on Frédéric Lordon's communist realism", *Radical Philosophy*, 2:12: 19–34, p. 27.

46 Matthew T. Huber (2022) *Climate Change as Class War*. London: Verso, p. 113.

47 The quote is from Hal Draper (1977) *Karl Marx's Theory of Revolution, Vol II: The Politics of Social Classes*. New York: Monthly Review Press.

48 Annie Ernaux (2003) *A Woman's Life*. New York: Seven Stories Press. p. 79; Didier Eribon (2019) *Returning to Reims*. London: Penguin Random House; Thomas Piketty (2020) *Capital and Ideology*. Cambridge, MA: Belknap Press.

49 Rebecca May Johnson (2022) *Small Fires: An Epic in the Kitchen*. London: Pushkin Press. p. 36. The quotes cited by Johnson are from Audre Lorde (1982) *Zami: A New Spelling of My Name*. Watertown, MA: Persephone Press.

50 *Ibid.*, p. 37.

51 *Ibid.*

52 "Brian Eno's BBC Music John Peel Lecture 2015".

53 *Ibid.*

54 *Ibid.*

55 Sebastian Olma (2016) *Autonomy and Weltbezug: Towards an Aesthetic of Performative Defiance*. Breda: Avans Hogeschool.

56 Wang Hui (2016) *China's Twentieth Century*. London: Verso, p. 49.

57 Michel Foucault (2005) *The Hermeneutics of the Subject: Lectures at the Collège de France, 1981–1982*. Translated by Graham Burchell. New York: Palgrave Macmillan. For critiques of the Stoics see Hägglund, *This Life* and Martha Nussbaum (1994) *The Therapy of Desire: Theory and Practice in Hellenistic Ethics*. Princeton, NJ: Princeton University Press. Both build on Hegel's critique in the *Phenomenology of Spirit*.

58 Williams, *The Long Revolution*, p. 59.

59 *Ibid.*

60 Bennett, *Culture*, p. 96.

61 The work of Axel Honneth, Charles Taylor, Richard Sennett, and Helmut Rosa come immediately to mind.

62 Raymond Williams (1977) *Marxism and Literature*. Oxford: Oxford University Press.

63 Helen Andrews (2021) *Boomers: The Men and Women Who Promised Freedom and Delivered Disaster.* New York: Sentinel; Nick Land (2023) "The open spiral", *Compact Magazine*, 8 March: "But what reigns in Babylon is the anti-canon, with its two immense pillars. Exoterically, the deconstructed and diversified new canon arises, through which students, children, and the public are to be guided by angels other than their own. Beside this, befogged in its own tactical opacity, but increasingly immodest in its public presentation, is the esoteric canon of destructive principles, and tools, by which subversion—and our ruin—is to be advanced."

64 Gillian Rose (1995) *Love's Work.* New York: New York Review Books, pp. 158–9, original emphasis.

65 Raymond Williams (2003) *Who Speaks for Wales?* Cardiff: University of Wales Press, pp. 10–11.

4 Culture and the social foundations

1 See, for example, the conclusion to Gary Gerstle (2022) *The Rise and Fall of the Neoliberal Order.* Oxford: Oxford University Press, pp. 292–293.

2 See their website: https://foundationaleconomy.com. The two key books are FEC (2018) *Foundational Economy: The Infrastructure of Everyday Life.* Manchester: Manchester University Press; and Luca Calafati, Julie Froud, Colin Haslam, Sukhdev Johal, and Karel Williams (2023) *When Nothing Works: From Cost of Living to Foundational Liveability.* Manchester: Manchester University Press. Cf. also: FEC (2020) *The Foundational Approach* https://foundationaleconomycom.files.wordpress.com/2020/08/fe-approach-2020.pdf; Richard Bärnthaler, Andreas Novy, and Leonhard Plank (2021) "The foundational economy as a cornerstone for a social–ecological trans-formation", *Sustainability*, 13. www.mdpicom/2071-1050/13/18/10460; Bertie Russell, David Beel, Ian Rees Jones, and Martin Jones (2022) "Placing the Foundational Economy: an emerging discourse for post-neoliberal economic development", *Economy and Space*, 54:6: 1069–1085; Jason Hickel (2023) "Universal public services: the power of de-commodifying survival". www.jasonhickel.org/blog/2023/3/18/universal-public-services.

3 Quoted in Marshall Auerback (2020) "Uber's dangerous drive to serfdom", *UnHerd*, 7 September. https://unherd.com/2020/09/ubers-dangerous-drive-to-serfdom.

Notes

4 Albena Azmanova (2020) *Capitalism on Edge: How Fighting Precarity Can Achieve Radical Change without Crisis or Utopia.* New York: Columbia University Press.

5 UNESCO (1982) "Mexico City Declaration on Cultural Policies". https://unesdoc.unesco.org/ark:/48223/pf0000052505.

6 John Hawkes (2001) *The Fourth Pillar of Sustainability.* Melbourne: Cultural Development Network. www.culturaldevelopment.net.au/ community/Downloads/HawkesJon%282001%29TheFourthPillar OfSustainability.pdf.

7 Jane Gleeson-White (2014, revised 2020) *Six Capitals.* Sydney: Allen & Unwin.

8 Michael Lind (2022) "The idiocy of Econ 101", *Compact* magazine, 21 June. https://compactmag.com/article/the-idiocy-of-econ-101.

9 Cf. Regen Melbourne (2021) *Towards a Regenerative Melbourne*, p. 5. www.lmcf.org.au/getmedia/432daf5b-f6fd-415b-b943-d557dbf89daa/ Towards-a-Regenerative-Melbourne-Report-April-2021.pdf.aspx. It is telling that this addition, according to the organisers, did not come from the policy expert group (which suspended its activities during the pandemic) but the "grassroots" community groups consulted.

10 In the draft declaration the multiple crises were deemed to "call, more than ever, for reinvesting in the transformative role of culture in public policies, for the full exercise of fundamental human rights". This phrase disappeared in the final adopted version. UNESCO (2023) "Modiacult: Final Declaration. Article 2". www.unesco.org/sites/ default/files/medias/fichiers/2022/10/6.MONDIACULT_EN_ DRAFT%20FINAL%20DECLARATION_FINAL_1.pdf.

11 Luca Calafati, Julie Froud, Colin Haslam, Sukhdev Johal, and Karel Williams (2023) *When Nothing Works: From Cost of Living to Foundational Liveability.* Manchester: Manchester University Press.

12 *Ibid.*, 221.

13 In this the FEC differ from Gibson-Graham and others who see post-capitalist enclaves as a space to expand alternative economies. The FEC are fully aware of how the local is always part of a wider social and economic system that involves more than just "transactional" exchanges, cf. J. K. Gibson-Graham (2006). *Postcapitalist Politics.* Minneapolis, MN: University of Minnesota Press; J. K. Gibson-Graham and Kelly Dombroski (2020) *The Handbook of Diverse Economies.* Cheltenham: Edgar Elgar.

Notes

14 Ernst Bloch (1994 [1959]) *The Principle of Hope*. Cambridge, MA: MIT Press; Ruth Levitas (1990) "Educated hope: Ernst Bloch on abstract and concrete utopia", *Utopian Studies*, 1:2: 13–26;cf. Jess Scully (2020) *Glimpses of Utopia*. Sydney: Pantera Press. pp. 21–23; Erik Olin Wright (2010) *Envisioning Real Utopias*. London: Verso.

15 "A form of profit-oriented activity in which returns are largely the result of the direct use of political power." Dylan Riley (2020) "Faultlines", *New Left Review*, 126: 35–52, p. 36; cf. also Brett Christophers (2020) *Rentier Capitalism*. London: Verso; Lisa Adkins, Melinda Cooper, and Martijn Konings (2020) *The Asset Economy*. Cambridge: Polity.

16 FEC, *Foundational Economy*.

17 This was born out by a recent survey conducted by the Reset team in Australia; cf. Justin O'Connor (2022) *Reset: Art, Culture and the Foundational Economy*. https://resetartsandculture.com/wp-content/uploads/2022/02/CP3-Working-Paper-Art-Culture-and-the-Foundational-Economy-2022.pdf. Manchester's 2018 Industrial Strategy suggests the foundational economy (without the "overlooked" sector) makes up 50 per cent of the city's employment. Manchester City Council (2018) *Our Manchester Industrial Strategy*. www.manchester.gov.uk/downloads/download/7156/our_manchester_industrial_strategy.

18 Isaac Stanley (2020) *Love's Labours Found: Industrial Strategy for Social Care and the Everyday Economy*. London: Nesta. https://media.nesta.org.uk/documents/Loves_Labours_Found.pdf; Calafati *et al.*, *When Nothing Works*.

19 Dani Rodrik (2022) "The new productivism paradigm", *Project Syndicate*, 5 July. www.project-syndicate.org/commentary/new-productivism-economic-policy-paradigm-by-dani-rodrik-2022-07. See also Aaron Benanav (2023) "A dissipating glut?" *New Left Review*, 140/141: 53–81.

20 Amy Kapczynski (2023) "What's beyond 'beyond neoliberalism'?" *LPE Project*. https://lpeproject.org/blog/whats-beyond-beyond-neoliberalism/. See also Thomas Meaney (2022) "Fortunes of the Green New Deal", *New Left Review*, 138: 79–102.

21 "It's been a long 3 years since the Green New Deal vision of public luxury has transmogrified into private homeowners making $150K getting tax credits to adorn their property with low carbon commodities." https://twitter.com/Matthuber78/status/1567490347479048195.

Notes

22 Henrietta Moore and Hannah Collins (2020) *Towards Prosperity: Re-invigorating Local Economies through Universal Basic Services*. London: Institute for Global Prosperity. www.researchgate.net/publication/341205239_Towards_prosperity_Reinvigorating_local_economies_through_Universal_Basic_Services.

23 Cf. Ana Kapczynski and Gregg Gonsalves (2020) "The new politics of care", *Boston Review*, 27 April. www.bostonreview.net/articles/gregg-gonsalves-amy-kapczynski-new-deal-public-health-we-need.

24 A local Greater Manchester head of innovation contrasted the planned hi-tech "Atom Valley" R&D zone which would bring produc-tive jobs with jobs in the "so-called foundational sectors – low-wage work such as taxi driving and hairdressing that exist to serve local residents". No mention here of health, education, infrastructure and so on. Larry Elliot (2023) "Atom Valley: Andy Burnham's vision for regenerating Manchester", *The Guardian*, 7 January. www.theguardian.com/business/2023/jan/07/atom-valley-andy-burnhams-vision-for-regenerating-great-manchester.

25 Julie Froud, Colin Haslam, Sukhdev Johal and Karel Williams (2020) "(How) does productivity matter in the foundational economy?" *Local Economy*, 35:4: 316–336.

26 Tom Haines-Doran (2022) *Derailed: How to Fix Britain's Broken Railways*. Manchester: Manchester University Press.

27 On the UK care sector, James Butler (2023) "This concerns everyone", *London Review of Books*, 2 March, pp. 11–15. On Australia, Rick Morten (2021) "Brutal cuts to NDIS sees some plans halved without consultation", *The Saturday Paper*, 21 August. www.thesaturdaypaper.com.au/news/politics/2021/08/14/brutal-cuts-ndis-see-some-plans-halved-with-out-consultation/162886320012270; Rick Morten (2021) "How private management consultants took over the public service", *The Saturday Paper*, 9 October. www.thesaturdaypaper.com.au/news/politics/2021/10/09/how-private-management-consultants-took-over-the-public-service.

28 On the NHS, see FEC (2020) Research Report: *When Systems Fail*. https://foundationaleconomycom.files.wordpress.com/2020/06/when-systems-fail-uk-acute-hospitals-and-public-health-after-covid-19.pdf.

29 I set aside debates about "de-growth" here.

30 FEC (2020) *What Comes after the Pandemic? A Ten-Point Platform for Foundational Renewal*, p. 7. https://foundationaleconomycom.files.wordpress.com/2020/03/what-comes-after-the-pandemic-fe-manifesto-005.pdf.

Notes

31 Stanley, *Love's Labours Found*; Rachel Reeves (2018) *The Everyday Economy*. www.scribd.com/document/374425087/Rachel-Reeves-The-Everyday-Economy.

32 Wolfgang Streeck (2012) "Citizens as customers: considerations on the new politics of consumption", *New Left Review*, 76: 27–48.

33 Cf. UNESCO (2009) Framework for Cultural Statistics. Figure 2. https://uis.unesco.org/en/files/unesco-framework-cultural-statistics-2009-en-pdf.

34 Anna Lowenhaupt Tsing (2015) *The Mushroom at End of the World: On the Possibility of Life in Capitalist Ruins*. Princeton, NJ: Princeton University Press.

35 Tony Judt (2009) "What is living and what is dead in social democracy?" *New York Review of Books*, 17 December. www.nybooks.com/articles/2009/12/17/what-is-living-and-what-is-dead-in-social-democrac/.

36 Gerstle, *The Rise and Fall of the Neoliberal Order*.

37 Michael Denning (2004) *Culture in the Age of Three Worlds*. London: Verso; Michael Denning (2010) *The Cultural Front: The Laboring of American Culture in the Twentieth Century*. London: Verso.

38 For Australia, see the brief portrait by Emma Webb (2023) "Bread and Roses", *Making and Breaking*, 3.

39 Nicolas Bourriaud (1998) *Relational Aesthetics*. Paris: Les Presses du Reel. For a critique, Claire Bishop (2012) *Artificial Hells: Participatory Art and the Politics of Spectatorship*. London: Verso.

40 Cf. Matthew Thompson (2020) "What's so new about the new municipalism?" *Progress in Human Geography*, 36:1: 25–43; Matthew Brown and Rhian Jones (2021) *Paint Your Town Red: How Preston Took Back Control and How Your Town Can Too*. London: Repeater Books; Owen Hatherley (2020) *Red Metropolis: Socialism and the Government of London*. London: Repeater Books.

41 Attributed in various publications to Jodi Dean (2018) *The Communist Horizon*. London: Verso.

42 The phrase is William Morris', from his preface to John Ruskin's "The Nature of the Gothic", *Stones of Venice*, Vol. 2. www.marxists.org/archive/morris/works/1892/ruskin.htm.

43 Kristin Ross (2015) *Communal Luxury: The Political Imaginary of the Paris Commune*. London: Verso. pp. 60–63. On "hair shirt" de-growth and culture cf. Mark Banks (2022) "The unanticipated pleasures of the future: degrowth, post-growth and popular cultural economies", *New Formations*, 107–108: 12–29.

Notes

5 Cultural infrastructures

1 Luca Calafati, Julie Froud, Colin Haslam, Sukhdev Johal, and Karel Williams (2023) *When Nothing Works: From Cost of Living to Foundational Liveability*. Manchester: Manchester University Press, p. 205.

2 *Ibid.*, p. 12.

3 *Ibid.*, p. 206.

4 *Ibid.*

5 For example, Orian Brook, Dave O'Brien, and Mark Taylor (2020) *Culture Is Bad for You*. Manchester: Manchester University Press.

6 Mark Banks (2023) "Cultural work and contributive justice", *Journal of Cultural Economy*, 16:1: 47–61. See also interview with Mark Banks by Amie Taylor (2023) "It's not just about the getting but the giving: Contributive justice in arts and culture". https://funpalaces.co.uk/its-not-just-about-the-getting-but-the-giving-contributive-justice-in-arts-and-culture.

7 Lisa Adkins, Melinda Cooper, and Martijn Konings (2020) *The Asset Economy*. Cambridge: Polity.

8 For an account of this view, see Neal Harris (2023) "Critical theory and Universal Basic Income", *Critical Sociology*. https://doi.org/10.1177/08969205231151562.

9 Indeed, it was the transformation of the nuclear family from the 1960s, and the new sets of demands placed on welfare outside that model family, that led to the attacks on welfare from both neo-conservative and neoliberal politicians. Cf. Melinda Cooper (2017) *Family Values: Between Neoliberalism and the New Social Conservatism*. New York: Zone Books.

10 Or we might look at the impact of IKEA, as discussed by Sam Johnson-Schlee. Their "chuck out the chintz" campaign involved the wholesale remaking of working-class interiors. From what previously involved a slow accumulation of furnishings often inherited or sourced locally, the home became a "house" reprogrammed by a corporate global behemoth. Local production and retail, as well as the generational circulation of furniture and decorative items, was replaced by out-of-town big box shopping. This at the same time the home became an "asset", to be hastily furnished and sold as financial requirements dictated. Cf. Sam Johnson-Schlee (2022) *Living Rooms*. London: Peninsular Press. "Chintz was too personal. Neutral tones allowed the market to keep working, magnolia meant that a house was always ready to go onto the market", p. 32.

Notes

11 Calafati *et al. When Nothing Works*, p. 206.

12 Robert Putnam suggested after the pandemic that there was no "correlation between internet usage and civic engagement", while "cyber-balkanization" and not "digital democracy" was the future, in Anton Jäger (2022) "From bowling alone to posting alone", *Jacobin* 12 May. https://jacobin.com/2022/12/from-bowling-alone-to-posting-alone.

13 See Chapter 2, notes 55 and 56.

14 David Hesmondhalgh (2019) *The Cultural Industries*, 4th edition. London: Sage.

15 Sharon Zuboff (2019) *Surveillance Capitalism: The Fight for a Human Future at the New Frontier of Power*. London: Profile Books; Nick Srnicek (2016) *Platform Capitalism*. Cambridge: Polity Press; Hesmondhalgh, *The Cultural Industries*; Jeremy Gilbert and Alex Williams (2022) *Hegemony Now: How Big Tech and Wall Street Won the World (and How We Win It Back)*. London: Verso.

16 Nick Couldry and Ulises A. Mejias (2019) *The Costs of Connection: How Data Is Colonizing Human Life and Appropriating It for Capitalism*. Redwood, CA: Stanford University Press.

17 Cf. *Theory Culture and Society* (2023) Special Issue: A New Structural Transformation of the Public Sphere? 39:4; William Davies (2023) "The reaction economy", *London Review of Books* 45:5, 2 March.

18 Jodi Dean (2020) "Neofeudalism: the end of capitalism?", *Los Angeles Review of Books*, 12 May. https://lareviewofbooks.org/article/neofeudalism-the-end-of-capitalism/; Jodi Dean (2023) "Feudalism by design: on Quinn Slobodian's 'crack-up capitalism'", *Los Angeles Review of Books*, 10 April. https://lareviewofbooks.org/article/feudalism-by-design-on-quinn-slobodians-crack-up-capitalism; Cédric Durand, "Scouting capitalism's frontiers", New Left Review, p. 29.

19 William Davies (2021) "Peter Thiel: Big Tech's dark prophet", *New Statesman*, 27 October. www.newstatesman.com/culture/books/2021/10/the-contrarian-peter-thiel-max-chafkin-review.

20 Eric Klinenberg (2018) *Palaces for the People: How Social Infrastructure Can Help Fight Inequality, Polarization, and the Decline of Civic Life*. New York: Crown Publishing Group; Tom Kelsey and Michael Kenny (2021) *The Value of Social Infrastructure*. Townscapes Policy Report. Bennett Institute for Public Policy. www.bennettinstitute.cam.ac.uk/wp-content/uploads/2020/12/Townscapes_The_value_of_infrastructure.pdf.

21 Jay Oldenberg (1989) *The Great Good Place*. St Paul, MN: Paragon House, p. 1.

Notes

22   Kelsey and Kenny, *The Value of Social Infrastructure*, p. 11.

23   Jäger, "From bowling alone to posting alone".

24   Cf. https://en.wikipedia.org/wiki/Crap_Towns.

25   "Seven years ago, the *Economist* summarised the logic of George Osborne's Northern Powerhouse as '[allowing] the failing places to fail, but [helping] people move to the boomtowns'." Grace Blakeley (2022) "'It's not rocket science – it's just community': radical Ffestiniog", *Tribune* magazine, 9 September. https://tribunemag. co.uk/2022/11/radical-ffestiniog.

26   Isaac Rose (2022) "Against the Manchester model", *Tribune* magazine, November. https://tribunemag.co.uk/2022/11/against-the-manchester-model.

27   Owen Hatherley (2010) *A Guide to the New Ruins of Great Britain.* London: Verso; Hatherley (2019) *Trans-Europe Express: Tours of the Lost Continent.* London: Penguin Random House; Rem Koolhaas (1995) "The generic city", in Rem Koolhaas and Bruce Mau (eds.), *S, M, L, XL.* New York: The Monacelli Press, 1248–1264; Marc Augé (1992) *Non-Places: An Introduction to an Anthropology of Supermodernity.* London: Verso.

28   Cf. Robert Hollands (2023) *Beyond the Neoliberal Creative City: Critique and Alternatives in the Urban Cultural Economy.* Bristol: Bristol University Press.

29   Hal Foster (2010) *The Art–Architecture Complex.* London: Verso.

30   Jess Pacella, Susan Luckman, and Justin O'Connor (2021) *Keeping Creative.* CP3 Working Paper #1. www.unisa.edu.au/contentassets/ 33e97267a93046f1987edca85823e7b1/cp3-working-paper-01.pdf.

31   Chandler Dandridge (2023) "'Manchester's music scene dragged the city out of postindustrial decline': an interview with Andy Spinoza", *Jacobin*, 6 April. https://jacobin.com/2023/04/manchester-unspun-book-interview-music-scene-joy-division-the-smiths-postindustrial-investment.

32   For example, Oli Mould and Roberta Comunian (2015) "Hung, drawn and cultural quartered: rethinking cultural quarter development policy in the UK", *European Planning Studies*, 23:12: 2356–2369.

33   Cf. the summary of Dan Hill's *Reset* presentation: https://resetarts andculture.com/2021/08/05/reset5-dan-hill-slowdown-reimagining-the-infrastructures-of-everyday-life and see the exhibition by Sweden's National Centre for Architecture: https://arkdes.se/wp-content/ uploads/2017/11/public-luxury_final2.pdf.

34   Kristin Ross (2015) *Communal Luxury: The Political Imaginary of the Paris Commune.* London: Verso.

35 See Christian Bason, Rowan Conway, Dan Hill, and Mariana Mazzucato (2021) *A New Bauhaus for a Green Deal*. www.ucl.ac.uk/bartlett/public-purpose/publications/2021/jan/new-bauhaus-green-deal.

36 Timothy Mitchell (2002) *Rule of Experts: Egypt, Techno-Politics, Modernity*. Berkeley, CA: University of California Press; Timothy Mitchell (2005) "The work of economics: how a discipline makes its world", *European Journal of Sociology*, 46:2: 297–320; Timothy Mitchell (2015) *Carbon Democracy: Political Power in the Age of Oil*. London: Verso; Timothy Mitchell (2008) "Rethinking economy", *Geoforum*, 39:3: 1116–1121; Michel Callon (1998) *Laws of Markets*. London: John Wiley and Sons.

37 David Hesmondhalgh (2021) "The infrastructural turn in media and internet research", in Paul McDonald (ed.), *The Routledge Companion to Media Industries*. London: Routledge, 132–142; David Hesmondhalgh, Raquel Campos Valverde, D. Bondy Valdovinos Kaye, and Zhongwei Li (2023) "Digital platforms and infrastructure in the realm of culture", *Media and Communication*, 11:2. https://doi.org/10.17645/mac.v11i2.6422.

38 Adam Greenfield (2013) *Against the Smart City*. New York: Do Editions; Adam Greenfield (2018) *Radical Technologies: The Design of Everyday Life*. London: Verso.

39 Dan Hill (2016) "The street as platform 2050". https://medium.com/butwhatwasthequestion/the-street-as-platform-2050-98bbb81016f4; Sarah Barnes (2020) *Platform Urbanism: Negotiating Platform Ecosystems in Connected Cities*. London: Palgrave Macmillan.

40 See Dan Hill's "The quietly radical importance of everyday infrastructure", *Slowdown Papers* #30. https://medium.com/slowdown-papers/30-the-quietly-radical-importance-of-everyday-infrastructures-f6e588d88d24.

41 Jo Guldi (2023) "The earth for man: redistributing land was once central to global development efforts – and it should be today", *Boston Review*, 3 May. www.bostonreview.net/articles/the-earth-for-man; Jo Guldi (2022) *The Long Land War: The Global Struggle for Occupancy Rights*. New Haven, CT: Yale University Press.

42 Brett Christophers (2018) *The New Enclosure: The Appropriation of Public Land in Neoliberal Britain*. London: Verso.

43 Cf. Burns Owens Partnership (n.d.) *Making Space for Culture*. www.worldcitiescultureforum.com/publications/making-space-for-culture.

44 For a policy overview, see Katie Warfield, Erin Schultz and Kelsey Johnson (2007) "Framing infrastructure in a cultural context: a national

and international policy scan", *Working Paper 3*. Creative City Network of Canada. www.academia.edu/8213745/Framing_Infrastructure_ in_a_Cultural_Context_A_National_and_International_Policy_ Scan_. For recent applied policy accounts: Create NSW (2019) *Cultural Infrastructure Plan*. https://create.nsw.gov.au/wp-content/uploads/ 2019/02/20190206_CIP2025.pdf; Government of Western Australia (2020) *Western Australian Cultural Infrastructure Framework 2030+*. www. dlgsc.wa.gov.au/docs/default-source/culture-and-the-arts/cultural-infrastructure-toolkit/cultural-infrastructure-framework-2030-summary-report---online-viewing.pdf?sfvrsn=7c45271_8.

45 On parks cf. Abigail Gilmore (2023) *Culture, Participation and Policy in the Urban Park*. Palgrave Studies in Cultural Participation. London: Palgrave Macmillan.

46 It is interesting that for a so called "apolitical" sector, recent events around football club ownership, golf circuits, cricketing authorities, and so on have given rise to far more political opposition than in much of the cultural sector.

47 Cf. Lea Fobel (2022) "Non-formal cultural infrastructure in peripheral regions: responsibility, resources, and regional disparities", *Urban Planning*, 7:4: 445–456.

48 See UNESCO's final declaration in September 2022: www.unesco.org/ sites/default/files/medias/fichiers/2022/10/6.MONDIACULT_EN_ DRAFT%20FINAL%20DECLARATION_FINAL_1.pdf.

49 Mariana Mazzucato (2018) *The Value of Everything: Making and Taking in the Global Economy*. London: Random House.

50 See, for example, Andreas Krüger (2023) "Financing non-extractive urban planning: a Berlin practice" and Dan Hill (2023) "Harbinger", both in Seb Olma and Justin O'Connor (eds.), *Making and Breaking III: Communal Luxury*. https://makingandbreaking.org.

51 For a recent overview of the use of impact studies, see Eleonora Belfiore (2022) "Is it really about the evidence? Argument, persuasion, and the power of ideas in cultural policy", *Cultural Trends*, 31:4: 293–310. For a general discussion, Julian Meyrick, Robert Phiddian, and Tully Barnett (2018) *What Matters: Talking Value in Australian Culture*. Melbourne: Monash University Press.

52 Alexander Zevin (2019) "Every penny a vote", *London Review of Books*, 41:16, 15 August.

53 UCLG Culture Committee – Team of the Secretariat, with Marta Llobet, Agnès Ruiz, Sarah Vieux, and Jordi Pascual (2023) "A cultural

boost in the achievement of the SDGs", in UCLG and GTF, *Towards the Localization of the SDGs*. For the 2022 Rome Charter for Cities, see www.agenda21culture.net/news/2020-rome-charter.

54 Judith White (2017) *Culture Heist: Art versus Money*. Sydney: Brandl & Schlesinger; Julian Meyrick, Justin O'Connor, and Tully Barnett (2021) "Circus Oz: a crisis in a crisis", *Artshub*, 22 December. www.artshub. com.au/news/opinions-analysis/circus-oz-a-crisis-in-a-crisis-2521777.

55 Andreas Novy and Bernhard Leubolt (2005) "Participatory budgeting in Porto Alegre: social innovation and the dialectical relationship of state and civil society", *Urban Studies*, 42:11: 2023–2036.

56 Matthew Thompson (2020) "What's so new about the new municipalism?" *Progress in Human Geography*, 36:1: 25–43; Matthew Brown and Rhian Jones (2021) *Paint Your Town Red: How Preston Took Back Control and How Your Town Can Too*. London: Repeater Books; Owen Hatherley (2020) *Red Metropolis: Socialism and the Government of London*. London: Repeater Books.

57 Quoted in Ian Penman (2022) "My God wears a durag", *London Review of Books*, 44:1, January.

58 Karel Williams summarises: "Restanza means choosing to stay in a place in a conscious active and proactive way by actively guarding it, being aware of the past while enhancing what remains with an impulse towards the future where a new community is possible. In this sense, staying is a dynamic concept, it is a form of journey." Blakeley, "'It's not rocket science – it's just community'". Cf. Lowri Cunningham Wynn, Julie Froud, and Karel Williams (2023) *A Way Ahead? Empowering Restanza in a Slate Valley*. Foundational Economy Research Limited. https://foundationaleconomycom.files.wordpress. com/2022/04/restanza-english-version-as-of-7-feb-2022.pdf.

59 Cf. Gretchen Coombs (2018) *The Lure of the Social: Encounters with Contemporary Artists*. Bristol: Intellect.

60 An organisation such as Trans-Europe Halles, which began as such a social and cultural infrastructure group, shifted into creative economy mode along with many others. Shifting back might be a way forward. https://teh.net.

61 Cf. Culture Commons (2022) *Creative Improvement Districts*. London. https://creativelandtrust.org/wp-content/uploads/2022/12/ 221114-Culture-Commons-Creative-Improvement-Districts- Nov-2022-published-1.pdf.

Notes

62 See, for example, the Waterside Workers Hall in Port Adelaide, Australia. Emma Webb (2023) "Crying through our singing", in Seb Olma and Justin O'Connor (eds.), *Making & Breaking III: Communal Luxury*. https:// makingandbreaking.org/article/crying-through-our-singing/.

63 Adam Greenfield's blog: https://speedbird.wordpress.com/2023/ 04/10/the-lifehouse-distributed-community-support-centers-for-the-long-emergency.

64 Simon Jenkins (2023) "The decline of churchgoing doesn't have to mean the decline of churches – they can help us level up", *The Guardian*, 7 April. www.theguardian.com/commentisfree/2023/apr/ 07/decline-churchgoing-english-churches-level-up.

65 Kim Stanley Robinson (2020) *The Ministry of the Future*. New York: Orbit Books; Justin O'Connor (2023) "UNESCO's 2005 Convention: from creative economy to sustainable prosperity?" in Chris Bailey, Elena Theodoulou Charalambous, and Geert Drion (eds.), *Cultural Governance in the 21st Century*. London: Routledge.

66 This was at a panel in 2002 organised by the Manchester Institute for Popular Culture, of which I was director at the time.

67 Mark Fisher (2014) *Ghosts of My Life: Writings on Depression, Hauntology and Lost Futures*. London: Zero Books; Phoebe Braithwaite (2019) "Mark Fisher's popular modernism", *Tribune* magazine, 18 January; Mark Fisher (2023) "Designer communism", in Seb Olma and Justin O'Connor (eds.), *Making & Breaking III: Communal Luxury*. https:// makingandbreaking.org/article/designer-communism.

68 Cf. William Harris (2023) "Ian Penman's *Fassbinder Thousands of Mirrors* is a love letter to postwar counterculture", *Jacobin*, 10 May. https://jacobin. com/2023/05/ian-penman-rainer-werner-fassbinder-thousands-of-mirrors-postwar-counterculture; Jon Savage (2015) *1966: The Year the Decade Exploded*. London: Faber and Faber. For how it is today, Alex Niven (2023) "Britain's ever-harsher welfare system means that now only the rich can afford to make art", *The Guardian*, 29 May. www.the guardian.com/commentisfree/2023/may/29/britain-welfare-rich-art-artists-housing-social-security.

69 John Merrick (2023) "England's north has been crushed by Thatcherism and austerity", *Jacobin*, 10 March. Review of Alex Niven (2023) *The North Will Rise Again: In Search of the Future in Northern Heartlands*. London: Bloomsbury. https://jacobin.com/2023/03/the-north-will-rise-again-alex-niven-book-review-thatcherism-england-industry.

70 Dandridge, "'Manchester's music scene dragged the city out of postindustrial decline'". Spinoza's contrast was with Liverpool. I once shared a platform with Tony Wilson in Liverpool, who claimed that the reason Manchester was more successful than them was that "we have enlightened despotism", referring to the city's long-serving chief executive, Howard Bernstein.

6 Culture and economy

1 UNESCO/Abu Dhabi Department of Culture and Tourism (2022) *Culture in Times of Covid 19: Resilience, Recovery and Revival.* https://unesdoc.unesco.org/ark:/48223/pf0000381524.locale=en.

2 Françoise Matarasso (2023) "Post-political arts policy", *A Selfless Art,* 29 May. https://arestlessart.com/2023/05/29/post-political-arts-policy.

3 Willian Baumol and William Bowen (1966) *Performing Arts: The Economic Dilemma. a study of problems common to theater, opera, music, and dance.* New York: Twentieth Century Fund.

4 Nicholas Hytner (2023) "The arts in Britain are teetering on the brink: here is my plan to save them", *The Guardian,* 17 May. www.theguardian.com/commentisfree/2023/may/17/arts-council-britain-plan-save-new-body.

5 According to the Statistica.com website. www.statista.com/statistics/298465/government-spending-uk/.

6 Jason Hickel (2023) "Universal public services: the power of decommodifying survival", *Jason Hickel blog,* 11 April. www.jasonhickel.org/blog/2023/3/18/universal-public-services.

7 Ben Spies-Butcher and Gareth Bryant (2023) "The history and future of the tax state II: financialisation of the state and fiscal hybridity", *Progress in Political Economy,* 6 June. www.ppesydney.net/the-history-and-future-of-the-tax-state-ii-financialisation-of-the-state-and-fiscal-hybridity.

8 Cf. the somewhat mainstream challenge to standard regeneration practices in Marcus Spiller (2020) "Reconceptualising local economic development strategies", *Economic Development Journal,* 14:1: 6–9. www.edaustralia.com.au/wp-content/uploads/2021/03/EDAJ_Vol14No1.pdf.

9 The Green New Deal for Europe (2019) *Blueprint for Europe's Just Transition.* https://report.gndforeurope.com/cms/wp-content/uploads/2020/01/Blueprint-for-Europes-Just-Transition-2nd-Ed.pdf; David Oks and

Henry Williams (2022) "The long, slow death of global development", *American Affairs*, 6:4. https://americanaffairsjournal.org/2022/11/the-long-slow-death-of-global-development.

10 Lars Coenen and Kevin Morgan (2020) "Evolving geographies of innovation: existing paradigms, critiques and possible alternatives", *Norsk Geografisk Tidsskrift*, 74:1: 13–24, pp. 16–17.

11 See overview by Dan Hill (2019) "Teams of teams, railways not sandwiches", *Dark Matter and Trojan Horses*. https://medium.com/dark-matter-and-trojan-horses/teams-of-teams-railways-not-sandwiches-4e901ce92787.

12 Geoff Mulgan (2014) *The Radical's Dilemma: An Overview of the Practice and Prospects of Social and Public Labs*. https://media.nesta.org.uk/documents/social_and_public_labs_-_and_the_radicals_dilemma.pdf.

13 See Mariana Mazzucato and Brian Eno in conversation: www.youtube.com/watch?v=FFbtFxgwZkA.

14 Cf. Coenen and Morgan, "Evolving geographies of innovation".

15 *Ibid.*; Dave Adamson and Mark Lang (2014) *Towards a New Settlement: A Deep Place Approach to Equitable and Sustainable Place*. Merthyr Tydfil: Crew Regeneration Wales. See also J. K. Gibson-Graham (2006) *Postcapitalist Politics*. Minneapolis, MN: University of Minnesota Press; J. K. Gibson-Graham and Kelly Dombroski (2020) *The Handbook of Diverse Economies*. Cheltenham: Edgar Elgar.

16 Al Rainnie (2023) "(Far) beyond smart specialisation to the foundational economy in Australia?" Unpublished paper.

17 Cf. Justin O'Connor (2004) "'A special kind of city knowledge': innovative clusters, tacit knowledge and the 'creative city'", *Media International Australia*, 112: 131–149; Justin O'Connor and Xin Gu (2010) "Developing a creative cluster in a post-industrial city: CIDS and Manchester", *The Information Society*, 26:2: 124–136.

18 Adamson and Lang, *Towards a New Settlement*, p. 4.

19 Larry Elliott (2023) "Atom Valley: Andy Burnham's vision for regenerating Greater Manchester", *The Guardian*, 8 January. www.theguardian.com/business/2023/jan/07/atom-valley-andy-burnhams-vision-for-regenerating-great-manchester.

20 Developers promoting hard cultural infrastructure often assume an endless supply of artists, just as those businesses that thrive on "vibrancy" take little responsibility for the ecosystem on which such vibrancy is based. Of course, when excess gentrification, online shopping, or events such as the pandemic threaten commercially usable

vibrancy, artists are asked to return to the city centre or retail strips, though usually on a temporary basis and with no thought of their increasingly desperate position. Cf. Kate Shaw (2021) "Can artists revive dead city centres? Without long-term tenancies it's window dressing", *The Conversation*, 27 October. https://theconversation.com/can-artists-revive-dead-city-centres-without-long-term-tenancies-its-window-dressing-169822.

21 Cf. Keir Milburn (2019) *Generation Left*. Cambridge: Polity Press; Alison Pennington (2023) *Gen F'd?: How Young Australians Can Reclaim Their Uncertain Futures*. Melbourne: Hardie Grant Books.

22 Roberta Comunian and Lauren England (2020) "Creative and cultural work without filters: Covid-19 and exposed precarity in the creative economy", *Cultural Trends*, 29:2: 112–128; Mark Banks and Justin O'Connor (2021) "'A plague on your howling': art and culture in the viral emergency", *Cultural Trends*, 30:1: 3–18; Alison Pennington and Ben Eltham (2021) *Creativity in Crisis: Rebooting Australia's Arts and Entertainment Sector after COVID*. Centre for Future Work, Australia Institute. https://futurework.org.au/report/creativity-in-crisis-rebooting-australias-arts-and-entertainment-sector-after-covid/; Katherine Power (2021) "The crisis of a career in culture", *The Conversation*, 6 December. https://theconversation.com/the-crisis-of-a-career-in-culture-why-sustaining-a-livelihood-in-the-arts-is-so-hard-171732.

23 Lisa Adkins, Melinda Cooper, and Martijn Konings (2020) *The Asset Economy*. Cambridge: Polity.

24 Xin Gu (2023) *Cultural Work and Creative Subjectivity: Recentralising the Artist Critique and Social Networks in the Cultural Industries*. London: Routledge.

25 Cf. Barbara Ehrenreich (1989) *Fear of Falling: The Inner Life of the Middle Class*. New York: Pantheon Books.

26 Matthew T. Huber (2022) *Climate Change as Class War*. London: Verso; Jenna Burrell and Marion Fourcade (2021) "The society of algorithms", *Annual Review of Sociology*, 47: 213–237. We can see a growing divide in the public cultural sector between the full-time paid professional administrators and creatives and the growing mass of impoverished culture workers outside of that system. A similar divide can be found between university administrators, lecturers, and casual staff.

27 Cornelia Dümcke (2021) "Five months under COVID-19 in the cultural sector: a German perspective", *Cultural Trends*, 30:1: 19–27.

28 See, for example, Nicola Countouris (2021) "Regulating digital work: from laisser-faire to fairness", *Social Europe*, 8 December.

Notes

https://socialeurope.eu/regulating-digital-work-from-laisser-faire-to-fairness; Kate Oakley and David Boyle (2018) *Co-operatives in the Creative Industries.* https://culturalworkersorganize.org/wp-content/uploads/2018/10/Cooperatives-and-Creative-Industries-Boyle-and-Oakley.pdf; Greig de Peuter, Bianca C. Dreyer, Marisol Sandoval, and Aleksandra Szaflarska (2020) *Sharing Like We Mean It: Working Co-operatively in the Cultural and Tech Sectors.* Cultural Workers Organize. https://culturalworkersorganize.org/wp-content/uploads/2021/01/Sharing-Like-We-Mean-It-Web.pdf; Annalisa Murgia and Sarah de Heusch (2020) "It started with the arts and now it concerns all sectors: the case of Smart, a cooperative of 'salaried autonomous workers'", in Stephanie Taylor and Susan Luckman (eds.), *Pathways into Creative Working Lives.* London: Palgrave Macmillan, pp. 211–230; EENCA (2020) *The Status and Working Conditions of Artists and Cultural and Creative Professionals.* https://eenca.com/eenca/assets/File/EENCA%20publications/Study%20on%20the%20status%20and%20working%20conditions%20of%20artists%20and%20creative%20professionals%20-%20Final%20report.pdf.

29 Pennington and Eltham, *Creativity in Crisis*; Power, "The crisis of a career in culture"; Kim Goodwin and Caitlin Vincent (2023) "Pay, safety and welfare: how the new Centre for Arts and Entertainment Workplaces can strengthen the arts sector", *The Conversation*, 31 January. https://theconversation.com/pay-safety-and-welfare-how-the-new-centre-for-arts-and-entertainment-workplaces-can-strengthen-the-arts-sector-198859.

30 Justin O'Connor and Ben Eltham (2020) *South Australian Creative Industries: A Census Snapshot.* www.unisa.edu.au/research/creative-people-products-places/news/south-australian-creative-industries-a-census-snapshot.

31 Power, "The crisis of a career in culture"; Jinghua Qian (2020) "I can't apply for another grant", *Unprojects.* https://unprojects.org.au/article/i-cant-apply-for-another-grant; Lauren Carroll Harris (2021) "The case for salaried artists', *Kill your Darlings*, 31 August. www.killyourdarlings.com.au/article/the-case-for-salaried-artists; International Labour Organisation (2013) "Decent work is a human right". www.ilo.org/newyork/speeches-and-statements/WCMS_229015/lang--en/index.htm.

32 Greig de Peuter, Kate Oakley, and Madison Trusolino (2023) "The pandemic politics of cultural work: collective responses to

the COVID-19 crisis", *International Journal of Cultural Policy*, 29:3: 377–392; Oakley and Boyle, *Co-operatives in the Creative Industries*; de Peuter, Dreyer, Sandoval, and Szaflarska, *Sharing Like We Mean It*; Murgia and de Heusch, "It started with the arts and now it concerns all sectors"; Angela McRobbie (2015) *Be Creative: Making a Living in the New Culture Industries*. Cambridge: Polity.

33 The 2022 Australian National Cultural Policy, Revive, radically reduced the culture-as-industry justifications, but set up a new Centre for Arts and Entertainment Workplaces to address issues such as the 45 per cent casualisation and gender pay gaps in the sector. Cf. Prime Minister's press release: www.pm.gov.au/media/revive-australias-new-national-cultural-policy.

34 Paul Redmond, Seamus McGuinness, and Klavs Ciprikis (2022) *A Universal Basic Income for Ireland: Lessons from the International Literature*. The Economic and Social Research Institute, Research Series 146. www.esri.ie/publications/a-universal-basic-income-for-ireland-lessons-from-the-international-literature; John O'Brien and Annette Clancy (2022) "A policy review of Basic Income for the Arts Pilot Scheme", *Irish Journal of Arts Management and Cultural Policy*, 9: 43–57.

35 Cf. Aaron Bastani (2023) "The left should champion universal basic services, not UBI", *New Statesman*, June. www.newstatesman.com/quickfire/2023/06/left-should-champion-universal-basic-services-income; Henrietta Moore and Hannah Collins (2020) *Towards Prosperity: Re-invigorating Local Economies through Universal Basic Services*. London: Institute for Global Prosperity; Daniel Zamora (2017) "The case against a basic income" *Jacobin* magazine 28 December; Anna Coote and Edanur Yazici (2019) *Universal Basic Income: A Union Perspective*. www.world-psi.org/sites/default/files/documents/research/en_ubi_full_report_2019.pdf; Anton Jäger and Daniel Zamora (2023) *Welfare for Markets: A Global History of Basic Income*. Chicago: University of Chicago Press; Anton Jäger and Daniel Zamora Vargas (2023) "The problem with universal basic income programs", *The Washington Post*, 14 June. www.washingtonpost.com/made-by-history/2023/06/14/universal-basic-income.

36 Anna Coote and Andrew Percy (2020) *The Case for Universal Basic Services*. Cambridge: Polity.

37 Alex Niven (2023) "Britain's ever-harsher welfare system means that now only the rich can afford to make art", *The Guardian*, 30 May.

Notes

www.theguardian.com/commentisfree/2023/may/29/britain-welfare-rich-art-artists-housing-social-security?CMP=share_btn_tw.

38 I once said this in a discussion in a bookstore in Ekaterinburg, Russia, in 2017. The young people told me "they'd tried communism and it doesn't work".

39 Neil Harris (2023) "Critical theory and Universal Basic Income", *Critical Sociology*. https://doi.org/10.1177/08969205231151562.

40 We might worry, as does Christie Offenbacher, editor of *Damage* magazine, about post-1968 sexual liberation in a neoliberal era. "Unions, local sports clubs, churches, community organisations – all of that has been thoroughly decimated in the last 50 years of unrestrained neoliberal rule … What do you do with lessening strictures on sexual action coexisting with degrees of atomisation unprecedented in human history?" Quoted in Nick Burn (2023) "Freud save America", *New Statesman*, 27 May.

41 Alex Gourevitch (2022) "Post-work socialism?" *Catalyst*, 6:2: Summer. https://catalyst-journal.com/2022/09/post-work-socialism.

42 Michael Young (1958) *The Rise of the Meritocracy 1870–2033: An Essay on Education and Society*. London: Thames and Hudson; Michael Sandel (2020) *The Tyranny of Merit: What's Become of the Common Good?* London: Allen Lane.

43 Arlene Goldbard and François Matarasso (2020) *The Arts and the State in Times of Crisis: The Prospect of a New WPA*. https://parliamentofdreams.files.wordpress.com/2020/10/the-arts-and-the-state-uk-29-09-2020.pdf; Pavlina R. Tcherneva (2020) *The Case for a Job Guarantee*. Cambridge: Polity; Power, "The crisis of a career in culture"; Jennifer Mills (2022) "A Liveable Income Guarantee should support artists—and artists should support a UBI", *Overland*, 28 March. https://overland.org.au/2022/03/a-liveable-income-guarantee-should-support-artists-and-artists-should-support-a-ubi.

44 Tony Judt (2011) *Ill Fares the Land*. London: Penguin.

45 Hill, "Teams of teams, railways not sandwiches". Original emphasis.

46 Andrew Ross (2003) *No-Collar: The Humane Workplace and Its Hidden Costs*. New York: Basic Books; Andrew Ross (2009) "The political economy of amateurism", *Television and New Media*, 10: 136–137.

47 Cf. Robert Hollands (2023) *Beyond the Neoliberal Creative City: Critique and Alternatives in the Urban Cultural Economy*. Bristol: Bristol University Press.

48 FEC (2019) *How an Ordinary Place Works: Understanding Morriston.* FEC research report, p. 39. https://foundationaleconomycom.files. wordpress.com/2019/05/morriston-report-v6-13-may-2019.pdf.

49 Richard Bärnthaler, Andreas Novy, and Leonhard Plank (2021) "The foundational economy as a cornerstone for a social-ecological transformation", *Sustainability*, 13, pp. 12–13.

50 Matthew Thompson (2020) "What's so new about the new municipalism?" *Progress in Human Geography*, 36:1: 25–43; Matthew Brown and Rhian Jones (2021) *Paint Your Town Red: How Preston Took Back Control and How Your Town Can Too.* London: Repeater Books; Joe Guigan and Martin O'Neil (2019) *The Case for Community Wealth Building.* Cambridge: Polity.

51 Harriet Sherwood (2023) "London's Roundhouse to train 15,000 young people in creative industries", *The Guardian*, 18 May. www. theguardian.com/society/2023/may/18/londons-roundhouse-to-train-15000-young-people-in-creative-industries.

52 For example, CRESC (2015) *What Wales Could Be.* https://foundational economycom.files.wordpress.com/2017/01/what-wales-could-be.pdf; Colleges Wales (2020) *Enabling Renewal.* https://foundationaleconomy com.files.wordpress.com/2021/02/enabling-renewal-final-report-feb-2021.pdf; Adamson and Lang, *Towards a New Settlement.*

53 For further discussion on this, see: O'Connor, "'A special kind of city knowledge'"; Justin O'Connor (2007) *The Cultural and Creative Industries: A Review of the Literature.* London: Creativity, Culture, Education; Justin O'Connor and Kate Shaw (2014) "What next for the creative city?" *City, Culture and Society*, 5:3: 165–70; Justin O'Connor and Kate Oakley (2015) "Cultural industries: an introduction", in Kate Oakley and Justin O'Connor (eds.), *The Routledge Companion to the Cultural Industries.* London: Routledge, 1–32.

54 Allen J. Scott (2004) "Cultural products industries and urban economic development: prospects for growth and market contestation in global context", *Urban Affairs Review*, 39:4: 461–490; Andy Pratt (2012) "The cultural and creative industries: organisational and spatial challenges to their governance", *Die Erde*, 143:4: 317–334; O'Connor and Shaw, "What next for the creative city?"

55 Andreas Reckwitz (2017) *The Invention of Creativity.* Cambridge: Polity.

56 David Hesmondhalgh (2019) *The Cultural Industries*, 4th edition. London: Sage, pp. 84–86.

Notes

57 Kuba Szreder (2021) *The ABC of the Projectariat: Living and Working in a Precarious Art World.* Manchester: Manchester University Press.

58 Amber A'Lee Frost (2019) "The WeWork con", *Jacobin* magazine, 25 November. www.jacobinmag.com/2019/11/wework-adam-neumann-con-artist-grifter-entrepreneur; Matthew Stewart (2019) "The real estate sector is using algorithms to work out the best places to gentrify", *Failed Architecture*, 11 February. https://failedarchitecture.com/the-extractive-growth-of-artificially-intelligent-real-estate/; Jed Rothstein (Dir.) (2021) *WeWork: Or the Making and Breaking of a $47 Billion Unicorn.* Documentary.

59 For an overview, see Shuwen Qu, David Hesmondhalgh, and Jian Xiao (2021) "Music streaming platforms and self-releasing musicians: the case of China", *Information, Communication & Society.* https://doi.org/10.1080/1369118X.2021.1971280; for the fate of digital workers or "hackers" themselves, see McKenzie Wark (2019) *Capital Is Dead.* London: Verso.

60 Fernand Braudel (1992) *Civilization and Capitalism, 15th–18th Century*, Vols. I–III. Berkeley, CA: University of California Press; Edward P. Thompson (1971) "The moral economy of the English Crown in the 18th century", *Past & Present*, 50: 76–136.

61 Filippo Barbera, Nicola Negri, and Angelo Salento (2018) "From individual choice to collective voice: foundational economy, local commons and citizenship", *Rassegna Italiana di Sociologia*, 2: 371–398. p. 374. https://doi.org/10.1423/90584.

62 New Economics Foundation (n.d.) *Co-operatives Unleashed: Doubling the Size of the UK's Co-operative Sector.* https://neweconomics.org/uploads/files/co-ops-unleashed.pdf; David Boyle and Kate Oakley (2018) *Co-operatives in the Creative Industries.* Co-ops UK. https://culturalworkers organize.org/wp-content/uploads/2018/10/Cooperatives-and-Creative-Industries-Boyle-and-Oakley.pdf; Guigan and O'Neil, *The Case for Community Wealth Building.*

63 Hesmondhalgh, *The Cultural Industries*; Richard E. Caves (2000) *Creative Industries: Contracts between Art and Commerce.* Cambridge, MA: Harvard University Press.

64 See Cecilia Rikap (2023) "Capitalism as usual? Implications of digital intellectual monopolies", *New Left Review*, 139: 145–160; Herman Schwartz (2022) "From Fordism to franchise: intellectual property and growth models in the Knowledge Economy", in Lucio Baccaro, Mark Blyth, and Jonas Pontusson (eds.), *Diminishing Returns: The New Politics*

of Growth and Stagnation. Oxford: Oxford University Press. https://uva.theopenscholar.com/files/hermanschwartz/files/schwartz-ch2-bbp.pdf.

65 Quote from Brett Christophers (2020). *Rentier Capitalism.* London: Verso. See good discussion in David Hesmondhalgh, Raquel Campos Valverde, D. Bondy Valdovinos Kaye, and Zhongwei Li (2023) "Digital platforms and infrastructure in the realm of culture", *Media and Communication,* 11:2. https://doi.org//10.17645/mac.v11i2.6422; Blake Durham and Georgina Born (2022) "Online music consumption and the formalisation of informality", in Georgina Born (ed.), *Music and Digital Media.* London: UCL Press, 171–219.

66 Schwartz, "From Fordism to franchise".

67 Harry Braverman (1974) *Labor and Monopoly Capital: The Degradation of Work in the Twentieth Century.* New York: Monthly Review Press.

68 Cf. Jairus Banaji (2020) *A Brief History of Commercial Capitalism.* London: Haymarket Books; Ackbar Abbas (2000) "Cosmopolitan descriptions: Shanghai and Hong Kong", *Public Culture,* 12:3: 769–786; Branko Milanović (2023) "The comprador intelligentsia", Global inequality blog. https://branko2f7.substack.com/p/the-comprador-intelligentsia.

69 Burrell and Fourcade, "The society of algorithms", p. 219.

70 *Ibid.*

71 Rebecca Giblin and Cory Doctorow (2022) *Chokepoint Capitalism: How Big Tech and Big Content Captured Creative Labor Markets and How We'll Win Them Back.* Boston, MA: Beacon Press, p. 1.

72 Justin O'Connor (2020) "Creative cities, creative classes and the global modern", in Xin Gu, Justin O'Connor, and Michael Kho Lim (eds.), *Re-imagining Creative Cities in 21st Century Asia.* London: Palgrave, 13–26.

73 Lydia Deloumeaux (2022) "Global flow of cultural goods and services: still a one-way trade", in UNESCO, *Reshaping Policies for Creativity: Addressing Culture as a Global Public Good.* UNESCO, 163–182. www.unesco.org/reports/reshaping-creativity/2022/en.

74 Burrell and Fourcade, "The society of algorithms", p. 219.

75 Ulla Carlsson (2017) "The rise and fall of NWICO", *Nordicom Review,* 24:2: 31–67; Colin Sparks and Chris Roach (1990) "Editorial: farewell to NWICO?" *Media, Culture & Society,* 12:3: 275–281.

76 Michael Franczak (2022) *Global Inequality and American Foreign Policy in the 1970s.* Ithaca, NY: Cornell University Press; Quinn Slobodian (2018) *Globalists: The End of Empire and the Birth of Neoliberalism.* Cambridge,

MA: Harvard University Press; Tim Barker (2019) "Other people's blood", *N+1*: Spring, Issue 34. www.nplusonemag.com/issue-34/reviews/other-peoples-blood-2/.

77   Ann Pettifor (2023) "The NIEO against financialisation", *Progressive International*, 20 January. https://progressive.international/blueprint/4110ecaf-7e69-48eb-ab6a-f98559ddb78c-pettifor-the-nieo-against-financialisation/en; Niles Gilman (2023) "The NIEO as usable past", *Progressive International*, 4 January. https://progressive.international/blueprint/e7bc30e1-d565-47de-a19f-80ad1bce9969-gilman-the-nieo-as-usable-past/en.

78   Cf. Jodi Dean (2023) "Feudalism by design: on Quinn Slobodian's 'crack-up capitalism'", *Los Angeles Review of Books*, 10 April. https://lareviewofbooks.org/article/feudalism-by-design-on-quinn-slobodians-crack-up-capitalism.

79   Joy Press and Natalie Jarvey (2023) "TV's streaming bubble has burst, a writers strike looms, and 'everybody is freaking out'", *Vanity Fair*, 1 May. www.vanityfair.com/hollywood/2023/05/tv-streaming-bubble-has-burst-writers-strike-looms.

80   Giblin and Doctorow, *Chokepoint Capitalism*, 258.

81   Neil Ascherson (2023) "Kings grew pale", *London Review of Books*, 45:11, 1 June. www.lrb.co.uk/the-paper/v45/n11/neal-ascherson/kings-grew-pale.

Bibliography

Abbas, Ackbar (2000) "Cosmopolitan de-scriptions: Shanghai and Hong Kong", *Public Culture*, 12:3, 769–786.

Adamson, Dave and Lang, Mark (2014) *Towards a New Settlement: A Deep Place Approach to Equitable and Sustainable Place*. Merthyr Tydfil: Crew. Regeneration Wales.

Adkins, Lisa, Cooper, Melinda, and Konings, Martijn (2020) *The Asset Economy*. Cambridge: Polity.

Adorno, Theodore, Pollock, Friedrich, and Adorno, Greta (2021 [1942]) "Theory of Needs", *New Left Review*, 128.

Alami, Ilias, Dixon, Adam D., and Mawdsley, Emma (2021) "State capitalism and the new global D/development regime, *Antipode*, 53:5, 1271–1595.

Anderson, Perry (1984) "Modernity and revolution", *New Left Review*, 144, 96–113.

Andrews, Helen (2021) *Boomers: The Men and Women Who Promised Freedom and Delivered Disaster*. New York: Sentinel.

Arendt, Hanna (1998 [1958]) *The Human Condition*. Chicago: University of Chicago Press.

Aronoff, Kate, Battistoni, Alyssa, Cohen, Daniel Aldana, and Riofrancos, Thea (2019) *A Planet to Win: Why We Need a Green New Deal*. London: Verso.

Ascherson, Neil (2023) "Kings grew pale", *London Review of Books*, 45:11.

Asia Development Bank Institute (2022) *Creative Economy 2030: Imagining and Delivering a Robust, Creative, Inclusive, and Sustainable Recovery*.

Augé, Marc (1992) *Non-Places: An Introduction to an Anthropology of Supermodernity*. London: Verso.

Azmanova, Albena (2020) *Capitalism on Edge: How Fighting Precarity Can Achieve Radical Change without Crisis or Utopia*. New York: Columbia University Press.

274

Bibliography

Banaji, Jairus (2020) *A Brief History of Commercial Capitalism*. London: Haymarket Books.

Banks, Mark (2007) *The Politics of Cultural Work*. London: Palgrave.

Banks, Mark (2017) *Creative Justice: Cultural Industries, Work and Inequality*. Lanham, MD: Rowman and Littlefield.

Banks, Mark (2023) "Cultural work and contributive justice", *Journal of Cultural Economy*, 16:1, 47–61.

Banks, Mark (2023) "The unanticipated pleasures of the future: degrowth, post-growth and popular cultural economies", *New Formations*, 107/108, 12–29.

Banks, Mark and O'Connor, Justin (2020) "'A plague on your howling': art and culture in the viral emergency", *Cultural Trends*, 30:1, 3–18.

Barbera, Filippo, Negri, N. and Salento, Angelo (2018) "From individual choice to collective voice: foundational economy, local commons and citizenship", *Rassegna Italiana di Sociologia*, 59, 371–97.

Barbrook, Richard and Cameron, Andy (1996) "The Californian ideology", *Science as Culture*, 6:1, 44–72.

Barnes, Sarah (2020) *Platform Urbanism: Negotiating Platform Ecosystems in Connected Cities*. London: Palgrave Macmillan.

Bärnthaler, Richard, Novy, Andreas, and Plank, Leonhard (2021) "The foundational economy as a cornerstone for a social-ecological transformation", *Sustainability*, 13.

Baumol, William and Bowen, William (1966) *Performing Arts: The Economic Dilemma. A Study of Problems Common to Theatre, Opera, Music, and Dance*. New York: Twentieth Century Fund.

Belfiore, Eleonora (2004) "Auditing culture: the subsidised cultural sector in the new public management", *International Journal of Cultural Policy*, 10:2, 183–202.

Belfiore, Eleonora (2009) "On bullshit in cultural policy practice and research: notes from the British case", *International Journal of Cultural Policy*, 15:3, 343–359.

Belfiore, Eleonora (2022) "Is it really about the evidence? Argument, persuasion, and the power of ideas in cultural policy", *Cultural Trends*, 31:4, 293–310.

Benanav, Aaron (2023) "A dissipating glut?" *New Left Review*, 140/141, 53–81.

Bennett, Tony (1998) *Culture: A Reformer's Science*. London: Sage.

Berman, Marshall (1983) *All That Is Solid Melts into Air: The Experience of Modernity*. London: Verso.

Bibliography

Bianchini, Franco (1987) "GLC R.I.P. 1981–1986", *New Formations*, 1, 103–117.

Binkley, Sam (2018) "The emotional logic of neoliberalism: reflexivity and instrumentality in three theoretical traditions", in Cahill, Damien, Cooper, Melinda, Konings, Martijn, and Primrose, David (eds.), *The Sage Handbook of Neoliberalism*. London: Sage, 580–595.

Bishop, Claire (2012) *Artificial Hells: Participatory Art and the Politics of Spectatorship*. London: Verso.

Bloch, Ernst (1991 [1935]) *Heritage of Our Times*. Cambridge: Polity Press.

Bloch, Ernst (1994 [1959]) *The Principle of Hope*. Cambridge, MA: MIT Press.

Boltanski, Luc and Chiapello, Eve (2005) *The New Spirit of Capitalism*. London: Verso.

Bourdieu, Pierre (1993) *The Field of Cultural Production: Essays on Art and Literature*, edited and introduced by Johnson, Randal. New York: Columbia University Press.

Bourriaud, Nicolas (1998) *Relational Aesthetics*. Paris: Les presses du reel.

Bowie, Andrew (2003) *Aesthetics and Subjectivity: From Kant to Nietzsche*. Manchester: Manchester University Press.

Bowie, Andrew (2013) *Aesthetics and Subjectivity*, 2nd edition. Manchester: Manchester University Press.

Braudel, Fernand (1992) *Civilization and Capitalism, 15th–18th Century*, Vols. I–III. Berkeley, CA: University of California Press.

Braverman, Harry (1974) *Labor and Monopoly Capital: The Degradation of Work in the Twentieth Century*. New York: Monthly Review Press.

Brook, Orian, O'Brien, Dave, and Taylor, Mark (2020) *Culture is Bad for You*. Manchester: Manchester University Press.

Brown, Matthew and Jones, Rhian E. (2021) *Paint Your Town Red: How Preston Took Back Control and How Your Town Can Too*. London: Repeater Books.

Brown, Wendy (2017) *Undoing the Demos: Neoliberalism's Stealth Revolution*. Princeton, NJ: Princeton University Press.

Burrell, Jenna and Fourcade, Marion (2021) "The society of algorithms", *Annual Review of Sociology*, 47, 213–237.

Calafati, Luca, Froud, Julie, Haslam, Colin, Johal, Sukhdev, and Williams, Karel (2023) *When Nothing Works: From Cost of Living to Foundational Liveability*. Manchester: Manchester University Press.

Caldwell, John T. (2023) *Specworld: Folds, Faults, and Fractures in Embedded Creator Industries*. Oakland, CA: University of California Press.

Callon, Michel (1998) *Laws of Markets*. London: John Wiley and Sons.

Carlsson, Ulla (2017) "The rise and fall of NWICO", *Nordicom Review*, 24:2, 31–67.

Bibliography

Caust, Jo (2003) "Putting the 'art' back into arts policy making: how arts policy has been 'captured' by the economists and the marketers", *International Journal of Cultural Policy*, 9:1, 51–63.

Caves, Richard E. (2000): *Creative Industries: Contracts between Art and Commerce.* Cambridge, MA: Harvard University Press.

Caygill, Howard (1990) *The Art of Judgement.* Oxford: Blackwell.

Chanan, Michael (2022) *From Printing to Streaming: Cultural Production under Capitalism.* London: Pluto Press.

Chiapello, Eve (2004) "Evolution and co-optation: the artistic critique of management and capitalism", *Third Text*, 18:6, 585–594.

Christophers, Brett (2018) *The New Enclosure: The Appropriation of Public Land in Neoliberal Britain.* London: Verso.

Christophers, Brett (2020) *Rentier Capitalism: Who Owns the Economy, and Who Pays for It?* London: Verso.

Clemens, Justin (2020) "Après moi le déluge: artists after art", *Arena Quarterly*, 3

Coenen, Lars and Morgan, Kevin (2020) "Evolving geographies of innovation: existing paradigms, critiques and possible alternatives", *Norsk Geografisk Tidsskrift*, 74:1, 13–24.

Colquhoun, Matt (2020) *Egress: On Mourning, Melancholy and Mark Fisher.* London: Repeater Books.

Comunian, Roberta and England, Lauren (2020) "Creative and cultural work without filters: Covid-19 and exposed precarity in the creative economy", *Cultural Trends*, 29:2, 112–128.

Coombs, Gretchen (2018) *The Lure of the Social: Encounters with Contemporary Artists.* Bristol: Intellect.

Cooper, Melinda (2017) *Family Values: Between Neoliberalism and the New Social Conservatism.* New York: Zone Books.

Coote, Anna and Percy, Andrew (2020) *The Case for Universal Basic Services.* Cambridge: Polity.

Couldry, Nick and Mejias, Ulises A. (2019) *The Costs of Connection: How Data Is Colonizing Human Life and Appropriating It for Capitalism.* Redwood, CA: Stanford University Press.

Crouch, Colin (2004) *Post-Democracy.* Hoboken, NJ: John Wiley.

Davies, William (2015) *The Limits of Neoliberalism: Authority, Sovereignty and the Logic of Competition.* London: Sage.

Dean, Jodi (2018) *The Communist Horizon.* London: Verso.

Denning, Michael (2004) *Culture in the Age of Three Worlds.* London: Verso.

Denning, Michael (2010) *The Cultural Front: The Laboring of American Culture in the Twentieth Century.* London: Verso.

Bibliography

Doctorow, Corey and Giblin, Rebecca (2022) *Chokepoint Capitalism: How Big Tech and Big Content Captured Creative Labor Markets and How We'll Win Them Back*. Boston, MA: Beacon Press.

Draper, Hal (1977) *Karl Marx's Theory of Revolution, Vol II: The Politics of Social Classes*. New York: Monthly Review Press.

Dümcke, Cornelia (2021) "Five months under COVID-19 in the cultural sector: a German perspective", *Cultural Trends*, 30:1, 19–27.

Duménil, Gérard and Lévy, Dominique (2011) *The Crisis of Neo-liberalism*. Cambridge, MA: Harvard University Press.

Durand, Cédric (2022) "Scouting capital's frontiers", *New Left Review*, 136.

Durham, Blake and Born, Georgina (2022) "Online music consumption and the formalisation of informality", in Born, Georgina (ed.), *Music and Digital Media*. London: UCL Press, 171–219.

Eagleton, Terry (1991) *Ideology of the Aesthetic*. Oxford: Blackwell.

Eagleton, Terry (2023) "What's Your Story?", *London Review of Books*, 45:4.

Edgerton, David (2018) *The Rise and Fall of the British Nation: A Twentieth-Century History*. London: Penguin.

Ehrenreich, Barbara (2020) *Fear of Falling: The Inner Life of the Middle Class*. New York: Pantheon Books.

Ehrenreich, Barbara and Ehrenreich, John (1979) "The professional-managerial class", in Walker, Pat (ed.), *Between Capital and Labor*. Boston, MA: South End Press, 5–45.

Eribon, Didier (2019) *Returning to Reims*. London: Penguin Random House.

Ernaux, Annie (2003) *A Woman's Life*. New York: Seven Stories Press.

Featherstone, Mike (1991) *Consumer Culture and Postmodernism*. London: Sage.

Feher, Michel (2018) *Rated Agency: Investee Politics in a Speculative Age*. Boston, MA: MIT Press.

Fisher, Mark (2009) *Capitalist Realism: Is There No Alternative?* London: Zero Books.

Fisher, Mark (2014) *Ghosts of My Life: Writings on Depression, Hauntology and Lost Futures*. London: Zero Books.

Fisher, Mark (2023) "Luxury communism", *Making and Breaking*, 3.

Florida, Richard (2002) *The Rise of the Creative Class*. New York: Basic Books.

Florida, Richard (2012) *The Rise of the Creative Class, Revisited*. New York: Basic Books.

Fobel, Lea (2022) "Non-formal cultural infrastructure in peripheral regions: responsibility, resources, and regional disparities", *Urban Planning*, 7:4, 445–456.

Foster, Hal (2010) *The Art–Architecture Complex*. London: Verso.

Bibliography

Foucault, Michel (2005) *The Hermeneutics of the Subject: Lectures at the Collège de France, 1981–1982* (trans. Graham Burchell). New York: Palgrave Macmillan.

Foundational Economy Collective (FEC) (2018) *Foundational Economy: The Infrastructure of Everyday Life*. Manchester: Manchester University Press.

Franczak, Michael (2022) *Global Inequality and American Foreign Policy in the 1970s*. Ithaca, NY: Cornell University Press.

Frank, Thomas (1997) *The Conquest of Cool: Business Culture, Counterculture and the Rise of Hip Consumerism*. Chicago: University of Chicago Press.

Frankfurt, Harry G. (2005) *On Bullshit*. Princeton, NJ/Oxford: Princeton University Press.

Fraser, Nancy (1990) "Rethinking the public sphere: a contribution to the critique of actually existing democracy", *Social Text*, 25/26, 56–80.

Fraser, Nancy (2017) "From progressive neoliberalism to Trump—and beyond", *American Affairs*, 1:4, 46–64.

Fraser, Nancy (2022) *Cannibal Capitalism*. London: Verso.

Fraser, Nancy and Honneth, Axel (2003) *Redistribution or Recognition: A Political–Philosophical Exchange*. London: Verso.

Froud, Julie, Haslam, Colin, Johal, Sukhdev, and Williams, Karel (2020) "(How) does productivity matter in the foundational economy?" *Local Economy*, 35:4, 316–336.

Fukuyama, Francis (1992) *The End of History and the Last Man*. New York: Free Press.

Gabor, Daniela (2021) "The Wall Street consensus", *Development and Change*, 52:3, 429–459.

Gare, Arran (2007/8), "The arts and radical enlightenment: gaining liberty to save the planet", *The Structuralist*, 47/48, 20–27.

Garnham, Nicholas (2000) *Emancipation, the Media and Modernity*. Oxford: Oxford University Press.

Gerbaudo, Paolo (2021) *The Great Recoil: Politics after Populism and the Pandemic*. London: Verso.

Gerstle, Gary (2022) *The Rise and Fall of the Neoliberal Order*. Oxford: Oxford University Press.

Ghosh, Amitav (2021) *The Nutmeg's Curse: Parables for a Planet in Crisis*. Chicago: University of Chicago Press.

Gibson-Graham, J. K. and Dombroski, Kelly (2020) *The Handbook of Diverse Economies*. Cheltenham: Edgar Elgar.

Gibson-Graham, J. K. (2006) *A Postcapitalist Politics*. Minneapolis, MN: University of Minnesota Press.

Bibliography

Giddens, Anthony (1991) *Modernity and Self-Identity*. Cambridge: Polity.

Gilbert, Jeremy and Williams, Alex (2022) *Hegemony Now: How Big Tech and Wall Street Won the World (and How We Win it Back)*. London: Verso.

Gilmore, Abigail (2023) *Culture, Participation and Policy in the Urban Park*. Palgrave Studies in Cultural Participation. London: Palgrave Macmillan.

Girard, August (1982) "Cultural industries: a handicap or a new opportunity for cultural development?", in UNESCO, *Cultural Industries: A Challenge for the Future of Culture*. Paris: UNESCO, 24–39.

Gleeson-White, Jane (2014. Revised 2020) *Six Capitals*. Sydney: Allen & Unwin.

Graeber, David (2015) *Bullshit Jobs: A Theory*. New York: Simon & Schuster.

Green, Toby and Fazi, Thomas (2023) *The Covid Consensus: The Global Assault on Democracy and the Poor – a Critique from the Left*. London: Hurst.

Greenfield, Adam (2013) *Against the Smart City*. New York: Do Editions.

Greenfield, Adam (2018) *Radical Technologies: The Design of Everyday Life*. London: Verso.

Gu, Xin (2023) *Cultural Work and Creative Subjectivity: Recentralising the Artist Critique and Social Networks in the Cultural Industries*. London: Routledge.

Guigan, Joe and O'Neil, Martin (2019) *The Case for Community Wealth Building*. Cambridge: Polity.

Guldi, Jo (2022) *The Long Land War: The Global Struggle for Occupancy Rights*. New Haven, CT: Yale University Press.

Habermas, Jurgen (1989) *The Structural Transformation of the Public Sphere*. Cambridge, MA: MIT Press.

Habermas, Jurgen (2023) *Theory, Culture and Society* Special Issue: A New Structural Transformation of the Public Sphere?, 39:4.

Hadley, Steven (2021) *Audience Development and Cultural Policy*. London: Palgrave Macmillan.

Hägglund, Martin (2019) *This Life: Why Mortality Makes Us Free*. London: Profile Books.

Haines-Doran, Tom (2022) *Derailed: How to Fix Britain's Broken Railways*. Manchester: Manchester University Press.

Hall, Stuart and Whannel, Paddy (2018 [1963]) *The Popular Arts*. Durham, NC: Duke University Press.

Harney, Stefano (2012) "Creative industries debate: unfinished business: labour, management, and the creative industries", in Hayward, Mark (ed.), *Cultural Studies and Finance Capitalism*. London: Routledge, 100–120.

Bibliography

Harris, John (2004) *The Last Party: Britpop, Blair and the Demise of English Rock*. London: Harper Perennial.

Harris, Neal (2023) "Critical theory and Universal Basic Income", *Critical Sociology*.

Hartley, John (1999) *Uses of Television*. London: Routledge.

Hatherley, Owen (2010) *A Guide to the New Ruins of Great Britain*. London: Verso.

Hatherley, Owen (2011) *Uncommon*. London: Zero Books.

Hatherley, Owen (2019) *Trans-Europe Express: Tours of the Lost Continent*. London: Penguin Random House.

Hatherley, Owen (2020) *Red Metropolis: Socialism and the Government of London*. London: Repeater Books.

Hatherley, Owen (2020) "The government of London", *New Left Review*, 122, 81–114.

Hesmondhalgh, David (2010) "Russell Keat, cultural goods and the limits of the market", *International Journal of Cultural Policy*, 16:1, 37–38.

Hesmondhalgh, David (2018) *The Cultural Industries*, 4th edition. London: Sage.

Hesmondhalgh, David (2021) "The infrastructural turn in media and internet research", in McDonald, Paul (ed.), *The Routledge Companion to Media Industries*. London: Routledge, 132–142.

Hesmondhalgh, David, Campos, Raquel Valverde, Kaye, Bondy Valdovinos and Li, Zhongwei (2023) "Digital platforms and infrastructure in the realm of culture", *Media and Communication*, 11:2, 296–306.

Hesmondhalgh, David, Oakley, Kate, Lee, David, and Nisbett, Melissa (2015) *Culture, Economy and Politics: The Case of New Labour*. London: Palgrave.

Hewison, Robert (2014) *Cultural Capital: The Rise and Fall of Creative Britain*. London: Verso.

Hochuli, Alex (2021) "The Brazilianization of the world", *American Affairs*, 5:2, 93–115.

Hochuli, Alex, Hoare, George and Cunliffe, Philip (2021) *The End of the End of History*. London: Zero Books.

Hoggart, Richard (1957) *The Uses of Literacy*. London: Penguin.

Holden, John (2004) *Capturing Cultural Value*. London: Demos.

Hollands, Robert (2023) *Beyond the Neoliberal Creative City: Critique and Alternatives in the Urban Cultural Economy*. Bristol: Bristol University Press.

Hood, Christopher (1991) "A public management for all seasons?", *Public Administration*, 69, 3–19.

Bibliography

Howkins, John (2001) *The Creative Economy: How People Make Money from Ideas*. London: Penguin.

Huber, Matthew (2022) *Climate Change as Class War*. London: Verso.

Hunt, Tristram (2005) *Building Jerusalem: The Rise and Fall of the Victorian City*. London: Metropolitan Books.

Hutton, William (2007) *The Writing on the Wall: China and the West in the 21st Century*. London: Little, Brown.

Inglehart, Ronald (1977) *The Silent Revolution: Changing Values and Political Styles among Western Publics*. Princeton, NJ: Princeton University Press.

Jackson, Tim (2021) *Post Growth: Life After Capitalism*. Hoboken, NJ: John Wiley.

Jäger, Anton and Zamora, Daniel (2023) *Welfare for Markets: A Global History of Basic Income*. Chicago: University of Chicago Press.

Jeffries, Stuart (2021) *Everything, All the Time, Everywhere: How We Became Postmodern*. London: Verso.

Joffe, Avril (2021) "Covid 19 and the African cultural economy: an opportunity to reimagine and reinvigorate?", *Cultural Trends*, 30:1, 28–39.

Johnson, Rebecca May (2022) *Small Fires: An Epic in the Kitchen*. London: Pushkin Press.

Johnson-Schlee, Sam (2022) *Living Rooms*. London: Peninsular Press.

Judt, Tony (2011) *Ill Fares the Land*. London: Penguin.

Kay, Jilly Boyce (2021) "A life lasts longer than the body through which it moves: an introduction to a special cultural commons section on Raymond Williams", *European Journal of Cultural Studies*, 24:4, 1009–1020.

Keat, Russell (2000) *Cultural Goods and the Limits of the Market*. Basingstoke: Macmillan.

Kelton, Stephanie (2020) *The Deficit Myth: How to Build a Better Economy*. London: John Murray.

Kevin, Kelly (1998) *New Rules for the New Economy*. London: Fourth Estate.

Klinenberg, Eric (2018) *Palaces for the People: How Social Infrastructure Can Help Fight Inequality, Polarization, and the Decline of Civic Life*. New York: Crown Publishing Group.

Koolhaas, Rem (1995) "The generic city", in Rem Koolhaas and Bruce Mau (eds.), *S, M, L, XL*. New York: The Monacelli Press, 1248–1264.

Lash, Scott and Urry, John (1994) *Economies of Signs and Space*. London: Sage.

Lazzarato, Maurizio (2014) *Signs and Machines: Capitalism and the Production of Subjectivity*. Los Angeles, CA: Semiotext.

Lazzarato, Maurizio (2017) *Experimental Politics: Work, Welfare and Creativity in the Neoliberal Age*. Cambridge, MA: MIT Press.

Bibliography

Lee, Hye-Kyung (2018) *Cultural Policy in South Korea: Making a New Patron State*. London: Routledge.

Leonard, Mark (1997) *Britain™: Renewing Our Identity*. London: Demos.

Levitas, Ruth (1990) "Educated hope: Ernst Bloch on abstract and concrete utopia", *Utopian Studies*, 1:2, 13–26.

Lewis, Justin and Miller, Toby (2003) *Critical Cultural Policy Studies: A Reader*. Oxford: Blackwell.

Littler, Jo (2017) *Against Meritocracy: Culture, Power and Myths of Mobility*. London: Routledge.

Liu, Catherine (2021) *Virtue Hoarders: The Case Against the Professional-Managerial Class*. Minneapolis, MN: University of Minnesota Press.

Mair, Peter (2013) *Ruling the Void: The Hollowing of Western Democracy*. London: Verso.

Mann, Geoff (2017) *In the Long Run: Keynesianism, Political Economy and Revolution*. London: Verso.

Marx, Karl and Engels, Friedrich (2022 [1846]) *The German Ideology*. London: Penguin.

Maslow, Abraham (1943) "A theory of human motivation", *Psychological Review*, 50, 370–396.

Matarasso, Françoise (1997) *Use or Ornament: The Social Impact of Participation in the Arts*. Stroud: Comedia.

Mazzucato, Mariana (2013) *The Entrepreneurial State*. New York: Anthem Press.

Mazzucato, Mariana (2018) *The Value of Everything: Making and Taking in the Global Economy*. London: Random House.

Mazzucato, Mariana (2021) "A new global economic consensus", *Project Syndicate*, 13 October.

Meaney, Thomas (2023) "Fortunes of the Green New Deal", *New Left Review*, 138, 79–102.

Meyercough, John (1988) *The Economic Importance of the Arts in Britain*. London: Policy Studies Institute.

Meyrick, Julian (2023) "Undoing Australian cultural policy: the 1976 IAC inquiry into the performing arts", *Performance Paradigm*, 17.

Meyrick, Julian, Barnett, Tully, and Phiddian, Robert (2018) *What Matters? Talking Value in Australian Culture*. Melbourne: Monash University Press.

Milanović, Branko (2019) *Capitalism, Alone*. Cambridge, MA: Harvard University Press.

Milburn, Keir (2019) *Generation Left*. Cambridge: Polity Press.

Miller, Toby and Yudice, George (2002) *Cultural Policy*. London: Sage.

Bibliography

Mitchell, Timothy (2002) *Rule of Experts: Egypt, Techno-Politics, Modernity*. Berkeley, CA: University of California Press.

Mitchell, Timothy (2005) "The work of economics: how a discipline makes its world", *European Journal of Sociology*, 46:2, 297–320.

Mitchell, Timothy (2008) "Rethinking economy", *Geoforum*, 39:3, 1116–1121.

Mitchell, Timothy (2015) *Carbon Democracy: Political Power in the Age of Oil*. London: Verso.

Moore, Henrietta and Collins, Hannah (2020) *Towards Prosperity: Reinvigorating Local Economies through Universal Basic Services*. London: Institute for Global Prosperity.

Morozov, Evgeny (2022) "Critique of techno-feudal reason", *New Left Review*, 133/134, 89–126.

Mould, Oli (2018) *Against Creativity*. London: Verso.

Mould, Oli and Comunian, Roberta (2015) "Hung, drawn and cultural quartered: rethinking cultural quarter development policy in the UK", *European Planning Studies*, 23:12, 2356–2369.

Nachtwey, Oliver (2018) *Germany's Hidden Crisis: Social Decline in the Heart of Europe*. London: Verso.

Negri, Antonio (2018) *From the Factory to the Metropolis*. Cambridge: Polity.

Negt, Oskar and Kluge, Alexander (1993 [1972]) *Public Sphere and Experience: Towards an Analysis of the Bourgeois and Proletarian Public Sphere*. Minneapolis, MN: University of Minnesota Press.

Novy, Andreas and Leubolt, Bernhard (2005) "Participatory budgeting in Porto Alegre: social innovation and the dialectical relationship of state and civil society", *Urban Studies*, 42:11, 2023–2036.

Nussbaum, Martha (1994) *The Therapy of Desire: Theory and Practice in Hellenistic Ethics*. Princeton, NJ: Princeton University Press.

Nussbaum, Martha (2011) *Creative Capabilities: The Human Development Approach*. Cambridge, MA: Harvard University Press.

O'Brien, John and Clancy, Annette (2022) "A policy review of basic income for the arts pilot scheme", *Irish Journal of Arts Management and Cultural Policy*, 9, 43–57.

O'Connor, Justin (2004) "'A special kind of city knowledge'": innovative clusters, tacit knowledge and the 'creative city'", *Media International Australia*, 112, 131–149.

O'Connor, Justin (2020) "Creative cities, creative classes and the global modern", in Gu, Xin, O'Connor, Justin, and Kho Lim, Michael (eds.), *Re-Imagining Creative Cities in 21st Century Asia*. London: Palgrave, 13–26.

Bibliography

O'Connor, Justin (2023) "UNESCO's 2005 Convention: from creative economy to sustainable prosperity?", in Bailey, Chris, Charalambous, Elena Theodoulou, and Drion, Geert (eds.), *Cultural Governance in the 21st Century*. London: Routledge.

O'Connor, Justin and Gu, Xin (2010) "Developing a creative cluster in a post-industrial city: CIDS and Manchester", *The Information Society*, 26:2, 124–136.

O'Connor, Justin and Shaw, Kate (2014) "What next for the creative city?" *City, Culture and Society*, 5:3, 165–70.

O'Connor, Justin and Oakley, Kate (2015) "Cultural industries: an introduction", in Oakley, Kate and O'Connor, Justin (eds.), *The Routledge Companion to the Cultural Industries*. London: Routledge, 1–32.

O'Connor, Justin and Gu, Xin (2020) *Red Creative: Culture and Modernity in Modern China*. Bristol: Intellect.

Oakley, Kate (2011) "In its own image: New Labour and the cultural workforce", *Cultural Trends*, 20, 281–289.

Oakley, Kate and O'Connor, Justin (2015) "Cultural industries: an introduction", in Oakley, Kate and O'Connor, Justin (eds.), *The Routledge Companion to the Cultural Industries*. London: Routledge, 1–32.

OECD Local Economic and Employment Development (2022) *The Culture Fix: Creative People, Places and Industries*.

Oldenberg, Jay (1989) *The Great Good Place*. St Paul, MN: Paragon House.

Olma, Sebastian (2016) *Autonomy and Weltbezug: Towards an Aesthetic of Performative Defiance*. Breda: Avans Hogeschool.

Pacella, Jessica, Luckman, Susan, and O'Connor, Justin (2020) "Fire, pestilence and the extractive economy: cultural policy after cultural policy", *Cultural Trends*, 30:1, 40–51.

Parrish, David (2007) *T-Shirts and Suits: A Guide to the Business of Creativity*. Liverpool: ACME.

Penman, Ian (2022) "My god wears a durag", *London Review of Books*, 44:1.

Pennington, Alison (2023) *Generation F'd*. Melbourne: Hardie Grant Books.

Peterson, Richard A. (1992) "Understanding audience segmentation: from elite and mass to omnivore and univore", *Poetics*, 21:4, 243–258.

Pettifor, Ann (2020) *The Case for the Green New Deal*. London: Verso.

Phiddian, Robert, Meyrick, Julian, Barnett, Tully, and Maltby, Richard (2017) "Counting culture to death: an Australian perspective on culture counts and quality metrics", *Cultural Trends*, 26:2, 174–180.

Piketty, Thomas (2020) *Capital and Ideology*. Cambridge, MA: Belknap Press.

Bibliography

Polanyi, Karl (1944) *The Great Transformation*. New York: Farrar and Rinehart.

Pope, Rob (2005) *Creativity: Theory, History, Practice*. London: Routledge.

Pratt, Andy (2012) "The cultural and creative industries: organisational and spatial challenges to their governance", *Die Erde*, 143:4, 317–334.

Putnam, Robert (2000) *Bowling Alone: The Collapse and Revival of American Community*. New York: Simon & Schuster Ltd.

Qu, Shuwen, Hesmondhalgh, David, and Xiao, Jian (2023) "Music streaming platforms and self-releasing musicians: the case of China", *Information, Communication and Society*, 26:4, 699–715.

Quiggin, John (2018) "Neoliberalism: rise, decline and future prospects", in Cahill, Damien, Cooper, Melinda, Konings, Martijn, and Primrose, David (eds.), *The Sage Handbook of Neoliberalism*. London: Sage, 143–153.

Rainnie, Al (2023) "(Far) beyond smart specialisation to the foundational economy in Australia?" Unpublished paper.

Raworth, Kate (2018) *Doughnut Economics: Seven Ways to Think Like a 21st Century Economist*. London: Random House.

Reckwitz, Andreas (2017) *The Invention of Creativity*. Cambridge: Polity.

Redhead, Steve (2004) "Creative modernity: the new cultural state", *Media International Australia*, 112:1, 9–27.

Reynolds, Simon (2011) *Retromania: Pop Culture's Addiction to Its Own Past*. London: Farrar, Straus and Giroux.

Rikap, Cecilia (2023) "Capitalism as usual? Implications of digital intellectual monopolies", *New Left Review*, 139, 145–160.

Riley, Dylan (2020) "Faultlines", *New Left Review*, 126, 35–52.

Riley, Dylan and Brenner, Robert (2022) "Seven theses on American politics", *New Left Review*, 138, 5–27, 6.

Robinson, Kim Stanley (2020) *The Ministry of the Future*. London: Orbit Books.

Rodgers, Daniel T. (2012) *Age of Fracture*. Cambridge, MA: Belknap Press.

Rosa, Hartmut (2013) *Social Acceleration: A New Theory of Modernity*. New York: Columbia University Press.

Rose, Gillian (1995) *Love's Work*. New York: New York Review Books.

Ross, Andrew (2004) *No-collar: The Humane Workplace and Its Hidden Costs*. Philadelphia, PA: Temple University Press.

Ross, Andrew (2009) "The political economy of amateurism", *Television and New Media*, 10, 136–137.

Ross, Kristin (2015) *Communal Luxury: The Political Imaginary of the Paris Commune*. London: Verso.

Bibliography

Russell, Bertie, Beel, David, Jones, Ian Rees, and Jones, Martin (2022) "Placing the Foundational Economy: an emerging discourse for post-neoliberal economic development", *Economy and Space*, 54:6, 1069–1085.

Sandbrook, Dominic (2016) *The Great British Dream Factory: The Strange History of Our National Imagination*. London: Allen Lane.

Sandel, Michael (2020) *The Tyranny of Merit: What's Become of the Common Good?* London: Allen Lane.

Savage, Jon (2015) *1966: The Year the Decade Exploded*. London: Faber and Faber.

Sawchuck, Kim (2001) "The cultural apparatus: C. Wright Mills' unfinished work", *The American Sociologist*, 32:1, 27–49.

Schlesinger, Philip (2017) "The creative economy: invention of a global orthodoxy", *Innovation: The European Journal of Social Science Research*, 30:1, 73–90.

Schwartz, Herman (2022) "From Fordism to franchise: intellectual property and growth models in the knowledge economy", in Baccaro, Lucio, Blyth, Mark, and Pontusson, Jonas (eds.), *Diminishing Returns: The New Politics of Growth and Stagnation*. Oxford: Oxford University Press.

Scott, Allen J. (2004) "Cultural products industries and urban economic development: prospects for growth and market contestation in global context", *Urban Affairs Review*, 39:4, 461–90.

Scully, Jess (2020) *Glimpses of Utopia*. Sydney: Pantera Press.

Sen, Amartya (1999) *Development as Freedom*. New York: Knopf.

Skeggs, Beverley (2011) "Imagining personhood differently: person value and autonomist working-class value practices", *Sociological Review*, 59:3, 496–513.

Skidelsky, Robert (2018) *Money and Government: A Challenge to Mainstream Economics*. London: Random House.

Slobodian, Quinn (2018) *Globalists: The End of Empire and the Birth of Neoliberalism*. Cambridge, MA: Harvard University Press.

Soper, Kate (2021) *Post-Growth Living: For an Alternative Hedonism*. London: Verso.

Sparks, Colin and Roach, Chris (1990) "Editorial: farewell to NWICO?", *Media, Culture & Society*, 12:3, 275–81.

Spiller, Marcus (2020) "Reconceptualising local economic development strategies", *Economic Development Journal*, 14:1, 6–9.

Srnicek, Nick (2016) *Platform Capitalism*. Cambridge: Polity Press.

Stedman Jones, Daniel (2018) "The neoliberal origins of the Third Way: how Chicago, Virginia and Bloomington shaped Clinton and

Bibliography

Blair", in Cahill, Damien, Cooper, Melinda, Konings, Martijn, and Primrose, David (eds.), *The Sage Handbook of Neoliberalism*. London: Sage, 167–178.

Streeck, Wolfgang (2012) "Citizens as customers: considerations on the new politics of consumption", *New Left Review*, 76, 27–48.

Streeck, Wolfgang (2014) *Buying Time: The Delayed Crisis of Democratic Capitalism*. London: Verso.

Streeck, Wolfgang (2016) *How Will Capitalism End?* London: Verso.

Streeck, Wolfgang (2021) "In the superstate", *London Review of Books*, 44:2.

Szreder, Kuba (2021) *The ABC of the Projectariat: Living and Working in a Precarious Art World*. Manchester: Manchester University Press.

Tcherneva, Pavlina R. (2020) *The Case for a Job Guarantee*. Cambridge: Polity.

Tether, Bruce S. (2022) "Creative clusters and sparse spaces: Manchester's creative industries and the geographies of deprivation and prosperity". Creative Industries Policy and Evidence Centre.

Therborn, Göran (2022) "The world and the left", *New Left Review*, 137, 23–73.

Thompson, Edward P. (1971) "The moral economy of the English crown in the 18th century", *Past & Present*, 50, 76–136.

Thompson, Matthew (2020), "What's so new about the new municipalism?" *Progress in Human Geography*, 36:1, 25–43.

Thompson, Noel (1996) "Supply side socialism: the political economy of New Labour", *New Left Review*, 1:216, 37–54.

Thompson, Noel (2002) *Left in the Wilderness: The Political Economy of British Democratic Socialism Since 1979*. Chesham: Acumen.

Throsby, David (2012) *The Economics of Cultural Policy*. Cambridge: Cambridge University Press.

Throsby, David (2017) "Culturally sustainable development: theoretical concept or practical policy instrument?", *International Journal of Cultural Policy*, 23:2, 133–147.

Tooze, Adam (2018) *Crashed: How a Decade of Financial Crises Changed the World*. London: Penguin Random House.

Tsing, Anna Lowenhaupt (2015) *The Mushroom at the End of the World: On the Possibility of Life in Capitalist Ruins*. Princeton, NJ: Princeton University Press.

UNCTAD (2022) *Creative Industry 4.0: Towards a New Globalized Creative Economy*.

Wang, Hui (2016) *China's Twentieth Century*. London: Verso.

Bibliography

Warde, Alan, Wright, David, and Gavo-Cal, Modesto (2007) "Understanding cultural omnivorousness: or, the myth of the cultural omnivore", *Cultural Sociology*, 1:2, 143–164.

Wark, McKenzie (2019) *Capital Is Dead*. London: Verso.

White, Judith (2017) *Culture Heist: Art Versus Money*. Sydney: Brandl and Schlesinger.

Williams, Raymond (1961) *The Long Revolution*. London: Chatto and Windus.

Williams, Raymond (1977) *Marxism and Literature*. Oxford: Oxford University Press.

Williams, Raymond (1981) *Culture*. London: Fontana.

Williams, Raymond (1983 [1976]) *Keywords: A Vocabulary of Culture and Society*, 2nd edition. London: Fontana.

Williams, Raymond (1989 [1958]) *Resources of Hope*. London: Verso.

Williams, Raymond (2003) *Who Speaks for Wales?* Cardiff: University of Wales Press.

Wolf, Martin (2023) *The Crisis of Democratic Capitalism*. London: Penguin Press.

Wright, Erik Olin (1978) "Intellectuals and the working class", *Critical Sociology*, 8:1, 5–18.

Wright, Erik Olin (2010) *Envisioning Real Utopias*. London: Verso.

Wulf, Andrea (2022) *Magnificent Rebels: The First Romantics and the Invention of the Self*. New York: Knopf.

Young, Michael (1958) *The Rise of the Meritocracy 1870–2033: An Essay on Education and Society*. London: Thames and Hudson.

Zevin, Alexander (2019) "Every penny a vote", *London Review of Books*, 41:16.

Žižek, Slavov (2002) *Welcome to the Desert of the Real*. London: Verso.

Zuboff, Sharon. (2019) *Surveillance Capitalism: The Fight for a Human Future at the New Frontier of Power*. London: Profile Books.

Index

Index

Index

Index

Index